Critical Perspectives on Global Englishes in Asia

NEW PERSPECTIVES ON LANGUAGE AND EDUCATION
Founding Editor: Viv Edwards, *University of Reading, UK*

Series Editors: Phan Le Ha, *University of Hawai'i at Mānoa, USA* and Joel Windle, *Monash University, Australia*

Two decades of research and development in language and literacy education have yielded a broad, multidisciplinary focus. Yet education systems face constant economic and technological change, with attendant issues of identity and power, community and culture. This series will feature critical and interpretive, disciplinary and multidisciplinary perspectives on teaching and learning, language and literacy in new times.

All books in this series are externally peer-reviewed.

Full details of all the books in this series and of all our other publications can be found on http://www.multilingual-matters.com, or by writing to Multilingual Matters, St Nicholas House, 31–34 High Street, Bristol BS1 2AW, UK.

NEW PERSPECTIVES ON LANGUAGE AND EDUCATION: 71

Critical Perspectives on Global Englishes in Asia

Language Policy, Curriculum, Pedagogy and Assessment

Edited by
**Fan Fang and
Handoyo Puji Widodo**

MULTILINGUAL MATTERS
Bristol • Blue Ridge Summit

DOI https://doi.org/10.21832/FANG4092
Library of Congress Cataloging in Publication Data
A catalog record for this book is available from the Library of Congress.
Names: Fang, Fan, 1984- | Widodo, Handoyo Puji.
Title: Critical Perspectives on Global Englishes in Asia: Language Policy,
   Curriculum, Pedagogy and Assessment/Edited by Fan Fang and
   Handoyo Puji Widodo.
Description: Bristol; Blue Ridge Summit: Multilingual Matters, [2019] |
   Series: New Perspectives on Language and Education: 71 |
   Includes bibliographical references and index.
Identifiers: LCCN 2018060944 (print) | LCCN 2019004525 (ebook) |
   ISBN 9781788924108 (pdf) | ISBN 9781788924115 (epub) |
   ISBN 9781788924122 (Kindle) | ISBN 9781788924092 (hbk : alk. paper)
Subjects: LCSH: English language—Study and teaching—Asia. |
   English language—Study and teaching—Asian speakers.
Classification: LCC PE1068.A7 (ebook) | LCC PE1068.A7 C75 2019 (print) |
   DDC 428.0071/05—dc23
LC record available at https://lccn.loc.gov/2018060944

British Library Cataloguing in Publication Data
A catalogue entry for this book is available from the British Library.

ISBN-13: 978-1-78892-409-2 (hbk)
ISBN-13: 978-1-78892-274-6 (pbk)

Multilingual Matters
UK: St Nicholas House, 31–34 High Street, Bristol BS1 2AW, UK.
USA: NBN, Blue Ridge Summit, PA, USA.

Website: www.multilingual-matters.com
Twitter: Multi_Ling_Mat
Facebook: https://www.facebook.com/multilingualmatters
Blog: www.channelviewpublications.wordpress.com

Copyright © 2019 Fan Fang, Handoyo Puji Widodo and the authors of individual chapters.

All rights reserved. No part of this work may be reproduced in any form or by any means without permission in writing from the publisher.
The policy of Multilingual Matters/Channel View Publications is to use papers that are natural, renewable and recyclable products, made from wood grown in sustainable forests. In the manufacturing process of our books, and to further support our policy, preference is given to printers that have FSC and PEFC Chain of Custody certification. The FSC and/or PEFC logos will appear on those books where full certification has been granted to the printer concerned.

Typeset by Nova Techset Private Limited, Bengaluru and Chennai, India.

Contents

	Contributors	vii
	Preface	xi
1	Critical Perspectives on Global Englishes in English Language Education *Fan (Gabriel) Fang and Handoyo Puji Widodo*	1
2	A Critical Examination of Common Beliefs about Language Teaching: From Research Insights to Professional Engagement *Ryuko Kubota*	10
3	English is the Default Language? A Study of International Students' Language Needs in the Chinese Higher Education Context *Ting Zhang and Yongyan Zheng*	27
4	Language Selection and Assessment in Brunei Darussalam *Ishamina Athirah Gardiner and David Deterding*	45
5	Global Englishes and the International Standardized English Language Proficiency Tests *James Dean Brown*	64
6	Looking through the Eyes of Global Englishes: Enhancing English Language Teaching in Multicultural Classrooms *Maria Luz Elena N. Canilao*	84
7	Contextualizing Teaching English as a Local/Global Language: A Bottom-up Sociolinguistic Investigation *Jim Chan*	104
8	From Learners to Users: Reframing a Japanese University Curriculum towards a 'World Englishes Enterprise'-Informed English as a Medium of Instruction Model *James D'Angelo*	123

9 Talking the Talk but Not Walking the Walk?
   Preparing Teachers for Global Englishes Pedagogy   141
   Ali Fuad Selvi

10 Practices of Teaching Englishes: Pedagogical Reflections
   and Implications   157
   Zhichang Xu

11 Reform and Opportunities: China English in Chinese
   Higher Education   176
   Yue Chen and Cong Zhang

12 Global Englishes-oriented English Language Education   194
   Handoyo Puji Widodo and Fan (Gabriel) Fang

   Index   201

Contributors

Maria Luz Elena N. Canilao is Assistant Professor at the Ateneo de Manila University (ADMU), the Philippines. She is the ADMU English Department's current Associate Chair for Language Programs. Her work focuses on multilingual education, language policy and materials development. She has worked as an ELT consultant for various institutions including the Ateneo Center for English Language Teaching (ACELT), Commission on Higher Education (CHED), Department of Education (DepEd) and British Council Philippines. Email: lcanilao@ateneo.edu

Jim Y.H. Chan is Assistant Professor in the Faculty of Education at the University of Hong Kong. His research interests include language policy, curriculum and teaching, language attitudes, World Englishes and English as a lingua franca. Some of his recent work has been published in *TESOL Quarterly*, *World Englishes*, *International Journal of Applied Linguistics*, *Language and Education*, *System*, *Journal of Multilingual and Multicultural Development*, *Journal of English as a Lingua Franca* and *Asian Englishes*. Email: egjim.chan@gmail.com

Yue Chen is a PhD candidate in second language studies/ESL at Purdue University, USA. With an MEd in TESOL, Chen has taught different classes from adult immigrants' ESL classes to first year composition at college level. Chen's research interests include second language writing, English education, writing programme administration and writing assessment. Email: chen1398@purdue.edu

James D'Angelo, PhD, is Chair of the graduate major in World Englishes, Chukyo University, Japan. His primary research area is ELF/EMI in the Japan context. He is Editor-in-Chief of the Routledge journal *Asian Englishes*, and is on the Editorial Advisory Board of the Routledge Studies in TEIL series. He has published in many journals and books, including 'The status of ELF in Japan' in the *Routledge Handbook of English as a Lingua Franca*. Email: dangelo@lets.chukyo-u.ac.jp

James Dean ('JD') Brown is Professor of Second Language Studies at the University of Hawai'i at Mānoa. He has taught courses and spoken in many countries ranging from Australia to Yugoslavia. He has also published numerous journal articles, book chapters and books – on language curriculum design, language testing, language research methods (including quantitative, qualitative and mixed-methods approaches) and connected speech. Email: brownj@hawaii.edu

David Deterding is a Professor at Universiti Brunei Darussalam, Brunei, where he teaches phonetics, forensic linguistics, Malay-English translation, history of English and research methods. His research focuses on the description of English pronunciation in southeast Asia, especially in Brunei, Singapore, Hong Kong and China. He has also completed a book on *Misunderstandings in English as a Lingua Franca* (Mouton de Gruyter, 2013). Email: david.deterding@ubd.edu.bn

Fan (Gabriel) Fang obtained his PhD at the University of Southampton, UK, and is currently Associate Professor in Applied Linguistics at Shantou University, China. His research interests include Global Englishes, language attitude and identity, intercultural communication, and ELT. He has published articles in journals including *Asian Englishes*, *ELT Journal*, *English Today*, *Language Teaching Research*, *System*, *Journal of Asia TEFL* and *Asian Journal of Applied Linguistics*. Email: ffang@stu.edu.cn

Ishamina Athirah Gardiner is a Lecturer in the Language Centre, Universiti Brunei Darussalam, Brunei. She has taught courses in phonetics, forensic linguistics, academic writing, and communication skills in English. Her research interests include intelligibility in English as a lingua franca interactions, describing Brunei English and pronunciation teaching. She has recently published papers in the *Routledge Handbook of English as a Lingua Franca*, the *Routledge Handbook of Contemporary English Pronunciation* and *Journal of Second Language Pronunciation*. Email: ishamina.athirah@gmail.com

Jennifer Jenkins is Professor of Global Englishes at Southampton University, UK. She has been researching English as a lingua franca for three decades and has published three monographs on the subject as well as a coursebook, *Global Englishes* (2015). She is Co-Editor of the *Routledge Handbook of ELF* (2018) and *Linguistic Diversity on the EMI Campus* (2019), and is Founding Editor of the book series 'Developments in English as a Lingua Franca'. Her current research focuses on language in higher education and issues of empowerment and disempowerment relating to ELF. Email: j.jenkins@soton.ac.uk

Ryuko Kubota is a Professor in the Department of Language and Literacy Education of the Faculty of Education at the University of British Columbia, Canada, where she teaches applied linguistics and teacher education in English as an additional language and modern languages. Her research draws on critical approaches to applied linguistics and second language education, focusing on race, culture and language ideology. Email: ryuko.kubota@ubc.ca

Ali Fuad Selvi is an Assistant Professor of TESOL and Applied Linguistics and the Chair of the Teaching English as a Foreign Language programme at Middle East Technical University, Northern Cyprus Campus, Turkey. His research interests include: Global Englishes and its implications for language learning, teaching, teacher education and language policy/planning; issues related to (in)equity, professionalism, marginalization and discrimination in TESOL; and second language teacher education. Email: selvi@metu.edu.tr

Handoyo Puji Widodo is currently affiliated with King Abdulaziz University (KAU) based in Jeddah, Saudi Arabia. He has taught English in China, Indonesia and the USA. Widodo has published extensively in refereed journals and edited volumes. His areas of specialization include language teaching methodology, language curriculum and materials development, systemic functional linguistics (SFL) in language education, and teacher professional development. His work has been grounded in sociosemiotic, sociocognitive, sociocultural and critical theories of language pedagogies. Email: handoyopw@yahoo.com

Zhichang Xu is Senior Lecturer in the School of Languages, Literatures, Cultures and Linguistics at Monash University, Australia, and Associate Editor for *English Today* (Cambridge University Press). He has extensive teaching experience in Beijing, Perth, Hong Kong and Melbourne. He has a disciplinary background in applied linguistics and intercultural education, and his research areas include World Englishes, applied linguistics, cultural linguistics, English as a lingua franca, intercultural communication and language education. Email: zhichang.xu@monash.edu

Cong Zhang is an Assistant Professor of Applied Linguistics in the School of Foreign Languages and Literature at Shandong University, China. Her research interests include second language writing, EFL teaching and learning, World Englishes and language testing. Her publications have appeared in *Journal of Second Language Writing*, *System* and *Chinese Journal of Applied Linguistics*. Email: zhangcong@sdu.edu.cn

Ting Zhang currently works as an English teacher at the Songjiang No. 2 High School, Shanghai, China. She gained her Master's in applied linguistics from Fudan University, Shanghai, China. Email: tingizhang@qq.com

Yongyan Zheng is Professor in the College of Foreign Languages and Literature, Fudan University, China. Her research interests include second language development, bilingual and multilingual education and academic literacy practices. Her recent publications have appeared in *Language Policy*, *System*, *Language Awareness*, *English Today* and *Journal of Scholarly Publishing*. Email: yongyanzheng@fudan.edu.cn

Preface

Global Englishes, the focus of this very timely volume, has become an increasingly hot topic over the past few decades. As readers may know, it all began in the late 1970s with two conferences focusing on the (then) new field of World Englishes. One of these conferences was organized by the late Larry Smith, the other by the late Braj Kachru, the founding fathers of World Englishes. Kachru's conference was subsequently published as an edited volume, *The Other Tongue: English Across Cultures*, originally in 1982, and republished in 1992 with a number of new chapters, including one on the rarely tackled subject of teaching World Englishes. Kachru's volume has remained a key text in the field of World Englishes ever since.

The establishment of World Englishes as an area of research was followed, in the 1990s, by the first published research into the phenomenon of English as a lingua franca (ELF), also known as English as an international language (EIL). Ideologically, ELF was very similar to World Englishes, and initially emulated it in so far as it focused on the use of forms that diverged from native English, aiming – like World Englishes research – to legitimize the use of these forms and bring about the abandoning of 'the whole mystique of native speaker [of English]', as Charles Ferguson put it in the Preface to Kachru's 1982 volume. A little later, ELF researchers began to move conceptually away from World Englishes. The reason for this was a difference between the two paradigms, whose effects had not initially been fully appreciated. That is, because ELF use transcends language boundaries, thus involving language use across rather than within boundaries, it is not possible to talk of 'varieties' of ELF in the same way as we can talk of varieties of World Englishes, Indian English, Nigerian English, and so on. Indeed, ELF's very variability became accepted as one of its defining characteristics, and any plans to codify ELF were dropped.

The two paradigms, World Englishes and ELF, nevertheless continued (and still continue) to share similar ideologies, according to which English use outside the small handful of mother tongue English countries (Kachru's 'inner circle'), can no longer be considered the property of its tiny minority of native speakers, and therefore the vast non-native English speaking majority are entitled to their own ways of using English.

The two paradigms, sadly, also share a second feature: that the uses of English which they document and analyze are still, to this day, criticized by those (including traditionally minded linguists) who have a limited understanding of language contact and change, and who continue to see the native English speaker as the rightful 'king' of English, rather than one that should have been deposed long ago. In this respect, the current volume, with its focus on language ideology in relation to English language teaching (ELT) policies and practices in a range of countries and educational settings/levels, provides a very important antidote to such outdated perspectives, especially at a time when not nearly enough has yet been said by scholars of ELF and even World Englishes about the implications of their research for English language teaching and testing, and for English use in educational settings.

Global Englishes, the focus of this volume, can thus be considered a cover term that includes both World Englishes and ELF. On the one hand, World Englishes refers to all the national varieties of English within in Kachru's three circles, i.e. inner (mother tongue Englishes), outer (postcolonial Englishes) and expanding (English use by speakers from countries that were not colonized by the British, in other words almost all those not included in the inner and outer circles). On the other hand, ELF means any use of English among speakers from any of these three circles who do not share a first language and choose to use English to communicate with each other. To put it another way, this means intercultural communication in which English is involved. The possible combinations of ELF users are thus immense and increasing year on year, particularly in the Asian region. It is therefore not at all surprising that the resulting use of English is not only diverse, but also emergent, and often unpredictable.

No doubt because of the potential diversity of English use, accommodation (which in Global Englishes often involves adjusting one's language to make it more intelligible for the specific interlocutor) has emerged as a key strategy, particularly in ELF interactions. And more recently, ELF has been reconceptualized to highlight the fact that the phenomenon would not exist in the first place without the multilingualism of the vast majority of its users (i.e. all but ELF's small minority of often-monolingual native English speakers). The backgrounding of the 'Englishness' of ELF and the foregrounding of its multilingualism has added substantially to researchers' understanding of ELF's complexity – a complexity that involves the natural influence of ELF users' first languages (or 'similects', as Anna Mauranen, 2012) has called them, along with mutual influences when speakers from different similects communicate with each other (Mauranen's 'second order contact'), the language of the locality, which is rarely English, and the use of other languages in ELF interactions. The latter factor led to a redefinition of ELF as 'multilingual communication in which English is available as a contact language of choice, but is not necessarily chosen' (Jenkins, 2015: 73).

As well as until recently marginalizing the other languages of speakers involved in ELF communication, ELF research has also tended to ignore Asian contexts, and to focus far more on communication in European settings and/or among European ELF users. This may have been the result of the European backgrounds of the earliest ELF researchers, but it nevertheless opens the field up to accusations of continuing Western hegemony, and even of racism. For whereas World Englishes scholars have provided plentiful descriptions and analyses of varieties of Asian Englishes, and critiques of policies and ELT practices according to the World Englishes paradigm, a focus on Asia has been seriously lacking according to the ELF paradigm. And while there are a few notable exceptions, such as the work of Kumiko Murata exploring ELF in Japanese academic and business settings, these have up to now been far from the rule. This, in turn, has meant that the field of Global Englishes as a whole has to a great extent (i.e. an ELF extent) neglected Asia. And even research within World Englishes has tended to sideline teaching and testing related issues.

These are both reasons why the current volume is so crucial. It fills a critical (in both senses) gap in the research literature by bringing together a number of key contributions by scholars in and/or from Asian settings, and from both World Englishes and ELF perspectives who engage with the implications of Global Englishes research in the educational domain. The authors demonstrate, chapter after chapter, how urgently the old ideologies of English language education and use need to be updated with reference to Global Englishes scholarship and, in the process, to move away from native-speakerist, essentialist, reductionist (mis)beliefs, and towards an understanding of the legitimate multiplicity of English use in today's diverse English-using, multilingual world. The editors are to be congratulated on having brought together this fascinating collection of chapters in a much-needed volume on Global Englishes in the Asian context.

Jennifer Jenkins
March 2018

References

Jenkins, J. (2015) Repositioning English and multilingualism in English as a lingua franca. *Englishes in Practice* 2 (3), 49–85.

Kachru, B. B. (1982/1992) *The Other Tongue: English Across Cultures*. Urbana: University of Illinois Press.

Mauranen, A. (2012) *Exploring ELF: Academic English Shaped by Non-native Speakers*. Cambridge: Cambridge University Press.

1 Critical Perspectives on Global Englishes in English Language Education

Fan (Gabriel) Fang and Handoyo Puji Widodo

In the areas of applied linguistics and English language teaching (ELT), recent years have witnessed the unprecedented growth of English as a global language in both educational and non-educational domains (Widodo *et al.*, 2017). For example, in language education, English has been included in school and university curricula in order to prepare learners to become competent users of the language outside the classroom (Widodo, 2016). In order to meet this educational goal, there have been many attempts (e.g. English-only policy, bilingual programs) to help learners enhance their English skills. As English is used by people from both English speaking and non-English speaking countries, the issue of how the English language should be perceived and taught in different contexts has become a hotly debated topic, particularly in the field of applied linguistics.

On the methodological surface, ELT seems to be a simple process in which language educators train language learners to listen, speak, read and write English. In this endeavor, language learners are supposed to reach a native speaker's level of English competence. In particular, so-called Standard British English and American English are viewed as providing the golden rules for English language instruction. However, when delving deeper and further, the traditional English as a foreign language (EFL) perspective is not akin to the current linguistic landscape of English as a global language and neglects the fact that the use of English does not exist in a vacuum. The spread and use of English in different contexts is in fact more complicated than what we have seen. For instance, in China and Indonesia (where the editors are currently based in) people use different languages and dialects, and such languages and dialects affect the use of English. To some degree, local accents may flavor the way people speak English. The question as to whether local dialect and language should be tolerated when speaking English has been debatable. From a multilingual perspective, however, a local language can be a resource for learning another language, such as English. With this in mind, English has been so differently adopted and adapted in various contexts that it is no longer viewed from a monolithic and unified perspective, and it is no longer owned merely by its native speakers (Widdowson, 1994).

This volume reflects the significance of moving beyond the traditional perspective of viewing English as a global language and therefore applies a critical perspective in negotiating the use of such a language. Particularly in the ELT industry, the increasingly multilingual and multicultural reality of today's English use in global communicative settings has also called for veering away from the native-speaker (NS) ideology to a more pluralistic view which acknowledges the diversity of English usage in different geographic contexts (Rose & Montakantiwong, 2018). From a critical perspective, Holliday (2006) and Kubota (this volume) contend that the standard NS ideology is a myth or a native speakerism fallacy and also prescriptive because this ideology does not recognize the creativity of English use from a user perspective.

This backdrop leads to a question for people who are involved in the field of applied linguistics and ELT in terms of what types of *English* should be taught and how *English* should be taught to cater for the various needs and goals of language learners in different geographic contexts (D'Angelo, this volume; Matsuda, 2012, 2016; Xu, this volume). In global communicative contexts, each user of English engages in a negotiation of meaning with other English users who may come from linguistically and culturally different backgrounds. This reality encourages English learners to learn how to communicate in such an environment (Rose & Montakantiwong, 2018). Along with this global use of English, Asia has been a strategic territory where there are a large number of people who use English for instrumental purposes, such as education, business and tourism (Widodo *et al.*, 2017). In response to this reality, this volume focuses on the Asian context where rich linguistic and cultural resources are mutually interwoven. The linguistic and cultural diversity of Asia as a multilingual and multicultural landscape has driven the socially fluid use of English where 'the use of English in Asian contexts has specific historical, social, and political particularities' (Fang, 2018: 16). English has been used in many Asian contexts for a long time with different purposes. From the paradigm of Global Englishes (GE), English is regarded as a postcolonial language in some Asian contexts where nativized varieties have been formed. From a broader range of the use of English, the paradigm of English as a lingua franca (ELF) moves beyond the description and codification of the varieties of English, but envisages the fluid and hybrid nature of English across borders (Jenkins, 2015; Seidlhofer, 2011).

Emboldened by a volume of proposals for the use of English as a global lingua franca, this edited book deals with language policy, curriculum, pedagogy and assessment from the paradigm of GE. The term 'Global Englishes' is adopted in this volume as the metamorphosis and fluid nature of the English language not within but transcending borders worldwide (Jenkins, 2015). We treat GE as a more inclusive term recognizing the varieties of English from the World Englishes (WE) paradigm as well as the diversity and fluidity of English use from the ELF paradigm (Galloway & Rose, 2018; Jenkins, 2015). In this respect, GE-driven policy, curriculum, pedagogy and assessment place greater emphasis on providing teachers and learners with more exposure and engagement with the diversity of English as a global lingua franca in authentic social interactions. This educational endeavor places more value on learners' multilingualism and orients learners towards reappropriating NS norms (McKay, 2012).

Overall, this volume includes several chapters that deal with debates and discussions about language policy, curriculum, pedagogy and assessment from the perspective of GE (see Brown, this volume; Kubota, this volume). It also features the contribution of GE to teacher training (Selvi, this volume), with some chapters discussing the English language ideologies and ELT in certain contexts where English is 'nativized', including the Philippines (Canilao, this volume), Brunei (Gardiner & Deterding, this volume) and Hong Kong (Chan, this volume). It also includes traditional contexts where English is regarded as a foreign language (EFL) and even as a native language (ENL). Two chapters focus on the context of Mainland China (Chen & Zhang, this volume; Zhang & Zheng, this volume) where more than 400 million English learners exist (Wei & Su, 2015), where one chapter introduces a GE-oriented course in Australia (Xu, this volume) and one focuses on a WE-informed curriculum in Japan (D'Angelo, this volume).

This Volume

This volume highlights the role of GE in language policy, curriculum, pedagogy and assessment. In Chapter 2, **A Critical Examination of Common Beliefs about Language Teaching: From Research Insights to Professional Engagement**, Kubota explores 10 common misperceived beliefs about language and language education, including the superiority of the native speaker, whiteness and the monolingual approach to pedagogy. Some taken-for-granted language ideologies and perceptions have been challenged, while a critical examination is important to 'engender an anti-racist, anti-essentialist, anti-Euro- and US-centric and anti-reductionist worldview'. Kubota has elaborated an overarching topic in relation to GE from a thorough perspective. These common misperceived beliefs are further explored and challenged by other contributions in this volume. Kubota's contribution to this volume provides language policy makers and curriculum developers with insights into national and institutional policy making which goes beyond native speakerism standards. This policy making may exert influence upon language pedagogy and assessment, which are addressed in the rest of the chapters in this volume.

In Chapter 3, **English is the Default Language? A Study of International Students' Language Needs in the Chinese Higher Education Context**, Zhang and Zheng reported a study on English as a medium of instruction (EMI) in a high-ranked Chinese university. Zhang and Zheng interviewed international students so as to examine their experiences of and attitudes towards EMI classrooms and their language needs when studying at a university in Mainland China. The findings challenge the assumption of English as the sole language used in EMI programs offered by international universities. As the participants reported, due to the varying language abilities of students, local languages in EMI classrooms are regarded as a key resource to facilitate content learning and classroom interaction. Therefore, Zhang and Zheng contend that it is important to recognize the multilingual needs of international students attending EMI programs or courses.

Chapter 4, **Language Selection and Assessment in Brunei Darussalam** by Gardiner and Deterding, reported an investigation into language selection and assessment in Brunei Darussalam. Gardiner and Deterding discuss some language policies enacted in Brunei Darussalam. They also show NS models of English usage as a popular discourse. By showing conversational data concerning misunderstandings of international communication, Gardiner and Deterding maintain that 'native-like patterns of pronunciation and lexical choices do not always ensure mutual intelligibility'. Hence, they emphasize that NS norms of pronunciation and lexis may not act as the only yardstick for assessment, and that ELF-based pedagogy should be promoted in the classroom. They lament, however, that ELF-based pedagogy is not widely accepted, and a native speakerism-oriented assessment model may continue to be dominant in English language assessment for some time.

The next chapter by Brown draws upon the issue of GE and international standardized tests. In Chapter 5, **Global Englishes and the International Standardized English Language Proficiency Tests**, Brown examines international standardized English language proficiency tests (ISELPT) such as TOEFL iBT, TOEIC and IELTS and their relationship with GE. Brown discusses five key questions: (1) What is English language proficiency (ELP) really? (2) Why is the so-called native-speaker standard a thing of the past? (3) What alternative models are there to the NS model for ELP? (4) Why is changing the ISELPT so difficult/slow? and (5) What strategies might prove useful for effecting change in the ISELPT? Brown suggests some alternative approaches to defining the ELP with strategies that EFL/ESL teachers can apply as key tools to revisit the LSELPT.

Canilao, in Chapter 6, **Looking through the Eyes of Global Englishes: Enhancing English Language Teaching in Multicultural Classrooms**, documented 10 PhD students' experiences of adopting GE in their language classrooms situated in the Philippines. Canilao shared her own experiences of her English learning journey in which Standard English (SE) was to be followed. In her autoethnography at the beginning of the chapter,

Canilao indicated that SE was her passport to academic success; however, she missed the wealth of her own mother tongue and local culture. The conflict between the use of SE and that of the forbidden use of mother tongue in class/school is 'an issue that teachers in multicultural teaching contexts need to confront seriously'. With this in mind, Canilao started to adopt the theories of WE and ELF. She also employed translanguaging and translingual practices in applied linguistics and incorporated the theories into her own ELT classes. In her study with these students, Canilao used a qualitative focus group interview with her own PhD students whose professional backgrounds were as teachers. She found a gap between Englishes and the rejection of regional accents. In reality, teachers were reluctant to incorporate GE principles into their classrooms, but they promoted SE solely because GE in their lessons might be seen as 'unacceptable' or might even cause harm to their positions (as English language teachers). As Canilao argued, this phenomenon reflects the issue of unequal Englishes (Tupas, 2015). She therefore calls for the importance of incorporating GE principles into language materials development and language pedagogies so as to raise students' awareness of GE.

In the Hong Kong context, in Chapter 7, **Contextualizing Teaching English as a Local/Global Language: A Bottom-up Sociolinguistic Investigation**, Chan addresses the possibility of a bottom-up approach to understanding local language needs and to formulating ELT goals. In his mixed-methods study, Chan explores three main issues in this chapter: (1) the use of spoken English in Hong Kong's sociolinguistic environment; (2) major stakeholders' attitudes towards English varieties and English learning; and (3) current practices in English language education. He found a mismatch between real-life language needs and current English language education. Therefore, he suggested the inclusion of local pronunciation features to better understand which features could enhance or impede intelligibility. The findings of Chan's study also showed that the overemphasis of the NS pronunciation model might not help learners when dealing with international communication. In this respect, learners will not benefit from non-authentic ELT activities for their future use of English. By focusing solely on the NS standard, students will not learn to cope with real-life challenges when using English with speakers who are mainly from different linguistic backgrounds. In sum, Chan maintains that language curricula and assessment should be oriented towards communicative proficiency in international English use rather than native correctness.

The next three chapters address three case studies: a WE-informed curriculum, teacher education, and practices of teaching Englishes. In Chapter 8, **From Learners to Users: Reframing a Japanese University Curriculum towards a 'World Englishes Enterprise'-Informed English as a Medium of Instruction Model**, D'Angelo introduces the background and contribution of WE research and discusses a program offered by the Department of World Englishes at Chukyo University in Nagoya, Japan.

With a detailed explanation of how the program runs and how students can benefit from the EMI program to prepare students to be effective ELF users, D'Angelo provides practical recommendations for curricular reforms in Japan for higher level students to develop their awareness of ELF and to become ELF users. The chapter concludes that traditional EFL approaches to ELT are outdated. D'Angelo also sums up the chapter by signaling the future of GE in language education.

The discussion of GE cannot be separated from teacher education and assessment in general. In Chapter 9, **Talking the Talk but Not Walking the Walk? Preparing Teachers for Global Englishes Pedagogy**, Selvi reviews some proposals for a GE-oriented teaching model in ELT practices. He stresses the importance of teacher education to equip English language teachers with an understanding of ELF-informed or ELF-aware language teaching. Selvi then chronicles teacher education programs in Turkey and Northern Cyprus. He reports that the majority of such programs did not have courses to provide student teachers with knowledge and understanding of GE principles. Drawing on a bottom-up observation, Selvi recognizes the gap between teacher education and GE pedagogy. For this reason, a more GE-oriented teacher education needs to be promoted. Based on the results of a national survey of teacher educators in the contexts of Turkey and Northern Cyprus, Selvi found that many teacher educators were aware of the GE pedagogy, while some teacher educators had already integrated GE into their teacher training programs. Selvi maintains that there should be GE-informed teacher education to align second language teacher education practices with the present-day sociolinguistic realities of the glocalized world.

In a similar vein, Xu showcases a study of the **Practices of Teaching Englishes: Pedagogical Reflections and Implications** in Chapter 10. He draws data from discussion forums, portfolios of lesson observations and teaching practices by the students of a postgraduate unit related to the curriculum, pedagogy and assessment from the WE perspective in an Australian university. In this chapter, Xu highlights the introduction and theoretical input of WE, a lesson observation practicum and a mini-lesson teaching practicum. In this unit, forums and portfolio-based reflections were adopted as part of assessment. Drawing on the data taken from the discussion forums and both domestic and international students' portfolios, Xu indicates a paradigm shift of teaching English for intercultural communication in multilingual and multicultural contexts. As reported in this chapter, the unit showcases the current theory of GE applicable to ELT practices. Xu emphasizes a need for revisiting and reconceptualizing the ELT curriculum, pedagogy and assessment to align with the paradigm shift from English to Englishes with a focus on teaching English as a glocal (global and local) language.

Chapter 11 pertains to the local variety of English in the Chinese context, GE and teacher education, and the reconceptualization of assessment from a GE perspective. In Chapter 11, **Reform and Opportunities: China English in Chinese Higher Education,** Chen and Zhang give a historical review of the development of English education in China with a conceptualization of China English as an emergent variety of English. They chronicle some linguistic features in China English, but they admit that the recognition of China English is still debatable. Chen and Zhang discuss the possibility of integrating China English into English education from three educational aspects: English curriculum, pedagogy and assessment. They also point out the necessity of codifying features of China English, and indicate that the integration of China English will promote ELT in a more effective and culturally meaningful way.

In sum, all the chapters in this volume stress the importance of incorporating GE into today's ELT world. From a critical perspective, GE scholars have pointed out the gap between language policy, curriculum, pedagogy and assessment in ELT classrooms, and the real-life language use from a sociolinguistic perspective. From a more optimistic standpoint, some chapters provide evidence regarding the successful application of GE-oriented curriculum and pedagogy in different contexts. With all the chapters in mind, readers will hopefully understand the twist and turn of GE in relation to language policy, curriculum, pedagogy and assessment.

In the last chapter, we address the importance of researching language policy, curriculum, pedagogy and assessment in the context of the GE paradigm. In the transition era of TESOL, we call for a need to incorporate GE into today's ELT, and bottom-up language policies to support GE-oriented English language education in multilingual contexts where English remains sociopolitically viewed as a foreign language. We also recognize the limited proposals that address GE-informed assessment and challenge the native speakerism-oriented international standard tests (see Jenkins & Leung, 2019; McNamara, 2012). We do, however, argue for the need to translate the concept of GE into assessment when certain language policies and curricula recognize GE (see Fang & Ren, 2018; Galloway & Rose, 2018; Sung, 2018), although this may still be a long way off. We are positive about this vision, given that the issue has been tackled by more researchers and practitioners, as reported in this volume.

Summing Up

This volume deals with various topics of GE from the critical perspective. As editors, we did not ask the contributors to strictly follow native norms in their writing; neither did we ask them to have their chapters proofread by native speakers before submission. Instead, in all the editing procedure, we strive to maintain intelligibility in this volume for a wider range of international readers. All the original local features of writing (if any) are all maintained in all the chapters. We believe that this is a good gesture of recognizing the identity of all the chapters to echo the theme of this volume: 'critical perspectives of Global Englishes'.

As language researchers and practitioners ourselves, we fully understand the fluidity and diversity of English as a global language being used in various contexts and we hope that people who are involved in language education will view the use of English in both educational and non-educational contexts from a critical perspective. The issues regarding the complexity of language ideologies, methodological debates and means of assessment are all prevalent in today's English language education. It is therefore important to cast a critical eye on the English language (Kubota, 2016, this volume; Kumaravadivelu, 2016). On the one hand, English does facilitate our communication and assist people in many fields. On the other hand, the dominance of English has led to some issues such as the privilege and marginalization of English and local languages (Yazan & Rudolph, 2018). Against the backdrop of globalization, it is hoped that people will understand various language ideologies in relation to English as a global language, and also take a critical stance when viewing language policy, curriculum, pedagogy and assessment related to the English language in the 21st century.

To sum up, the English language entails various ideologies and people's attitudes towards the use of the language in different sociopolitical landscapes. This volume addresses issues of language policy, curriculum, pedagogy and assessment related to the ideologies, attitudes and identities situated in English language education. It is important to note that this volume only represents a number of Asian contexts, although many findings and discussions can resonate in other similar contexts. But, with all the contributions of this volume, it will serve as a useful reference for policy-makers, researchers and practitioners, as well as students of English. It provides them with a critical perspective from which to interrogate English as a global language in today's globalized world. From here, we would like to encourage people to explore the use of English in different contexts from a sociocultural and sociopolitical stance. We hope that this volume will provide another venue for people who study and research the English language, in particular Global Englishes, to have further food for thought.

References

Fang, F. (2018) Ideology and identity debate of English in China: Past, present and future. *Asian Englishes* 20 (1), 15–26.
Fang, F. and Ren, W. (2018) Developing students' awareness of Global Englishes. *ELT Journal* 72 (4), 384–394.
Galloway, N. and Rose, H. (2018) Incorporating Global Englishes into the ELT classroom. *ELT Journal* 72 (1), 3–14.
Holliday, A. (2006) Native-speakerism. *ELT Journal* 60 (4), 385–387.
Jenkins, J. (2015) Repositioning English and multilingualism in English as a lingua franca. *Englishes in Practice* 2 (3), 49–85.

Jenkins, J. and Leung, C. (2019) From mythical 'standard' to standard reality: The need for alternatives to standardized English language tests. *Language Teaching* 52 (1), 86–110.

Kubota, R. (2016) The multi/plural turn, postcolonial theory, and neoliberal multiculturalism: Complicities and implications for applied linguistics. *Applied Linguistics* 37 (4), 474–494.

Kumaravadivelu, B. (2016) The decolonial option in English teaching: Can the subaltern act? *TESOL Quarterly* 50 (1), 66–85.

Matsuda, A. (ed.) (2012) *Principles and Practices of Teaching English as an International Language*. Bristol: Multilingual Matters.

Matsuda, A. (ed.) (2016) *Preparing Teachers to Teach English as an International Language*. Bristol: Multilingual Matters.

McKay, S.L. (2012) Teaching materials for English as an international language. In A. Matsuda (ed.) *Principles and Practices of Teaching English as an International Language* (pp. 70–83). Bristol: Multilingual Matters.

McNamara, T. (2012) English as a lingua franca: The challenge for language testing. *Journal of English as a Lingua Franca* 1 (1), 199–202.

Rose, H. and Montakantiwong, A. (2018) A tale of two teachers: A duoethnography of the realistic and idealistic successes and failures of teaching English as an international language. *RELC Journal* 49 (1), 88–101.

Seidlhofer, B. (2011) *Understanding English as a Lingua Franca*. Oxford: Oxford University Press.

Sung, C.C.M. (2018) Out-of-class communication and awareness of English as a lingua franca. *ELT Journal* 72 (1), 15–25.

Tupas, R. (ed.) (2015) *Unequal Englishes: The Politics of Englishes Today*. Basingstoke: Palgrave Macmillan.

Wei, R. and Su, J. (2015) Surveying the English language across China. *World Englishes* 34 (2), 175–189.

Widdowson, H. (1994) The ownership of English. *TESOL Quarterly* 28, 377–389.

Widodo, H.P. (2016) Language policy in practice: Reframing the English language curriculum in the Indonesian secondary education sector. In R. Kirkpatrick (ed.) *English Education Policy in Asia* (pp. 127–151). New York: Springer.

Widodo, H.P., Wood, A. and Gupta, D. (eds) (2017) *Asian English Language Classrooms: Where Theory and Practice Meet*. New York: Routledge.

Yazan, B. and Rudolph, N. (eds) (2018) *Criticality, Teacher Identity, and (In)equity in English Language Teaching: Issues and Implications*. Dordrecht: Springer.

2 A Critical Examination of Common Beliefs about Language Teaching: From Research Insights to Professional Engagement[1]

Ryuko Kubota

Language education is situated in a political and ideological space, in which certain beliefs about language, language speakers, cultures and language teaching and learning are produced and reproduced. These beliefs constitute language ideology. The ideological and political facets of English language teaching have been scrutinized and debated in our field for almost 30 years. However, little has changed towards a more just and equitable direction in policies and practices reflected in language curricula, instruction, materials and teacher education. Focusing on 10 common beliefs related to language teaching and learning, I will review insights generated by previous research and discuss how we can think differently and critically for change. Specifically, I will focus on language ideology constituted by beliefs about: (1) legitimate varieties of English, (2) native speakerness, (3) whiteness, (4) Euro- and US-centrism, (5) cultural essentialism, (6) English as an international language, (7) English competence for economic success, (8) early learning of English, (9) the monolingual approach to pedagogy, and (10) the ideal learner and learning. Questioning language ideology requires a worldview that is anti-racist, anti-essentialist, anti-Eurocentric and anti-reductionist as well as a perspective that affirms multiplicity, fluidity and intellectual ways of understanding. These critical views are developed through constantly questioning assumptions, reflecting on one's own biases, and making informed judgments.

Introduction

In the last several decades, the field of teaching English as a foreign language (TEFL) has witnessed changes in pedagogical beliefs and practices. A previous belief about language pedagogy influenced by behaviorism, for instance, has been replaced by communicative language teaching with a focus on negotiation of meaning. Beliefs about legitimate varieties of English and English speakers are slowly changing as the field has begun to question linguistic normativism. At the same time, other beliefs about language teaching and learning have emerged or become stronger. For instance, increased economic globalization has strengthened the notion of English as a global language and as a promise of economic prosperity, creating a greater urgency to develop competence in English. This has compelled many governments, institutions and individuals to increase opportunities for English language learning. These conditions and beliefs shape instructional practices and language education policies. Just as some ideologies in our society tend to persist, language ideologies – beliefs about language and language education – continue to influence TEFL. Although not all beliefs about language are harmful, some beliefs, such as the superiority of native speakers, standardized language and whiteness, need to be scrutinized, since they perpetuate unequal relations of power among diverse users of English.

Language education, which aims to foster competent global citizens, can contribute to achieving greater equality and justice in our society. In order to encourage learners of English to develop the skills, awareness and attitudes necessary to become global citizens, teachers should critically examine existing beliefs about English, English speakers and English language learning, and understand their ideological nature.

Focusing on 10 common beliefs about language teaching and learning, this chapter will discuss how these beliefs can be debunked and how alternative knowledge can inform educational practices. Critical examinations of these beliefs will invite teachers to affirm diversity, recognize the contextual nature of language teaching and learning, and seek greater equity and justice. Due to this pedagogical concern as the main impetus of this chapter, the purpose of this chapter is more about raising awareness among language professionals than making a scholarly contribution.

Ten Beliefs about Language Teaching and Learning

In TEFL, the following 10 topics reflect major beliefs that influence educational practices: (1) legitimate varieties of English, (2) native speakerness, (3) whiteness, (4) Euro- and US-centrism, (5) cultural essentialism, (6) English as an international language, (7) English competence for economic success, (8) early learning of English, (9) the monolingual approach to pedagogy, and (10) the ideal learner and learning. Common beliefs about these topics have been problematized in recent scholarly discussions. As will become evident in the following discussion, these topics and issues are complex, contextual and interrelated, indicating the need for language teachers to be always vigilant about the ideological nature of any perspective – even a tentative solution of a problem.

(1) Legitimate varieties of English

In TEFL as well as in everyday situations, people typically believe that standardized English is the most acceptable variety for oral and written use. Using the term *myths* in discussing language ideologies of English, Watts (2011) refers to this belief as the *legitimate language myth*. This belief has influenced language pedagogy as reflected in teaching materials (e.g. textbooks, audio-recordings) and assessment.

However, the *legitimate language myth* has been challenged by research on World Englishes (WE). Questioning the superior status of standardized English used in inner circle countries (i.e. the USA, the UK, Canada, Australia and New Zealand), scholars have shed light on other varieties of English (Bolton & Kachru, 2006; Kachru & Smith, 2008; Kachru et al., 2009; Kirkpatrick, 2007). Research on WE regards Englishes used in outer circle countries (former British and American colonies) and expanding circle countries (those where English is mainly taught as a foreign language) as a legitimate means of communication. EFL learners, who will be interacting with users of English from various parts of the world, must affirm linguistic diversity.

Paralleling WE's attention to linguistic diversity, research on English as a lingua franca (ELF) has examined the linguistic and pragmatic features of English used by people from diverse linguistic backgrounds (Jenkins, 2014; Seidlhofer, 2011). Initially focusing on communication exclusively between non-native users of English but later including native speakers of English, ELF scholars have been investigating how these users negotiate meaning and what linguistic forms are essential for such negotiation. The research offers several pedagogical implications. First, strict adherence to the inner circle norm is unnecessary in communicating in ELF. Secondly, effective communication is enabled not so much by linguistic accuracy as it is by intelligibility, which is supported by communicative strategies. Thirdly, learners of English should be provided with opportunities to practice interacting with diverse speakers of ELF. ELF invites teachers and administrators to reconsider their instructional and curricular foci.

Although WE and ELF offer alternative views, the conventional idea about legitimate varieties of English persists due to constraints imposed by language assessment, fixed conventions for formal writing, and media influence. First, as Brown (2014) summarizes, incorporating WE, for instance, in large-scale tests will pose a challenge of establishing construct validity and fairness. In other words, if a particular variety of English is to be used in a test, a thorough description of the variety needs to exist, and all test takers should be familiar with that variety. Even for locally developed achievement tests, all stakeholders, including parents, would need to buy into the underlying concept of WE.

Secondly, similar to the issue of language assessment, learners' writing performance is usually judged against established expectations, especially for high-stakes academic writing (Heng Hartse & Kubota, 2014). To transgress such fixed conventions and express oneself more creatively and flexibly, translingual practices using multilingual repertoires have been advocated (Canagarajah, 2013; Horner *et al.*, 2011). However, such translingual approaches tend to sidetrack real-world demands imposed by institutional expectations (Heng Hartse & Kubota, 2014). In general, currently popular pluralistic approaches (e.g. multilingualism, plurilingualism, translingualism) are conceptually parallel to the multiplicity and flexibility valorized by neoliberalism, which supports free market economy on the one hand and widens economic and educational gaps on the other (Flores, 2013; Kubota, 2016). It is necessary to understand this ideological tension and contradiction between fixed conventions and pluralistic approaches.

Thirdly, the media also perpetuate linguistic norms. Despite vast linguistic diversity, news anchors on TV tend to speak in a standardized variety of English rather than a locally dominant variety. This further reinforces the idea of legitimate English.

These realities indicate that transforming the *legitimate English myth* is not simply a matter of changing classroom practices; rather, it involves a transformation of beliefs and institutional practices in the broader society.

(2) Native speakerness

The belief about legitimate varieties of English is closely associated with the legitimacy attached to the native speaker of English. Native speakers are often viewed as ideal teachers equipped with complete knowledge and skills of the language to provide best instructions. Phillipson (1992) calls this belief the *native speaker fallacy* and Holliday (2006, 2008) calls it *native speakerism*. The persistence of this ideology is reflected in the continued preference for native English speaking teachers for employment.

However, many scholars have challenged this assumption since the 1990s, as seen in the growing popularity of research on issues of non-native English speaking teachers (NNESTs) (e.g. Braine, 1999, 2010; Kamhi-Stein, 2004; Mahboob, 2010). Research on NNESTs has illuminated the positive traits of NNESTs, including being able to serve as a good second language (L2) user model, providing learners with effective instruction on grammar and learning strategies and empathizing with them (Moussu & Llurda, 2008). The advocacy role of the NNESTs movement is represented in TESOL's 2006 'Position statement against discrimination of nonnative speakers of English in the field of TESOL'.[2]

Despite active scholarly discussions on NNESTs, the status of NNESTs in educational institutions has not drastically improved. Kumaravadivelu (2016) argues that the problem is partly due to NNESTs' complicity with the West-based knowledge system. Specifically, NNESTs and researchers tend to support the existing West-based framework for pedagogy and research, rather than fundamentally challenging the status quo. To break the dependency on the center-based framework of knowing and doing, Kumaravadivelu (2016: 81) urges non-native teachers and scholars to engage in 'result-oriented strategic action' to transform the existing colonial relations of power.

Another issue to consider in understanding non-native speakerness is diversity within the category. NNESTs do not form a homogeneous group; rather, they come from diverse backgrounds with regard to gender, race, nationality, age and sexual identity, all of which impact individual teachers' experiences. Indeed, non-native speakerness should not be essentialized; it should be viewed not as an objective and essentialist category but as a fluid, hybrid and yet contentious identity (Faez, 2011; Park, 2012; Yazen & Rudolph, 2018). Of the social categories mentioned above, race is closely linked to the belief about native speakers and legitimate speakers of English. Issues of race will be discussed below.

(3) Whiteness

There is an implicit assumption in TEFL that equates *native speakers* and *standardized English speakers* with *white people* (Kubota & Lin, 2009). This ideological formula tends to position non-white teachers of English – native or non-native – as inferior. For instance, native English speaking American teachers of Japanese descent working in Japan have experienced alienation, marginalization and discrimination (Kubota & Fujimoto, 2013). According to an experimental study on the effects of teacher attributes on Japanese university students' preferences for English language teachers (Rivers & Ross, 2013), the white race was significantly preferred.

Similar to the first two beliefs discussed thus far, the ideology that assigns superiority to whiteness is deeply ingrained in everyday life, yet it is rarely noticed or discussed. For example, we typically do not notice the predominance of the images of white teachers in English language textbooks or advertisements for English language institutes (see Takahashi, 2013; Yamada, 2015). This type of racial bias reflects *institutional racism*, as opposed to *individual racism* experienced by individuals.

Individual racism constitutes a large part of *racial micro-aggressions*, defined as 'brief and commonplace daily verbal, behavioral, and environmental indignities, whether intentional or unintentional, that communicate hostile, derogatory, or negative racial slights and insults to the target person or group' (Sue *et al.*, 2007: 273). For example, an Asian female native English speaking teacher working at a private language institute in Canada may frequently be asked, 'Where are you *really* from?', be mistaken for a student, or have her photo placed on the student photo page rather than on the instructor page (Lee & Simon-Maeda, 2006). Such racial micro-aggressions as a covert form of individual racism are as damaging and injurious as overt racism.

Another category of racism is *epistemological racism* (Scheurich, 1997). Epistemological racism is seen in superior values assigned to a certain racial group in our knowledge system. For example, in Western societies, white European cultural perspectives tend to predominate in school curricula and textbooks over non-white histories or ways of knowing. This leads to the next topic.

(4) Euro- and US-centrism

White-dominant epistemological racism parallels the Euro- and US-centric beliefs observed in TEFL. Related to the previous three topics, Euro- and US-centrism is manifested in the predominance of Western culture in the curricular content and programmatic foci. The belief that the legitimate English is British or American standardized English and that the legitimate English language teacher is a white native speaker of English privileges Western culture.

We can see how this belief is reflected in EFL textbooks by analyzing whose culture (e.g. European, American, Asian, African, Indigenous) is represented in the lesson topics and illustrations of human characters (Yamada, 2015). It is also reflected in the destinations of study abroad. Inner circle countries are predominantly chosen as locations for intensive language study. Some students certainly seek unique opportunities to learn English in outer circle countries such as Singapore and the Philippines. However, a study by Kobayashi (2011) revealed that Japanese student sojourners in Singapore still preferred white native speakers and standardized English.

Euro- and US-centric beliefs are also reflected in broader political interests, as seen in overseas professional development programs for English language teachers sponsored by central or local governments in Japan. One program implemented from 2011 to 2013 was called 'Japan-U.S. Training and Exchange Program for English Language Teachers (JUSTE)'.[3] The aim was for the participating teachers to understand the United States better through person-to-person exchange and homestay. Although engaging in professional development in the United States does not necessarily reinforce Euro- and US-centric ideas, the location is likely to impact participants' worldview (Kubota, 2018).

Euro- and US-centrism in TEFL also diverts teachers' and students' attention away from diversity and socio-economic disparity within a country or region where English is predominantly used. Euro- and US-centric knowledge associated with the superiority of white native speakers of standardized English evokes the economic wealth attached to certain types of English and English speakers. In fact, ideas about English and socio-economic conditions are interrelated. For instance, educated English speakers in outer circle countries typically manipulate an inner circle variety of English, and they are economic elites who embrace a Euro- or US-centric worldview. This is contrasted with undereducated users of English in the same country (see Tupas, 2004, for the case of the Philippines). Critical teachers must recognize political, economic, linguistic and cultural relations of power that produce and legitimate unequal Englishes and unequal human relations (Tupas, 2015).

(5) Cultural essentialism

Culture has multiple dimensions and manifestations, reflecting and producing certain beliefs in TEFL. One challenge for teachers is how to conceptualize culture. A common belief is that each culture – often understood as a national or ethnic culture – is distinct with a unique history and characteristics, and thus homogeneous and resistant to change. However, postmodern and postcolonial conceptualizations of culture underscore its diverse, dynamic and hybrid nature (Kubota, 2014). For example, great cultural diversity exists within a nation in terms of geographical, ethnic, linguistic, socio-economic and generational differences, among others. Furthermore, cultural traditions that are commonly regarded as century old are often recent inventions (Hobsbawm, 1983).

Nonetheless, the fixed, static and homogeneous understanding of culture persists. This is partly due to the political nature of culture. In discussing the historical processes of establishing modern nation states, Anderson (1983) introduced the notion of *imagined communities* to explain the forces of nationalism (e.g. standardization of the national language), through which a sense of a shared community was established for people who previously belonged to culturally and linguistically diverse communities. It is necessary for teachers to critically examine the political and ideological meanings behind taken-for-granted representations of a certain culture.

One topic often discussed in TEFL is cultural difference in writing practices. It is commonly believed that writers of English generally state the main idea at the beginning and organize the subsequent supporting arguments in a logical and clear manner. Students are frequently told that writing in their native language is the opposite of this deductive style of English texts and that the reason their L2 texts written in English often sound awkward is because they apply their first language (L1) conventions to L2 writing. This understanding used to correspond to the findings of contrastive rhetoric (CR) research. However, many studies have critiqued this conceptual framework of CR (Atkinson, 2012; Kubota, 2010). Specifically, research indicates that the perceived quality of L2 texts is affected by students' L1 writing expertise, L2 proficiency and writer identity. Cultural differences in textual features are also difficult to establish. Furthermore, conventions for certain genres (e.g. academic, journalistic) are being merged across cultures due to global influences. Critics also argue that the previous CR framework ideologically parallels the colonial dichotomy of cultural images between the colonizer and the colonized (Kubota & Lehner, 2004).

It is necessary for teachers and learners to approach cultural difference critically so that they will not fall easily into cultural essentialism, which can lead to cultural stereotyping and racial micro-aggressions. However, not all discourses on cultural uniqueness and homogeneity are problematic. To treat culture as a stable and bounded category can help marginalized groups preserve their cultures. Such strategic essentialism can support counter-hegemonic resistance. It is thus important to recognize the situated meanings of culture.

(6) English as an international language

In many parts of the world, learning English is increasingly stressed in formal and non-formal education. This trend stems from the belief that English functions everywhere in the world as a universal language for international communication. Together with the next belief on the perceived economic benefit of English competence, the belief about English as an international lingua franca has become a strong motivation to develop English language skills as an integral part of neoliberal *human capital* (Block *et al.*, 2012; Flores, 2013; Kubota, 2011a). The concept of *human capital* is defined as people's knowledge and ability required for success in the new economy (Keeley, 2007). Enhancing students' skills in English through quality instruction and assessment has indeed become an educational priority for many governments and educational institutions.

English is no doubt useful. According to Graddol (2006), one-fourth of the world population are English speakers. However, this also means that three-quarters of the world population are not English speakers. Even within inner circle countries, the language used in workplaces is not necessarily English (Block, 2007; Duff *et al.*, 2000; Kramsch & Whiteside, 2007, 2008). In expanding circle countries, multiple languages are used for intercultural communication. For instance, in a qualitative study on Japanese transnational corporate workers' communication in workplaces abroad (Kubota, 2013, 2015), the language they reported to have used in China, Thailand and South Korea was not always English. Interviews revealed that the Japanese workers' linguistic choice was influenced by various factors, including the work type, the availability of local workers with Japanese proficiency, the linguistic distance between the local language and Japanese, and individual differences. These workers also underscored the *ability to communicate* rather than linguistic skills per se. They placed importance on non-linguistic dimensions, such as communicative strategies, willingness to communicate, mutual accommodation and communicative dispositions (e.g. respect for difference; non-discriminatory attitudes; cultural, political and historical knowledge).

Both the myth of the absolute universality of English and the significance of non-linguistic competence for cross-cultural communication provide several pedagogical implications. First, teachers and learners of English need to acknowledge multilingualism in society and become willing to learn and use languages other than English. Secondly, learners should be encouraged to develop plurilingual competence or the ability to mobilize their available multiple linguistic and non-linguistic resources as repertories in order to accomplish communicative tasks. This departs from a previous understanding of language use, which presumes complete knowledge of a language system that is distinct from another language (Marshall & Moore, 2013). Thirdly, more pedagogical attention should be paid to the strategic and dispositional aspects of communication, including a variety of communicative strategies, willingness to communicate, affirmation of all kinds of diversity and support for social justice.

(7) English competence for economic success

It is believed that acquiring English language proficiency is essential for individual and national economic success. This belief, which is referred to as the *economic benefit myth* (Watts, 2011), has become a strong justification for promoting English language teaching and learning (Kubota, 2011a; Park, 2011). Yet, this myth can be scrutinized by examining empirical research and socio-economic issues.

According to a synthesis of empirical studies in Québec and Switzerland on the effects of language proficiency on individual incomes (Grin *et al.*, 2010), individuals' language proficiency generally correlated with higher earnings, even when the level of education and experience was statistically controlled. Yet, the data indicated that the economic value attached to a particular language varied according to geographical regions and types of industrial sectors. Conversely, an analysis of Japanese public survey data demonstrated no statistically significant correlation between self-reported English language skills and income, when taking into account the actual need to use English for work (Terasawa, 2015). Due to a large number of variables and contextual issues under consideration, it seems difficult to come to a universal conclusion regarding the individual economic benefit of English language skills.

The very fact that the statistical analysis described in Grin *et al.* (2010) had to control the level of education in order to see the correlation between language skills and income indicates that those who have a higher level of education are more likely to be proficient in an additional language and have better paying jobs. This raises the question of who has access to education (Lorente & Tupas, 2013). The promotion of TEFL driven by the *economic benefit myth* is predicated on neoliberal ideology, as seen in increased competition and reduced social safety nets which have created larger economic gaps almost everywhere in the world. English language teachers must recognize how TEFL, which is purported to bring people from diverse linguistic backgrounds together, may actually be separating people along socio-economic lines, generating the English divide (Terasawa, 2017).

(8) Early learning of English

The neoliberal impetus for English language learning is linked to the *more and earlier* premise, reflecting the belief that English opens doors to future opportunities, as discussed above (Sayer, 2015). Phillipson (1992) calls this premise the *early-start fallacy*. Indeed, people tend to believe that the earlier children start learning a language, the better results they obtain. This belief partly stems from the critical period hypothesis, which posits that people lose their natural ability to acquire native-like proficiency after puberty. However, second language acquisition (SLA) research has shown that, in naturalistic settings such as immigrants' SLA, older children or adolescents are more efficient learners than younger children due to their cognitive maturity. Today, scholars generally support the tenet, *the older the faster, the younger the better*, or the difference between *rate of acquisition* versus *ultimate attainment* (see Muñoz, 2008, 2014).

In contrast, research focused on *foreign language* instructional settings has yielded slightly different results. While older learners still outperform younger learners with regard to the rate of learning, younger starters' advantage for ultimate attainment has not been found; instead, older starters generally outperform younger starters given the same number of instructional hours in schools over the years (García Mayo & García Lecumberri, 2003; Muñoz, 2006; Pfenninger & Singleton, 2017). According to Muñoz (2011, 2014), what matters is not so much the starting age as the cumulative amount of exposure (e.g. watching films and TV, writing emails, extensive reading) and the quality of input (e.g. studying abroad and interacting with speakers of the target language).

The research indicates that lowering the starting age of foreign language learning does not necessarily yield higher attainment; rather, providing a large amount of quality input leads to the development of proficiency. This means that the validity of the current language education policy, which promotes early learning of English for only a couple of hours per week in the classroom, is questionable if the purpose is to enhance language proficiency. Although teachers may not be able to change the policy, they can inform parents by sharing scholarly knowledge to adjust their expectations for their children.

(9) The monolingual approach to pedagogy

The *more and earlier* approach (Sayer, 2015) also relates to what Phillipson (1992) calls the *monolingual fallacy*, which posits that English is best taught solely in English. The assumption is that the goal of language learning is to be able to use the language like a monolingual native speaker and that the monolingual approach will boost exposure to and use of the target language. However, research in both second and foreign language contexts rejects this premise.

In L2 learning settings, the positive role of the L1 is empirically supported by the effectiveness of maintenance bilingual education (e.g. dual-language programs, in which immigrant students learn both the heritage language and the L2 to become bilingual and biliterate) compared to the monolingual teaching of the L2 (e.g. the ESL pullout program, which views students' L1 as a barrier in L2 learning) (Cummins, 2000, 2007; Genesee *et al.*, 2006; Thomas & Collier, 2002). The advantage of maintenance bilingual instruction is theoretically explained by the linguistic interdependence principle. Cummins (2000) explains that proficiencies in two or more languages are operated by a common underlying proficiency, rather than separate language-specific competencies that function in a zero-sum manner. This corroborates the concept of multicompetence – L2 users' knowledge of two or more languages in the same mind (Cook, 2005). According to this theory, maintaining and developing the L1 does not impede L2 learning but rather promotes it via crosslinguistic transfer. Pedagogically, Cummins (2007) supports the important role of the L1 in L2 learning even in immersion education, which has traditionally shunned translation and code-switching/mixing. Overall, scholars advocate replacing monolingual teaching with approaches that promote bi/multilingual practices, including code-switching, as seen in translanguaging (e.g. García & Li, 2014) and translingual approaches (e.g. Canagarajah, 2013; Horner *et al.*, 2011).[4]

In foreign language teaching, research has also raised skepticism about the effectiveness of monolingual teaching (Hall & Cook, 2012). It has been found that L1 use serves important pedagogical functions, including teaching grammar, classroom management and meeting the social and affective needs of learners (e.g. communicating empathy, reducing anxiety, respecting learner identity). The social and affective function is significant especially in contexts where English language learning is mandatory for all learners. Although the superior learning outcome of L1 use over monolingual approaches still needs to be substantiated, Lee and Macaro (2013) found that L1 use was more effective than a monolingual approach in vocabulary learning among young and older Korean learners, with a greater benefit found in the younger group. Zhao and Macaro (2014) found a similar result among Chinese adult learners of English. However, further empirical evidence needs to be sought beyond vocabulary learning.

With regard to implications for pedagogy, scholars propose several strategies, such as the judicious and purposeful use of the L1 (Butzkamm & Caldwell, 2009), using translation for developing language awareness and responding to learner needs (Cook, 2010; Witte et al., 2009) and fostering multilingual awareness beyond L1/L2 use (Levine, 2013).

(10) The ideal learner and learning

Many language teachers teach in schools, universities or private language institutes. A common image or schema of foreign language learning in the classroom includes physical objects such as textbooks, dictionaries and worksheets, and activities such as memorization, pair/group practice and language tests. In these contexts, ideal learners are seen to have integrative motivation and, under neoliberal ideology, invest in learning in order to gain cultural capital, which is convertible into economic capital (e.g. higher earnings) or social capital (e.g. higher social status).

However, many alternative learning opportunities and purposes exist both inside and outside of the classroom. For instance, adults of all ages learn English and other languages at community centers or in private spaces (Kubota, 2011b; Kubota & McKay, 2009). These learners do not necessarily wish to obtain cultural capital through language learning, but rather they often learn a language as a leisure activity or hobby (Kubota, 2011b). Furthermore, learning a language with peers frequently becomes a social activity for enjoyment to consume. Learning in these instances can be more aptly described by *consumption* of pleasure generated by socializing and escaping everyday routine. Although learning English in this way often reinforces the superiority of whiteness (Appleby, 2013; Kubota, 2011b; Takahashi, 2013), diverse meanings and desires attached to learning a foreign language need to be recognized (Motha & Lin, 2013).

Learning for consumption of pleasure also implies that learners in traditional classrooms are likely to have diverse desires. For instance, a survey with students learning Japanese as a foreign language in Australian universities revealed that many of them began enrolling in a Japanese language course because they were drawn by J-pop culture (e.g. anime, manga, music). This sometimes created a gap between the students' interest and traditional curriculum and instruction (Northwood & Thomson, 2012). Another example is an anecdote told by a friend of mine, who was teaching students with special needs at a Japanese junior high school. One girl with Asperger syndrome was an avid learner of English grammar. In fact, her favorite subject was English. However, her disability caused panic reactions when she encountered irregular English structures, and her teacher struggled to deal with the tension between her desire to learn English and ideal learning strategies.

It is often challenging for teachers to fill a gap between learner desires and curriculum mandates. However, recognizing multiple desires and simultaneously negotiating contextual demands will bring about well-being for the learners.

Conclusion

Multiple beliefs about TEFL are under scholarly scrutiny. Some of the beliefs are part of contested broader ideologies, while others are empirically unsupported by SLA research. The beliefs about legitimate varieties of English and native speakerness are rooted in language ideology mobilized to establish modern nation-states. The beliefs about Euro- and US-centrism, cultural essentialism and whiteness are related to the ideology of colonialism. The more recent ideology of neoliberalism reflects and constitutes beliefs about English as an international language, English competence for economic success, early learning of English and the monolingual approach to pedagogy. Beliefs about the early learning of English and the monolingual approach to pedagogy have been empirically challenged by SLA research. Furthermore, a critical examination of the belief about the ideal learner and learning encourages us to affirm learners' diverse desires and reconsider taken-for-granted approaches to teaching.

Multiple beliefs and assumptions held by teachers, learners, parents and institutions ultimately influence the ways our learners interact with people from diverse linguistic and cultural backgrounds. Critical appraisals of these beliefs will support an anti-racist, anti-essentialist, anti-Euro- and US-centric and anti-reductionist worldview. They will also foster attitudes to affirm diversity and value empirical knowledge. Teachers are encouraged to make informed judgments by constantly questioning assumptions, understanding contextual meanings and reflecting on their own biases.

Notes

(1) This is a revised version of the publication: Kubota, R. (2016) A critical examination of common beliefs about language teaching: From research insights to professional engagement. In Y.-N. Leung (ed.) *Epoch Making in English Language Teaching and Learning* (pp. 348–365). Taipei: English Teachers' Association-Republic of China (ETA-ROC).
(2) See http://www.tesol.org/docs/pdf/5889.pdf.
(3) See http://www.mext.go.jp/a_menu/kokusai/culcon/__icsFiles/afieldfile/2015/03/05/1355548_02.pdf and http://www.mext.go.jp/a_menu/shotou/haken/index.htm.
(4) It is necessary to recognize the complicity of translingual approaches with neoliberal ideology, as discussed earlier.

References

Anderson, B. (1983) *Imagined Communities: Reflections on the Origin and Spread of Nationalism*. London: Verso.

Appleby, R. (2013) Desire in translation: White masculinity and TESOL. *TESOL Quarterly* 47, 122–147.

Atkinson, D. (2012) Intercultural rhetoric and intercultural communication. In J. Jackson (ed.) *The Routledge Handbook of Language and Intercultural Communication* (pp. 116–129). London and New York: Routledge.

Block, D. (2007) Niche lingual francas: An ignored phenomenon. *TESOL Quarterly* 41, 561–566.

Block, D., Gray, J. and Holborow, M. (2012) *Neoliberalism and Applied Linguistics*. Abingdon: Routledge.

Bolton, K. and Kachru, B.B. (2006) *World Englishes: Critical Concepts in Linguistics*. London: Routledge.

Braine, G. (ed.) (1999) *Non-native Educators in English Language Teaching*. Mahwah, NJ: Lawrence Erlbaum.

Braine, G. (2010) *Nonnative Speaker English Teachers: Research, Pedagogy, and Professional Growth*. New York: Routledge.

Brown, J.D. (2014) The future of World Englishes in language testing. *Language Assessment Quarterly* 11, 5–26.

Butzkamm, W. and Caldwell, J. (2009) *The Bilingual Reform: A Paradigm Shift in Foreign Language Teaching*. Tübingen: Narr Studienbücher.

Canagarajah, S. (2013) *Translingual Practice: Global Englishes and Cosmopolitan Relations*. London: Routledge.

Cook, G. (2010) *Translation in Language Teaching: An Argument for Reassessment*. Oxford: Oxford University Press.

Cook, V. (2005) Basing teaching on the L2 user. In E. Llurda (ed.) *Non-native Language Teachers: Perceptions, Challenges and Contribution to the Profession* (pp. 47–61). New York: Springer.

Cummins, J. (2000) *Language, Power and Pedagogy: Bilingual Children in the Crossfire*. Clevedon: Multilingual Matters.

Cummins, J. (2007) Rethinking monolingual instructional strategies in multilingual classrooms. *Canadian Journal of Applied Linguistics* 10, 221–240.

Duff, P., Wong, P. and Early, M. (2000) Learning language for work and life: The linguistic socialization of immigrant Canadians seeking careers in health care. *Canadian Modern Language Review* 57, 9–57.

Faez, F. (2011) Reconceptualizing the native/nonnative speaker dichotomy. *Journal of Language, Identity & Education* 10, 231–249.

Flores, N. (2013) The unexamined relationship between neoliberalism and plurilingualism: A cautionary tale. *TESOL Quarterly* 47, 500–520.

García, O. and Li, W. (2014) *Translanguaging: Language, Bilingualism and Education*. New York: Palgrave Macmillan.

García Mayo, M. del P. and García Lecumberri, M.L. (eds) (2003) *Age and the Acquisition of English as a Foreign Language*. Clevedon: Multilingual Matters.

Genesee, F., Lindholm-Leary, K., Saunders, W. and Christian, D. (eds) (2006) *Educating English Language Learners: A Synthesis of Empirical Evidence*. New York: Cambridge University Press.

Graddol, D. (2006) *English Next: Why Global English May Mean the End of 'English as a Foreign Language'*. London: British Council.

Grin, F., Sfreddo, C. and Vaillancourt, F. (2010) *The Economics of the Multilingual Workplace*. New York: Routledge.

Hall, G. and Cook, G. (2012) Own-language use in language teaching and learning. *Language Teaching* 45, 271–308.

Heng Hartse, J. and Kubota, R. (2014) Pluralizing English? Variation in high-stakes academic writing. *Journal of Second Language Writing* 24, 71–82.
Hobsbawm, E.J. (1983) Introduction: Invention of tradition. In E.J. Hobsbawm and T. Ranger (eds) *The Invention of Tradition* (1–14). Cambridge: Cambridge University Press.
Holliday, A. (2006) Native-speakerism. *ELT Journal* 60, 385–387.
Holliday, A. (2008) Standards of English and politics of inclusion. *Language Teaching* 41, 119–130.
Horner, B., Lu, M., Royster, J. and Trimbur, J. (2011) Language difference in writing: Toward a translingual approach. *College English* 73, 303–321.
Jenkins, J. (2014) *English as a Lingua Franca in the International University: The Politics of Academic English Language Policy*. London: Routledge.
Kachru, B.B., Kachru, Y. and Nelson, C. (2009) *The Handbook of World Englishes*. Malden, MA: Wiley-Blackwell.
Kachru, Y. and Smith, L. (2008) *Cultures, Contexts and World Englishes*. New York: Routledge.
Kamhi-Stein, L. (ed.) (2004) *Learning and Teaching from Experience: Perspectives on Nonnative English-speaking Professionals*. Ann Arbor, MI: University of Michigan Press.
Keeley, B. (2007) *Human Capital: How What You Know Shapes Your Life*. Paris: OECD Publishing.
Kirkpatrick, A. (2007) *World Englishes: Implications for International Communication and English Language Teaching*. Cambridge: Cambridge University Press.
Kobayashi, Y. (2011) Expanding-circle students learning 'standard English' in the outer-circle Asia. *Journal of Multilingual and Multicultural Development* 32, 235–248.
Kramsch, C. and Whiteside, A. (2007) Three fundamental concepts in second language acquisition and their relevance in multilingual contexts. *The Modern Language Journal* 91, 907–922.
Kramsch, C. and Whiteside, A. (2008) Language ecology in multilingual settings. Towards a theory of symbolic competence. *Applied Linguistics* 29, 645–671.
Kubota, R. (2010) Cross-cultural perspectives on writing: Contrastive rhetoric. In N.H. Hornberger and S.L. McKay (eds) *Sociolinguistics and Language Education* (pp. 265–289). Bristol: Multilingual Matters.
Kubota, R. (2011a) Questioning linguistic instrumentalism: English, neoliberalism, and language tests in Japan. *Linguistics and Education* 22, 248–260.
Kubota, R. (2011b) Learning a foreign language as leisure and consumption: Enjoyment, desire, and the business of *eikaiwa*. *International Journal of Bilingual Education and Bilingualism* 14, 473–488.
Kubota, R. (2013) 'Language is only a tool': Japanese expatriates working in China and implications for language teaching. *Multilingual Education* 3 (4). doi:10.1186/2191-5059-3-4
Kubota, R. (2014) Standardization of language and culture. In S. Sato and N. Doerr (eds) *Rethinking Language and Culture in Japanese Education: Beyond the Standard* (pp. 19–34). Bristol: Multilingual Matters.
Kubota, R. (2015) Questioning language myths in English language teaching: Toward border-crossing communication. *Selected Papers from the Twenty-fourth International Symposium on English Teaching* (pp. 44–57). Taipei: English Teachers' Association-Republic of China (ETA-ROC).
Kubota, R. (2016) The multi/plural turn, postcolonial theory, and neoliberal multiculturalism: Complicities and implications for applied linguistics. *Applied Linguistics* 37, 474–494.
Kubota, R. (2018) *Eigo kyōiku gensō [Myths about English Language Teaching]*. Tokyo: Chikuma Shobō.
Kubota, R. and Fujimoto, D. (2013) Racialized native-speakers: Voices of Japanese American English language professionals. In S.A. Houghton and D.J. Rivers (eds) *Native-speakerism in Japan: Intergroup Dynamics in Foreign Language Education* (pp. 196–206). Bristol: Multilingual Matters.

Kubota, R. and Lehner, A. (2004) Toward critical contrastive rhetoric. *Journal of Second Language Writing* 13, 7–27.

Kubota, R. and Lin, A. (eds) (2009) *Race, Culture, and Identity in Second Language Education: Exploring Critically Engaged Practice*. New York: Routledge.

Kubota, R. and McKay, S. (2009) Globalization and language learning in rural Japan: The role of English in the local linguistic ecology. *TESOL Quarterly* 43, 593–619.

Kumaravadivelu, B. (2016) The decolonial option in English teaching: Can the subaltern act? *TESOL Quarterly* 50, 66–85.

Lee, E. and Simon-Maeda, A. (2006) Racialized research identities in ESL/EFL research. *TESOL Quarterly* 40, 573–594.

Lee, J.H. and Macaro, E. (2013) Investigating age in the use of L1 or English-only instruction: Vocabulary acquisition by Korean EFL learners. *The Modern Language Journal* 97, 887–901.

Levine, G.S. (2013) The case for a multilingual approach to language classroom communication. *Language and Linguistics Compass* 7/8, 423–436.

Lorente, B.P. and Tupas, T.R.F. (2013) (Un)emancipatory hybridity: Selling English in an unequal world. In R. Rubdy and L. Alsagoff (eds) *The Global-Local Interface and Hybridity: Exploring Language and Identity* (pp. 66–82). Bristol: Multilingual Matters.

Mahboob, A. (ed.) (2010) *The NNEST Lens: Non Native English Speakers in TESOL*. Newcastle upon Tyne: Cambridge Scholars.

Marshall, S. and Moore, D. (2013) 2B or not 2B plurilingual? Navigating languages literacies, and plurilingual competence in postsecondary education in Canada. *TESOL Quarterly* 47, 472–499.

Motha, S. and Lin, A. (2013) 'Non-coercive rearrangements': Theorizing desire in TESOL. *TESOL Quarterly* 48, 331–359.

Moussu, L. and Llurda, E. (2008) Non-native English-speaking English language teachers: History and research. *Language Teaching* 41, 315–348.

Muñoz, C. (2006) The effects of age on foreign language learning. In C. Muñoz (ed.) *Age and the Rate of Foreign Language Learning* (pp. 1–40). Clevedon: Multilingual Matters.

Muñoz, C. (2008) Symmetries and asymmetries of age effects in naturalist and instructed L2 learning. *Applied Linguistics* 29, 578–596.

Muñoz, C. (2011) Input and long-term effects of starting age in foreign language learning. *International Review of Applied Linguistics in Language Teaching* 49, 113–133.

Muñoz, C. (2014) Starting age and other influential factors: Insights from learner interviews. *Studies in Second Language Learning and Teaching* 4, 465–484.

Northwood, B. and Thomson, C.K. (2012) What keeps them going? Investigating ongoing learners of Japanese in Australian universities. *Japanese Studies* 32, 335–355.

Park, G. (2012) 'I am never afraid of being recognized as an NNES': One teacher's journey in claiming and embracing her nonnative speaker identity. *TESOL Quarterly* 46, 127–151.

Park, J.S.-Y. (2011) The promise of English: Linguistic capital and the neoliberal worker in the South Korean job market. *International Journal of Bilingual Education and Bilingualism* 14, 443–455.

Pfenninger, S.E. and Singleton, D. (2017) *Beyond Age Effects in Instructional L2 Learning: Revisiting the Age Factor*. Bristol: Multilingual Matters.

Phillipson, R. (1992) *Linguistic Imperialism*. Oxford: Oxford University Press.

Rivers, D.J. and Ross, A.S. (2013) Idealized English teachers: The implicit influence of race in Japan. *Journal of Language, Identity & Education* 12, 321–339.

Sayer, P. (2015) 'More & earlier': Neoliberalism and primary English education in Mexican public schools. *L2 Journal* 7, 40–56.

Scheurich, J.J. (1997) *Research Method in the Postmodern*. London: Falmer Press.

Seidlhofer, B. (2011) *Understanding English as a Lingua Franca*. Oxford: Oxford University Press.

Sue, D.W., Capodilupo, C.M., Torino, G.C., Bucceri, J.M., Holder, A.M.B., Nadal, K.L. and Esquilin, M. (2007) Racial microaggressions in everyday life. *American Psychologist* 62 (4), 271–286.

Takahashi, K. (2013) *Language Learning, Gender and Desire: Japanese Women on the Move.* Bristol: Multilingual Matters.

Terasawa, T. (2015) *'Nihonjin to eigo' no shakai gaku: Naze eigo kyôiku wa gokai darake nano ka* [*Sociology of English for the Japanese: Fallacies of the Discourses of English Language Teaching*]. Tokyo: Kenkyûsha.

Terasawa, T. (2017) Has socioeconomic development reduced the English divide? A statistical analysis of access to English skills in Japan. *Journal of Multilingual and Multicultural Development* 38, 671–685.

Thomas, W. and Collier, V. (2002) *A National Study of School Effectiveness for Language Minority Students' Long-term Academic Achievement.* Santa Cruz, CA: Center for Research on Education, Diversity and Excellence.

Tupas, R. (2004) The politics of Philippine English: Neocolonialism, global politics, and the problem of postcolonialism. *World Englishes* 23, 47–58.

Tupas, R. (ed.) (2015) *Unequal Englishes: The Politics of Englishes Today.* Basingstoke: Palgrave.

Watts, R.J. (2011) *Language Myths and the History of English.* New York: Oxford University Press.

Witte, A., Harden, T. and Harden, A.R.O. (eds) (2009) *Translation in Second Language Learning and Teaching.* New York: Peter Lang.

Yamada, M. (2015) *The Role of English Teaching in Modern Japan: Diversity and Multiculturalism Through English Language Education in a Globalized Era.* New York: Routledge.

Yazen, B. and Rudolph, N. (eds) (2018) *Criticality, Teacher Identity, and (In)equity in English Language Teaching: Issues and Implications.* Cham: Springer.

Zhao, T. and Macaro, E. (2014) What works better for the learning of concrete and abstract words: Teachers' use of L2-only explanations? *International Journal of Applied Linguistics* 26 (1), 75–98.

3 English is the Default Language? A Study of International Students' Language Needs in the Chinese Higher Education Context

Ting Zhang and Yongyan Zheng

This chapter reports on the findings of a small-scale qualitative study which aimed to explore the language needs of international students who choose to study in a high-ranked Chinese university. The study aimed to unpack the assumption of English as the default language of instruction for the heterogeneous body of international students in the multilingual/multicultural university setting. Semi-structured interviews were conducted to probe into 13 participants' attitudes towards English and other languages, their experiences in English as the medium of instruction classrooms, and their language needs in the local setting. Qualitative data analysis revealed that code-switching was adopted in English-medium classrooms, and international students attached high value to learning Chinese. Some participants expressed the need for academic English training to better equip themselves for English as the medium of instruction courses. These findings throw new light on choosing English as a default language for instruction in higher education, calling for universities to attend to international students' language needs.

Introduction

The effects of globalization and internationalization have been manifested in a myriad of fields. As an essential part of the global knowledge economy, higher education in the 21st century has undergone tremendous transformation, during which English has developed into a world lingua franca (Graddol, 2006), particularly for academic communication purposes in the higher education setting (Lillis & Curry, 2010; Mauranen et al., 2010). As a crucial part of the use of English in the academic setting, English as the medium instruction (EMI) has become an ever-growing global phenomenon (Dearden, 2015).[1] As such, EMI may be viewed as one of the most tangible manifestations of globalization's effect on internationalization (Earls, 2016: 65). Among the many driving forces behind the adoption of EMI, national governments and universities use it as an important strategy for higher education internationalization in order to gain access to cutting-edge knowledge and participate in global knowledge competition, raise the university profile and attract more international students and academics as a new source of revenue (Coleman, 2006; Hu, 2007; Wilkinson, 2013).

The body of research on EMI has grown substantially in recent decades. As international higher education usually features a bi-/multilingual environment, English is generally used within a highly heterogeneous milieu. Topics of interest include the rationale of adopting EMI (McKay, 2014; Shohamy, 2013; Wilkinson, 2005), implementation and practices (Airey & Linder, 2007; Earls, 2016; Sercu, 2004; Vinke et al., 1998), and students' and teachers' attitudes and perceptions (Ball & Lindsay, 2013; Bolton & Kuteeva, 2012; Costa & Coleman, 2013; Doiz et al., 2014; Tong & Shi, 2012). Among these studies, the choice of EMI is usually uncritically embraced by students and teachers who tend to have overwhelmingly positive attitudes towards EMI as they see it as providing opportunities for social mobility and educational opportunities (e.g. Costa & Coleman, 2013). Yet, several studies have revealed a discrepancy between the students' actual practices and the EMI language policy implemented at the institutional level, as the students choose to use languages other than English in either study-related situations or their social interactions (Hu et al., 2014; Lindström, 2012; Ljosland, 2008; Mortenson, 2014).

The observed competition between languages has drawn attention to the phenomenon of code-switching in EMI classrooms. Researchers have found that local languages have an important role to play in EMI classrooms (Söderlundh, 2012). Students and teachers adapt their choice of language to local needs and conditions. Hence, language choice at a bi-/multilingual university is not something that is 'simple and easy, once and for all, and subsequently taken-for-granted, but rather is oriented to by participants throughout, and is dependent on moment-to-moment interactional contingencies for speaker designation and participation' (Neville & Wagner, 2008: 168). However, most of the studies were based in Europe, and it is not clear whether findings on EMI in European countries can also apply to Asian countries, especially considering the different cultural, linguistic and social configurations.

International Students in China and Language Choice

Traditionally, Anglophone countries such as the United States, the United Kingdom, Australia, Canada and New Zealand are favorable destinations because of their inner circle status (Kachru, 1992), attracting a large number of overseas students. However, these traditional leading study destinations are gradually losing their appeal. The rise of EMI courses and programs all over the world seems to have diffused the attractiveness of English speaking countries. For example, European higher education has witnessed a rapid growth of EMI, with the number of EMI programs rising from 700 in 2002 to more than 2400 in 2007, a remarkable threefold increase (Wächter & Maiworm, 2008). The number of EMI programs has also surged dramatically in Asian higher education institutions. Postcolonial contexts such as Singapore, Malaysia, India, Hong Kong and other Asian countries such as China, Japan, Korea and Israel have also been actively engaged in implementing EMI policies (e.g. Byun *et al.*, 2011; Lo & Lo, 2014; Tsuneyoshi, 2005; Yeh, 2014). This phenomenon is attested to by recent book-length discussions on EMI programs in Asian contexts (e.g. Barnard & Hasim, 2018; Fenton-Smith *et al.*, 2017).

The case of China is particularly interesting. The Study in China Program indicates that China will become the largest study abroad destination in Asia.[2] According to statistics released by China's Ministry of Education in 2016, a total of 442,773 international students from 205 countries and regions study at 829 colleges, universities, research institutions and other teaching institutions in Mainland China, an increase of 45,138 people compared with that in 2015 (11.35% increase).[3] It is expected that by the end of 2020 the number of international students who come to China to study will reach 500,000, among whom 150,000 foreign students receive higher education. The top three nationalities of international students are Korean, American and Thai. European countries such as France and Germany are another major source of students coming to study in China. In addition to learning the Chinese language, a rapidly increasing number of international students study for academic degrees at Chinese universities. In 2016, 210,000 international students pursued bachelor degrees in China, accounting for 47.4% of the total international students studying in China. The students who extended their study to master's or doctoral level reached 64,000, accounting for 14.4% of the total – a 19.22% increase compared with 2015. It is no exaggeration to say that China has become a regional education hub in the shifting landscape of higher education internationalization.

Although English is not an official language but only a foreign language in China, its status as an academic lingua franca at international universities has made it a default choice as the medium of instruction for Chinese universities when offering courses to international students. The overwhelming bulk of studies on EMI are based on European higher education institutions, but research attention to EMI in the Chinese context is increasing (Botha, 2016; Hu & Lei, 2014; Hu *et al.*, 2014; Tong & Shi, 2012). In particular, Hu and colleagues (Hu & Lei, 2014; Hu *et al.*, 2014) took a critical perspective and began to question the indiscriminating acceptance of English as the natural or neutral choice of language in higher education settings. Hu and Lei (2014: 562) pointed out that due to the lack of academic English proficiency of both the instructors and students in the focal university, 'EMI was adulterated and Chinese was also frequently used as a medium of instruction in the EMI classroom'.

In summary, the preceding literature review reveals several limitations in current research on EMI. First, the majority of EMI research is conducted in the European context. It is questionable whether the experience of Europe can be transplanted to other contexts irrespective of the sociopolitical, cultural and linguistic parameters that are involved in language policy implementation. The prevalence of EMI programs around the world calls for studies to be undertaken in diverse contexts in order to shed light on the status quo and offer first-hand insights. Secondly, the multilingual needs of international students in the EMI programs in China have received scant attention. The limited number of EMI studies in China have focused on domestic Chinese students while leaving international students largely unaddressed, despite the fact that EMI courses were offered to meet the needs of international students in the first place. The presence of a large body of international students implies an inherently multilingual nature of communication in the academic setting. In this vein, EMI courses and programs have made an already diverse linguistic landscape more complex.

As such, this study aims to explore the language needs of international students who choose to study in a high-ranked Chinese university and to unpack the assumption of English as the default choice of instruction medium in the multilingual/multicultural university setting. We formulated the following research questions:

(1) Is English the sole language used in EMI classrooms composed of a heterogeneous body of international students? If not, what role do other language(s) play in EMI classrooms?
(2) What are the multilingual needs of international students in a high-ranked Chinese university?

The Study

This study is part of a larger project which investigated the EMI implementations for international students in a focal university. The findings reported in this chapter mainly explore the viewpoints of international students. To fully address the situatedness of the issue of EMI we opted for a qualitative approach. In applied linguistics there has been a considerable increase in qualitative research conducted in the social sciences and education (Duff, 2008). Gall *et al.* (2003: 436) explicate that the main advantage of qualitative research in education is its ability to carry out 'the in-depth study of instances of a phenomenon in its natural context and from the perspective of the participants involved in the phenomenon'. From this perspective, it is imperative to conduct an in-depth examination of international students' language beliefs and practices in the EMI program in a local context.

Research site

This study was conducted at a focal university anonymized as GHU, one of the top universities in China. It is located in a cosmopolitan city – Shanghai, one of the most important global financial, shipping and trading hubs. Established more than 100 years ago, GHU comprises 17 schools (including 66 study majors) and four departments. It has 68 majors for bachelor students, 209 specialties for master's students and 157 specialties for doctoral students. The university now has nearly 44,300 students, including full-time students and students in continuing education or network education, as well as overseas students.

GHU boasts the largest group of international students in China's comprehensive universities. Every year around 7000 international students from 120 countries and regions come to the university to receive higher education. Forty-two percent of the entire international student population are enrolled in degree programs and the rest are enrolled in non-degree or exchange programs. Although it mainly uses Chinese Mandarin as the medium of instruction, GHU offers 22 EMI degree programs in total, including one bachelor degree program in clinical medicine, 15 master's degree programs and six PhD degree programs.

Participants

The participants in this study were 13 international students studying at GHU during 2015 and 2016. They were recruited following the principle of maximum variation sampling coupled with snowball sampling. Among the 13 students, S7 was recommended by S5, and S7 later recommended S6 to the first author. Then S6 invited S11 to participate in our study. Although three of them were from the same department, they were from different countries, and one of them was an exchange student. The other seven students were recruited in similar ways. In order to ensure maximum variation, all the participants were carefully selected based on their nationalities and majors. The demographic diversity of students enabled us to explore diversity and commonality in their language needs. Detailed information is presented in Table 3.1.

Table 3.1 Summary of the participants' demographics

Participant	Gender	Nationality	Type	Grade	Major/Department
S1	Female	French	Exchange	Third-year	Business
S2	Female	American	Exchange	Third-year	Environmental science
S3	Female	American	Exchange	Third-year	Global Asia studies
S4	Male	Mexican	Degree	Master	English literature
S5	Female	Thai	Degree	Master	Chinese language and literature
S6	Male	American	Degree	Doctoral	Chinese philosophy
S7	Male	Dutch	Degree	Second-year	Chinese philosophy
S8	Female	Bangladeshi	Degree	Master	Medicine
S9	Male	Thai	Degree	Master	Chinese politics and diplomacy
S10	Female	Korean	Degree	Master	Chinese politics and diplomacy
S11	Female	Danish	Exchange	Doctoral	Chinese philosophy
S12	Male	German	Exchange	Master	Finance
S13	Male	Swiss	Exchange	Master	Finance

Data collection and data analysis

Semi-structured interviews were used to collect data. A set of core prompt questions (see Appendix) were used to guide the interviews. Because semi-structured interviews are open-ended they encourage the interviewees to elaborate on the issues discussed (Dörnyei, 2007: 136). Thirteen interviews were conducted by the first author, with each interview lasting for about 30 minutes. All the interviews were recorded and transcribed word for word. Prior to the recording, we explained the reasons for the interview and assured each interviewee of the confidentiality of the data in order to clear up their doubts and gain their verbal consent so as to facilitate better responses. In addition, some small talk was made before the formal interviews in an attempt to establish rapport and collect some basic information from the interviewees including their names, majors, nationalities, previous learning experiences, English score such as IELTS or TOEFL, and their use of English in daily life. All the interviewees were given the choice of using English or Chinese to conduct the interview, and all of them chose to use English. The core prompt questions revolved around four aspects: the participants' language practices in EMI classrooms; their attitudes towards English as an academic lingua franca; the language support they received from the institution; and thoughts and suggestions for the current EMI courses or programs.

The qualitative data were analyzed using NVivo 11.0. After the completion of each interview, the first author transcribed it in English while the second author checked the accuracy of the transcription. When we met difficulties in transcribing and understanding the interview data, we would double-check with our interviewees so as to ensure the trustworthiness of our study (Lincoln & Guba, 1985). The coding started from four aspects of the core prompt questions as first-level codes. Then we randomly chose three interview transcripts and independently read them line by line, assigning second-level codes under each of the first-level codes. After comparing our categorization, we agreed on the coding scheme, and the first author finished analyzing the rest of the data.

Findings and Discussion

Code-switching as a means of intercultural communication

The interview data showed that most Chinese instructors at GHU delivered English courses competently. For example:

> I've liked [the English-taught courses] so far. The class instructions are very clear. I don't see any major differences between the English-taught courses here and those in my home university. I think it is pretty seamless. Like my teacher for the course Chinese Commercial Culture and Practice, she is very engaging and asks students a lot of questions. Her English is fantastic! But she's a native Chinese speaker. (Interview with S3)

S3 was an exchange student from the United States, and her comments illustrate that the English proficiency of her instructors of various courses lived up to her expectations, as she described it as 'seamless' with the courses from her home country. Most other participants agreed on this point as they considered that their instructors were able to deliver content competently in English.

Even though English proficiency did not seem to be a major problem, code-switching was an often-employed strategy in the classroom. Code-switching refers to a strategy where the speaker switches or mixes other language(s) with English. One reason for code-switching was not due to the teachers' lack of English proficiency, but for better understanding of the content.

> I think that the switch of language is for the students, not because the professor's lack of English proficiency in our department. […] Everyone can express him or herself in a more than satisfactory manner. (Interview with S4)

S11, a student of Chinese philosophy, concurred with S4's view that making the content understood by the students was the primary reason for code-switching. It emerged that the acceptance of code-switching contrasts with the English-only medium of instruction.

Past research has shown that teachers use code-switching as a principle strategy to facilitate learning, engage students and manage student–teacher relationships in EMI classrooms (Hahl *et al.*, 2016; Yeh, 2012). Wilkinson (2005) observed that content teaching through the medium of English could be effective if code-switching was allowed. Our finding confirms the use of English and the local language Chinese in a classroom composed of students from different language backgrounds. In contrast to previous studies reporting a lack of English proficiency on the part of EMI instructors in China (Botha, 2016; Hu & Lei, 2014), the participants in our study did not consider code-switching to be a compensatory strategy for a lack of English proficiency.

In addition to facilitating content learning, code-switching between English and Chinese was viewed as an opportunity to gain insights into Chinese culture.

> What was interesting was that certain Chinese translation of English words has slightly different meaning, so the professor will explain to us international students why the Chinese translation is slightly different, which gives us good insights into the Chinese culture. (Interview with S13)

Intercultural communication arises naturally from a diverse international student body. The provision of EMI programs in higher educational institutions is regarded as a potential platform for intercultural exchange (Hultgren *et al.*, 2014). Similarly to those at European universities, the participants in our study reported active intercultural communication in the EMI classroom, and they frequently regarded the intercultural environment as a benefit of studying in EMI classrooms. For example, S8 believed that studying in a 'multi-culture or multi-diversified class can help you become more flexible in terms of language and also in terms of the culture', and S10 considered that studying in an EMI classroom can 'get you think out of the box and learn how to think in a sense of global perspective'. In this respect, the participants viewed classroom discussion as an opportunity to engage with other students – a process in which they could familiarize themselves with multifarious cultures, become more flexible, gain new insights and think more critically. In other words, the participants' acceptance of switching to Chinese now and then in the EMI classroom can be partly explained by their positive attitudes towards intercultural communication and their willingness to learn Chinese.

Apart from switching to Chinese, there were instances when teachers switched to a language which was the mother tongue of the majority of the students in the class. S3, an American student in Global Asia Studies, took an EMI course tailored for Mexican students. She reported:

> In my marketing intelligence course, the class is part of ITESM, specifically for students from Mexico. And sometimes when students cannot understand, he (the teacher) speaks Spanish to them. (Interview with S3)

Although it might be a single case, this instance illustrates the multilingual repertoire employed by the instructor at the focal university. It is interesting to see that two foreign languages, English and Spanish, were employed simultaneously in the EMI classroom in a Chinese university.

Code-switching was also often adopted among students within the project group itself. For example, S5 reported:

> Sometimes we switch to Chinese. Some technical words. But let's say there is a German classmate together. Sometimes they do not know how to express the term in English, they talk to each other in German to help each other to translate. (Interview with S5)

Similar to Mortensen's (2014) finding in a Danish university, our study showed that English was not the only language used in the Chinese EMI classroom context. Teachers and students switched to other languages, either the local language Chinese or the language shared among the students, in order to facilitate content learning and enhance intercultural communication in the multilingual classroom. Mortensen (2013) considered international student cohorts to be prime examples of a 'transient multilingual community'. Our findings illustrate such a transient multilingual community in each EMI classroom where international students' language choice was not restricted to English which was presumed to be the default language in the EMI classroom. Rather, the EMI program could provide them with potential opportunities for multilingual and multicultural development.

English as a global language and Chinese as an added skill

With regard to language attitudes, the findings showed that the participants acknowledged English as a lingua franca and accorded high prestige to English, but in the meantime some international students also voiced their concern over the hegemonic status of English in academic communication and expressed a desire to learn Chinese. On the one hand, most of the participants believed that English is a global language that people are obliged to master. The participants employed such adjectives as 'global', 'universal', 'major' and 'compulsory' to describe the English language. For instance, S5 noted that:

> English is a universal language that everyone needs to know by now in the 21st century. English is compulsory if you want to communicate with foreigners. (Interview with S5)

Some participants also noticed the presence of English in other domains, especially international business. S13 observed that 'English is going to be the only language spoken in certain contexts, such as business contexts'. S6 viewed English as 'an access to a lot of resources mediated by the English language'. These comments suggest that the participants generally acknowledged the extensive use of English in academic and business domains (Jenkins, 2014). By the same token, it seems that the international students who seek higher education in a Chinese university in a non-Anglophone context hold positive attitudes towards English as an academic lingua franca in higher education similar to other contexts (e.g. Bolton & Kuteeva, 2012; Botha, 2016; Costa & Coleman, 2013; Jenkins, 2014).

However, due to the global spread of English, the participants also became aware that a mastery of English is no longer an added skill. Instead, English is taken for granted as a basic skill that everyone should have. This further arouses a desire to acquire a third language on the part of some participants. For instance, S9 commented:

> In my generation, English is not enough. A third language is necessary ... I study Chinese four hours a week. (Interview with S9)

S9, a student from Thailand, situated a need for a third language in a new social context where English could not completely satisfy people's needs. S13 expressed a similar concern when he recounted his job-seeking experience in Shanghai.

> Interviewer: Do you plan to work here in Shanghai or back to your country?
> S13: I talked to three companies, but they all told me that they only take Chinese speaking students here in Shanghai, at least on junior level. So I have to go back to Switzerland.
> Interviewer: So if you can't speak Chinese, it is quite hard for you to get a job in Shanghai.
> S13: It is easier to get a job in the industrial companies that are from Europe. But I wanted to do management consulting, where you need to speak local languages. And I also met some friends who work for BCG (Boston Consulting Group) and Roland Berger in Shanghai. They all have to learn Chinese.

For S13 and other international students, the local language was a prerequisite for them to land a satisfactory job in Shanghai. Chinese proficiency is instrumental for them to obtain potential career opportunities after they finish their degree programs. As a result, some participants required the university to offer more Chinese language courses. For example, S10 commented:

> I think that [GHU] should offer more Chinese language courses, because I knew some students who already graduated, but who could never speak fluent Chinese. It's because they never have chance to speak Chinese. (Interview with S10)

S10's observation that the international students had limited chances to speak Chinese was shared by S5, who complained about devoting most of the time to using English and being deprived of the opportunity to speak and improve his Chinese. He referred to it as 'the negative part' of EMI.

> Disadvantage one is that we don't get to improve our Chinese. That's the negative part of English-taught courses. We are in China. We expect to speak Chinese, but we learn everything in English. The majority of our time is devoted to reading in English, writing English papers, and there's not much time to use Chinese. Most of the classmates are not Chinese. So you don't get to practice in Chinese. (Interview with S5)

It seems that overstressing the use of English in the EMI program has resulted in a reality that English becomes the *only* medium of instruction, which obscures international students' need to learn Chinese. As stipulated by GHU policy, non-degree international students are not required to take Chinese language courses, so it is a personal choice regarding Chinese learning, while for degree-seeking international students, only students engaged in Chinese-related programs are obliged to learn Chinese. Other students choose Chinese language as an elective course.

Those participants who were willing to take Chinese language courses were somewhat dissatisfied with the courses available. This dissatisfaction centered on a lack of Chinese language courses accessible to international students at different proficiency levels. During the interview, S11 complained about a lack of beginners' and in-between course. Similarly, S5 described in detail her friend's and her own frustration and bewilderment at the process of choosing a Chinese language course corresponding to their Chinese level.

> We need to take one of them (Chinese language courses), but since there was only five, at first I chose intermediate at first. ... [On meeting for the first time] the teacher said my Chinese was quite good. Why don't you go to the advanced class? Ok, I went to the advanced, but it was too difficult for me. All the other classmates were in the advanced level. I feel I don't understand anything. I went back to the intermediate. And another friend of mine, an American-Korean, she also sat with me in the intermediate class, but she felt like it was too hard for her. She goes to the basic one, but the basic one starts with pinyin. There is no class in between. (Interview with S5)

The multilingual needs of international students have been noted in several other studies in the European context (Lindström, 2012; Mortensen, 2014; Söderlundh, 2012). As Mortensen (2014: 438) argued, 'international education is always anchored locally', and the integration of the local language into the international students' linguistic repertoire can be a desirable part of international education. It seems that GHU, as a Chinese university that has the largest international student body, has acknowledged international students' need for Chinese language courses and made efforts to satisfy their needs, an effort valued by the students. However, our findings also suggested that the Chinese language courses were not fine-tuned to the students' diverse proficiency levels and there was no placement test to gauge the international students' Chinese proficiency level. Consequently, they were disoriented when choosing the appropriate class, and their willingness to learn Chinese was thwarted.

Need for academic English training

Our findings revealed that most participants were quite satisfied with their international classmates' English proficiency. For example, S13 thought highly of European students' English abilities, commenting that 'they have good English to have a vivid discussion in the class'. S7 even noted that his classmates' English was 'sometimes, maybe all the time, better than the teachers'.

Despite this, however, the international students' abilities to use English for academic communication varied, particularly depending on their native-language backgrounds. The data showed that the participants from non-English countries considered that native English speakers had an advantage over them in class discussion, oral presentations, reading and academic writing. S9, a Thai student, found it difficult to ask questions in class because he had to 'think about it longer'. S1, a French student, conceded that 'for oral presentations, they [native English speakers] might be more energetic, and they can be funny'. S12, a German student, found that 'it took longer time to write an essay' because he had to 'look up some words'. S10, a Korean student, lamented that: 'I have to spend more time reading English materials. They [native-English speakers] only need one hour or two but I have to spend a whole day.'

The varying academic English abilities generated quite different responses to the EMI course.

> Some courses go too slow. (Interview with S2)

> It almost seems like an introductory course to Chinese philosophy. However, it is labelled as a master's program. I myself also think it should be a little bit higher. It's very slow. The pace is very very slow. This is already the sixth week. We haven't really done anything. (Interview with S6)

> The level which requires us to do is much too low. For a master degree, it's much too low. They want us to write papers which are so short, about seven to nine pages. (Interview with S7)

> Especially the native speakers like American and British, they expect to be fast, fast, fast, but for Thai, for other Europeans, the pace is fine. I heard a lot of complaints from native speakers. They feel that the class is going slow. (Interview with S5)

We can see from the above excerpts that the views of S2, S6 and S7 contrasted markedly with that of S5. S2 and S6, the two American students, and S7, a Dutch student, expected the courses to be much more intensive, while S5, a Thai student, felt comfortable with the pace of the course. As pointed out by Airey (2004), different English proficiencies in one classroom give rise to concern over surface learning. Limited English proficiency in the EMI implementation was found to lead to a dearth of classroom interaction (Webb, 2002), compromise on content learning and teaching (Hu & Lei, 2014), and even resistance to EMI (Doiz et al., 2013). In this sense, the default choice of EMI for international students in the Chinese context needs to be problematized as it neglects the multilingual backgrounds and varying academic English abilities of the heterogeneous international student body.

To compensate for her inadequacy in academic English, S10 voluntarily took a course in English academic writing. However, she observed that although 'the materials are good, there are a lot of different majors in the class so it is not very effective' (Interview with S10) as far as her own need was concerned. Since the course was specifically designed for Chinese students it did not cater to the needs of international students for academic English improvement. GHU offers a range of academic English courses, but all are designed for local Chinese students, and although international students have access to these courses and learning resources, there is no specific academic English course designed for international students and it is a personal choice whether to take any of these courses. It seems that international students were by no means a homogeneous body whose academic English proficiency could be universally assumed in the EMI practices. If this point was not sufficiently attended to, EMI programs would fall short of the content and language learning goals envisioned by the institution or the students.

Conclusion

This qualitative study probed 13 international students' experiences and attitudes towards English and other languages situated in the EMI courses and programs in GHU, China. Although this is a small sample, and the findings could not be easily generalized to other contexts, the analysis sheds some light on the international students' multilingual needs anchored in the Chinese higher education context.

In line with previous studies conducted in European contexts (Lindström, 2012; Mortensen, 2014; Söderlundh, 2012), our findings stressed the crucial role of local languages in the EMI classroom, while acknowledging the dominant role of English in international universities. Teachers switched to Chinese or other languages to facilitate communication and knowledge construction, and the students considered code-switching 'a platform of intercultural exchange' (Hultgren et al., 2014). Therefore, our findings defied the assumption of English as the sole language used in EMI programs offered by international universities.

Instead, the use of English should be explored as situated in a multilingual ecosystem in which the local language occupies an important niche.

Two types of language needs on the part of international students emerged from our findings. First, Chinese is embraced by the participants as a legitimate type of linguistic capital (Bourdieu, 1991) which can convert to economic capital (e.g. securing a decent job) and cultural capital (e.g. pursuing further study in China) (Bourdieu, 1986). This is inherently related to the rising influence and economic prosperity of China in recent decades. International students come to China not only to receive quality higher education or to encounter Chinese culture, but to seek potential career opportunities and to participate in China's high-speed economic development. These incentives impel the students to learn Chinese. Our findings suggest that it is incumbent on the institution to offer sufficient and fine-tuned Chinese language courses to cater for the students of different Chinese language levels.

Secondly, the international students voiced their need for courses in English for academic purposes (EAP). The assumed equation between international students and good English abilities tends to ignore the heterogeneity of international students, and the effective implementation of EMI programs hinges on sufficient EAP support. Without it, the students from Anglophone countries would suffer a compromise of content learning and the students from non-Anglophone countries would be sidelined and even marginalized in the EMI classroom. As Tollefson and Tsui (2004: 2) forcefully argued, 'medium-of-instruction policy determines which social and linguistic groups have access to political and economic opportunities, and which groups are disenfranchised'. In today's globalized age, the spread of English as an academic lingua franca in higher education settings seems to be an irreversible trend. However, policy makers should be mindful when English is chosen as the default medium of instruction, because EMI does not mean that English is the exclusive language of use in the academic setting. Rather, EMI may provide a platform for intercultural communication and multilingual learning. International universities aiming to elbow their way into the higher education internationalization drive and to provide quality education to international students should attend to the multilingual needs of the highly diverse group of international students engaged in EMI courses or programs. Language should be treated with greater sensitivity, so that the EMI policy can better serve the benefits and needs of international students regardless of their country of origin and native languages.

Appendix: Core Prompt Interview Questions

(1) How would you comment on the global status of English in today's world? Do you believe that English should be the language used for

instruction in the university here? Is there any need to choose other languages?
(2) Why do you come to study at GHU instead of other universities in other countries? Have you had any study abroad experience before coming to China?
(3) How many English-taught courses have you taken at GHU? How would you describe your experience? How would you compare the English-taught courses you've taken at GHU with the courses you took before? Are you satisfied with the English-taught courses at GHU?
(4) Do you think native English speakers have more advantages than you in the academic study? If you can choose your teacher, who would you prefer, native speakers of English or non-native speakers? How would you describe the language competence of your classmates? Are there any differences between and among students from different parts of the world?
(5) What's your plan after you complete your program here at GHU?
(6) Is there anything that you want to add?

Notes

(1) According to the EMI Oxford Center, EMI refers to the use of the English language to teach academic subjects (other than English itself) in countries or jurisdictions in which the majority of the population's first language is not English (Macaro, 2017).
(2) See http://www.moe.edu.cn/publicfiles/business/htmlfiles/moe/moe_850/201009/xxgk_108815.html.
(3) See http://www.moe.gov.cn/jyb_xwfb/xw_fbh/moe_2069/xwfbh_2017n/xwfb_170301/170301_sjtj/201703/t20170301_297677.html.

References

Airey, J. (2004) Can you teach it in English? Aspects of the language choice debate in Swedish higher education. In R. Wilkinson (ed.) *Integrating Content and Language: Meeting the Challenge of a Multilingual Higher Education* (pp. 97–108). Maastricht: Maastricht University Press.
Airey, J. and Linder, C. (2007) Disciplinary learning in a second language: A case study from university physics. In R. Wilkinson and V. Zegers (eds) *Researching Content and Language Integration in Higher Education* (pp. 161–171). Maastricht: Maastricht University Language Center.
Ball, P. and Lindsay, D. (2013) Language demands and support for English-medium instruction in tertiary education. Learning from a specific context. In A. Doiz, D. Lasagabaster and J. Sierra (eds) *English-Medium Instruction at Universities: Global Challenges* (pp. 44–66). Bristol: Multilingual Matters.
Barnard, R. and Hasim, Z. (2018) *English Medium of Instruction Programmes: Perspectives from Southeast Asian Universities*. London: Routledge.
Bolton, K. and Kuteeva, M. (2012) English as an academic language at a Swedish university: Parallel language use and the 'threat' of English. *Journal of Multilingual and Multicultural Development* 33, 429–447.
Botha, W. (2016) English and international students in China today. *English Today* 32 (1), 41–47.

Bourdieu, P. (1986) The forms of capital. In J.G. Richardson (ed.) *Handbook of Theory and Research in the Sociology of Education* (pp. 241–258). New York: Greenwood Press.

Bourdieu, P. (1991) *Language and Symbolic Power* (G. Raymond and M. Adamson, trans.). Cambridge, MA: Harvard University Press.

Byun, K., Chu, H., Kim, M., Park, I., Kim, S. and Jung, J. (2011) English-medium teaching in Korean higher education: Policy debates and reality. *Higher Education* 62, 431–449.

Coleman, J.A. (2006) English-medium teaching in European higher education. *Language Teaching* 39, 1–14.

Costa, F. and Coleman, J.A. (2013) A survey of English-medium instruction in Italian higher education. *International Journal of Bilingual Education and Bilingualism* 16 (1), 3–19.

Dearden, J. (2015) *English as a Medium of Instruction: A Growing Global Phenomenon*. London: British Council.

Doiz, A., Lasagabaster, D. and Sierra, J.M. (2013) English as L3 at a bilingual university in the Basque Country, Spain. In A. Doiz, D. Lasagabaster, and J. Sierra (eds) *English-Medium Instruction at Universities: Global Challenges* (pp. 84–105). Bristol: Multilingual Matters.

Doiz, A., Lasagabaster, D. and Sierra, J.M. (2014) Language friction and multilingual policies in higher education: The stakeholders' view. *Journal of Multilingual and Multicultural Development* 35, 345–360.

Dörnyei, Z. (2007) *Research Methods in Applied Linguistics: Quantitative, Qualitative, and Mixed Methodologies*. Oxford: Oxford University Press.

Duff, P. (2008) *Case Study Research in Applied Linguistics*. New York: Lawrence Erlbaum.

Earls, C.W. (2016) *Evolving Agendas in European English-medium Higher Education: Interculturality, Multilingualism and Language Policy*. London: Palgrave Macmillan.

Fenton-Smith, B., Humphreys, P. and Walkinshaw, I. (2017) *English Medium Instruction in Higher Education in Asia-Pacific: From Policy to Pedagogy*. Cham: Springer.

Gall, M.D., Gall, J.P. and Borg, W.T. (2003) *Educational Research* (7th edn). White Plains, NY: Pearson Education.

Graddol, D. (2006) *English Next: Why Global English Can Mean the End of 'English as a Foreign Language'*. London: British Council.

Hahl, K., Järvinen, H.M. and Juuti, K. (2016) Accommodating to English-medium instruction in teacher education in Finland. *International Journal of Applied Linguistics* 26, 291–310.

Hu, G.W. (2007) The juggernaut of Chinese-English bilingual education. In A. Feng (ed.) *Bilingual Education in China: Practices, Policies and Concepts* (pp. 94–125). Clevedon: Multilingual Matters.

Hu, G.W. and Lei, J. (2014) English-medium instruction in Chinese higher education: A case study. *Higher Education* 67, 551–567.

Hu, G.W., Li, L. and Lei, J. (2014) English-medium instruction at a Chinese University: Rhetoric and reality. *Language Policy* 13 (1), 21–40.

Hultgren, A.K., Gregersen, F. and Thøgersen, J. (eds) (2014) *English in Nordic Universities: Ideologies and Practices*. Amsterdam: Johns Benjamins.

Jenkins, J. (2014) *English as a Lingua Franca in the International University: The Politics of Academic English Language Policy*. New York: Routledge.

Kachru, B.B. (1992) Models for non-native Englishes. In B.B. Kachru (ed.) *The Other Tongue: English Across Cultures* (2nd edn) (pp. 48–74). Chicago, IL: University of Illinois Press.

Lillis, T. and Curry, M.J. (2010) *Academic Writing in a Global Context: The Politics and Practices of Publishing in English*. London: Routledge.

Lincoln, Y.S. and Guba, E.G. (1985) *Naturalistic Inquiry*. Thousand Oaks, CA: Sage.

Lindström, J. (2012) Different languages, one mission? Outcomes of language policies in a multilingual university context. *International Journal of the Sociology of Language* 216, 33–54.

Ljosland, R. (2008) Lingua franca, prestisje språk og forestilt fellesskap: Om engelsk som akademisk språk i Norge. Et kasusstudium i bred kontekst [Lingua franca, prestige language and imagined communities: On English as an academic language in Norway. A case study in its broader context]. Dissertation, Norwegian University of Science and Technology.

Lo, Y.Y. and Lo, E.S.C. (2014) A meta-analysis of the effectiveness of English-medium education in Hong Kong. *Review of Educational Research* 84 (1), 47–73.

Macaro, E. (2017) English medium instruction: Global views and countries in focus. Introduction to the symposium held at the Department of Education, University of Oxford on Wednesday 4 November 2015. *Language Teaching* 50 (3), 1–18. doi:10.1017/S0261444816000380

Mauranen, A., Hynninen, N. and Ranta, E. (2010) English as an academic lingua franca: The ELFA project. *English for Specific Purposes* 29, 183–190.

McKay, S.L. (2014) Commentary: English-medium education in the global society – findings and implications. *International Review of Applied Linguistics in Language Teaching* 52, 221–228.

Mortensen, J. (2013) Notes on the use of English as a lingua franca as an object of study. *Journal of English as a Lingua Franca* 2 (1), 25–46.

Mortensen, J. (2014) Language policy from below: Language choice in student project groups in a multilingual university setting. *Journal of Multilingual and Multicultural Development* 35, 425–442.

Nevile, M. and Wagner, J. (2008) Managing languages and participation in a multilingual group examination. In H. Haberland, J. Mortensen, A. Fabricius and S. Kjærbeck (eds) *Higher Education in the Global Village* (pp. 149–174). Roskilde: Institut for Kultur og Identitet, Roskilde Universitet.

Sercu, L. (2004) The introduction of English-medium instruction in university: A comparison of Flemish lecturers' and students' language skills, perceptions and attitudes. In R. Wilkinson (ed.) *Integrating Content and Language: Meeting the Challenge of a Multilingual Higher Education* (pp. 547–555). Maastricht: Maastricht University Press.

Shohamy, E. (2013) A critical perspective on the use of English as a medium of instruction at universities. In A. Doiz, D. Lasagabaster and J. Sierra (eds) *English-Medium Instruction at Universities: Global Challenges* (pp. 196–210). Bristol: Multilingual Matters.

Söderlundh, H. (2012) Global policies and local norms: Sociolinguistic awareness and language choice at an international university. *International Journal of the Sociology of Language* 216, 87–109.

Tollefson, J.W. and Tsui, A.B.M. (eds) (2004) *Medium of Instruction Policies: Which Agenda? Whose Agenda?* Mahwah, NJ: Lawrence Erlbaum.

Tong, F. and Shi, Q. (2012) Chinese–English bilingual education in China: A case study of college science majors. *International Journal of Bilingual Education and Bilingualism* 15, 165–182.

Tsuneyoshi, R. (2005) Internationalization strategies in Japan: The dilemmas and possibilities of study abroad programs using English. *Journal of Research in International Education* 4 (1), 65–86.

Vinke, A.A., Snippe, J. and Jochems, W. (1998) English-medium content courses in non-English higher education: A study of lecturer experiences and teaching behaviours. *Teaching in Higher Education* 3, 383–394.

Wächter, B. and Maiworm, F. (2008) *English-taught Programmes in European Higher Education: The Picture in 2007.* Bonn: Lemmens.

Webb, V. (2002) English as a second language in South Africa's tertiary institutions: A case study at the University of Pretoria. *World Englishes* 21 (1), 49–61.

Wilkinson, R. (2005) The impact of language on teaching content: Views from the content teacher. Paper presented at the *Conference on Bi- and Multilingual Universities – Challenges and Future Prospects*, Helsinki.

Wilkinson, R. (2013) English-medium instruction at a Dutch university: Challenges and pitfalls. In A. Doiz, D. Lasagabaster and J.M. Sierra (eds) *English-Medium Instruction at Universities: Global Challenges* (pp. 3–24). Bristol: Multilingual Matters.

Yeh, C.C. (2012) Instructors' perspectives on English-medium instruction in Taiwanese universities. *Curriculum Instruction Quarterly* 16 (1), 209–232.

Yeh, C.C. (2014) Taiwanese students' experiences and attitudes towards English-medium courses in tertiary education. *RELC Journal* 45, 305–319.

4 Language Selection and Assessment in Brunei Darussalam

Ishamina Athirah Gardiner and David Deterding

In the past, the variety of English promoted in the education system and how the language is assessed have usually involved a choice between Standard British or American English. In recent studies, two alternatives have been proposed: nativized varieties that are influenced by indigenous languages in each country (influenced by the World Englishes paradigm); and English as a lingua franca based teaching that pays more attention to international intelligibility than adherence to any fixed standard. In Brunei Darussalam, British English is officially promoted, and indeed all 'O' level examination papers have been graded in the UK, indicating a continuing orientation towards British usage which school students are ill-advised to ignore. However, there has been a remarkable increase in American features of pronunciation in recent years, and there also seems to be quite widespread use of American lexis by Bruneians. Quite apart from this choice between British and American usage, it is not clear that adopting native-speaker styles of pronunciation or idiomatic usage is constructive in enhancing international intelligibility, and recent data confirm that misunderstandings can arise when Bruneian speakers adhere too closely to native-speaker norms in international communication. In this chapter, we explore evidence that native-speaker patterns of pronunciation and lexical choice can interfere with intelligibility, based on a recent study of a total of 152 misunderstandings in English as a lingua franca conversations that occurred in Brunei. This is then followed by a discussion on the implications of this for the models of speech that are promoted in schools and how language assessment is addressed.

Introduction

The burgeoning use of English in Asia in the modern globalized world raises a fundamental issue about which variety of English should be promoted in the education system and how it should be assessed. Traditionally, native-speaker varieties have been favoured, usually involving a choice between Standard British or American English. Although teaching and testing based on such native-speaker models are still prevalent throughout the world, various scholars have questioned whether this should continue (e.g. Jenkins, 2000; Seidlhofer, 2011). In recent years, two alternatives for language teaching have been proposed: adoption of a nativized model of English that is influenced by the indigenous languages in each country, following the World Englishes paradigm (Kirkpatrick, 2006); and an English as a lingua franca (ELF) approach that pays more attention to international intelligibility than to adherence to fixed standards (Fang, 2017; Jenkins, 2007; Walker, 2010).

This chapter provides a brief overview of current issues concerning the assessment of English, and it explores arguments about the suitability of native-speaker based testing in the outer and expanding circles (using the three circles model proposed by Kachru, 1992). It then discusses the situation in Brunei Darussalam by first describing the bilingual education system that was implemented in 1985, and then considering changes in assessment following the implementation of a new system of education in 2009. Next, it presents evidence that adopting native-speaker styles of pronunciation, lexis and idiomatic usage is not always constructive in enhancing the intelligibility of interactions in international settings. The chapter finally discusses the implications of this for the models of speech that are promoted in education and how the language of school children is assessed.

Current Issues in Pedagogy and Assessment

Despite the increasing use of English as a global language to facilitate communication in international settings and the acceptance of nativized varieties of English as models for teaching in some places in the outer circle, many countries continue to try to enforce standard varieties of speech based on inner circle usage in their education systems. Learners are still often assessed on their ability to use British or American English, and they may be penalized for not being able to speak or write like a native speaker (Tomlinson, 2010: 609). For example, carefully controlled, standardized English language tests such as IELTS and TOEFL are widely adopted to assess the English proficiency of international students from non-English speaking backgrounds, and they constitute the entry requirements to higher institutions, as the scores of such tests are believed to be linked to learners' potential academic performance. Indeed, Bayliss (2006) suggests that the validity of ratings in IELTS tests is relatively positive, reporting that IELTS scores can accurately predict the language behaviour of foreign students in Australia. However, other studies question the validity of standardized tests as a predictor of academic success, reporting no significant correlation between test scores and academic performance (Cotton & Conrow, 1998; EduCo, 2016).

Native-speaker models remain popular in education and among policy makers, largely because they are codified as standard varieties of English, with reference books such as dictionaries and a wide range of pedagogical materials. Furthermore, there is a widespread belief that native-speaker models can ensure international intelligibility, and that not conforming to native-speaker norms endangers successful communication (Kirkpatrick, 2006). However, Tomlinson (2010: 609) argues that the idealized standard varieties of English, especially in their spoken forms, do not actually exist, and furthermore that non-native speakers should not be penalized for 'mistakes' that native speakers often make. Pedagogy and testing should therefore reflect an actual use of English which is appropriate and effective in the contexts that learners find themselves in.

One possible model proposed by Kirkpatrick (2006) is the nativized model based on the local variety of English used in each country. He suggests that such a model is advantageous, particularly for outer circle countries, as it can provide an appropriate set of rules for language teaching based on indigenous norms. Moreover, local English teachers can be highly valued as role models for learners, as they have the ability to empathize with their students and understand their needs. However, Kirkpatrick acknowledges that such a model is not widely accepted, especially in expanding circle countries.

An alternative suggestion is to replace native-speaker based pedagogy and assessment with ELF-informed teaching (Fang, 2017; Leung *et al.*, 2016). This kind of teaching is more flexible in the sense that learners are encouraged to use English to suit their needs rather than adhering to irrelevant native-speaker rules and patterns of usage, and Kirkpatrick (2006: 81) notes that a lingua franca model is especially appropriate for learners whose main reason for learning English is to facilitate communication with non-native speakers.

Leung *et al.* (2016: 68) argue that there is a need to reconceptualize standardized large-scale tests and instead adopt small-scale assessments that reflect local demands and usage. First, they suggest that assessment in English for academic purposes (EAP) should focus on communicative effectiveness and on improving communication strategies among non-native speakers rather than assessing students on the accuracy of their native-speaker usage. Secondly, assessment should be context specific, reflecting the specific situations and language use that students are likely to encounter. O'Sullivan (2011: 270) further asserts that testing is only of value if it is adapted for a specific domain. Therefore, English language teaching and assessment should be more focused on how learners use the language to fulfil tasks with different goals in academic and non-academic settings (Fang, 2017: 65).

However, the concept of adopting an ELF-based approach in English language teaching and assessment has yet to be accepted by the majority of teachers and education policy makers. There have been concerns that the approach is not based on clearly defined standards, and furthermore that it would lower standards if what are perceived to be errors in native speech are regarded as acceptable (Walker, 2010: 51). Svartvik and Leech (2006: 234) add that, if the concept of ELF-based teaching ever gains acceptance, it will take a long time to overcome the general preference for standard native-speaker norms that are especially evident in pedagogy.

We should also consider the different motivations that some learners have for wanting to achieve native-speaker proficiency, especially when this includes seeking respect when participating in international forums or living in an inner circle country. Elsewhere, we have suggested that ELF-informed teaching is only appropriate in some language teaching contexts, so the approach that is adopted must always involve evaluating learners' needs (Deterding & Gardiner, 2018).

Pedagogy and Assessment in Brunei

Prior to 1984, most schools in Brunei were either Malay medium or English medium, and students sat for separate examinations administered by Malaysia based on their medium of instruction. At secondary five and upper sixth levels, Malay-medium students sat for the *Sijil Pelajaran Malaysia* (SPM; 'Malaysia Certificate of Education') and *Sijil Tinggi Pelajaran Malaysia* (STPM; 'Malaysia Higher Certificate of Education') examinations, while English-medium students sat for the Malaysia Certificate of Education (MCE) and Higher School Certificate (HSE) examinations (Ministry of Education, 2009: 10). In 1974, the Brunei Examination Board was established to administer all public examinations, and the joint Brunei-Cambridge 'O' and 'A' level examinations were introduced for upper secondary and sixth form students (Gunn, 1997: 154).

After gaining independence in 1984, there was a call for integration of all schools into a single education system (Gunn, 1997: 155). The bilingual education system or *dwibahasa* ('dual languages') was introduced in 1985 for all schools in Brunei except international and religious schools, with the aim of maintaining the mother tongue (Malay) and at the same time promoting English (Jones, 1996: 123). As a result, schools were no longer segregated into Malay and English medium, and the goal was to offer equal opportunities for all school children (Jones, 2007: 246). Under this system, all subjects at lower primary level, except English language, were taught in Malay, but English was used as the medium of instruction for most subjects from the fourth year of primary school onwards (Martin & Poedjosoedarmo, 1996: 4).

In 2009 a new system of education, called *Sistem Pendidikan Negara Abad Ke-21* (SPN21; 'National Education System for the 21st Century'), was introduced, aiming to prepare pupils to face the social and economic challenges of the modern world. Concern about low levels of proficiency in English was one rationale for the new system (Ministry of Education, 2009: 15), and a significant change involved adopting English as the medium of instruction for mathematics and science from the first year of primary school (Jones, 2012), underlining the perceived importance of English.

However, a preliminary evaluation of the SPN21 curriculum raised concerns about overemphasis on examinations and continuous assessment which can undermine good teaching (Mundia, 2010). Indeed, there has been an increase in the number and type of assessments, such as the Student Progress Assessment (SPA) and the Student Progress Examination (SPE) in addition to the continued use of Cambridge GCE 'O' and 'A' level examinations (Ministry of Education, 2007). Clearly, the culture of testing and examinations continues to dominate the education system in Brunei, and this assessment is generally based on native-speaker norms.

One issue concerns the suitability of the 'O' level English examination for Bruneian students with limited ability in English (Nicol, 2005). The exam is regarded as outdated, and furthermore it is designed for native speakers of English, with the result that many pupils in Brunei have problems in understanding difficult words and idioms widely occurring in the texts. As a result, barely 50% of pupils nationwide have been obtaining a 'Credit' pass in this exam, the grade needed for entry to Universiti Brunei Darussalam (UBD), although the percentage has apparently been slowly improving year on year.

Table 4.1 shows the results over a seven-year span, from 2010 to 2016. While the percentage obtaining a Credit has improved every year, one factor is that an increasing number of students are taking an alternative IGCSE ESL (English as a second language) exam instead of this 'O' level exam, so it is not clear whether achievement in English really is improving. One may note the steady decrease in the number of students taking the English 'O' level, while there is no such decrease in the numbers taking

Table 4.1 Number of students obtaining Credit for GCE 'O' level English from 2010 to 2016

Year	No. of candidates	Credit (A–C)	%
2010	6362	2172	34.1%
2011	7134	3067	43.0%
2012	5986	2688	44.9%
2013	4881	2210	45.3%
2014	4494	2296	51.1%
2015	4514	2421	53.6%
2016	4236	2290	54.1%

the Malay 'O' level. Indeed, while the percentage obtaining a Credit grade has steadily improved, the number of students achieving this shows no such change. In conclusion, the standard of English in Brunei, as reflected in this native-speaker 'O' level exam, actually shows no evidence of improvement over this seven-year period.

At about the same time as SPN21 was implemented, in 2009 UBD introduced a new undergraduate degree called GenNEXT, involving revised bachelor degrees in arts, business, health sciences and science. Elsewhere we have shown that the new programme seems to favour English as the medium of instruction in two ways (Ishamina & Deterding, 2017). First, there is now an entry requirement for all students to have at least a Credit in 'O' level English, a B grade in the IGCSE ESL exam or an IELTS score of 6.0, whereas in the pre-GenNEXT programmes, applicants for Malay-medium degrees were not subject to this requirement. Secondly, the figures for English- and Malay-medium graduating students in 2006 (pre-GenNEXT) and 2014 (GenNEXT) show that there was an increase in the number of English-medium graduates from 66.5% in 2006 to 82.4% in 2014, while the number of Malay-medium graduates dropped correspondingly from 33.5% to 17.6%. The increase in the number of students taking English-medium degrees suggests that students now realize the importance of having an English-medium degree for their future career and also if they want to pursue their studies abroad.

Clearly, there is a continuing insistence on students in Brunei passing English proficiency exams that are based on native-speaker models of usage. However, it is not clear that such usage always ensures a high level of intelligibility in interactions in an international setting. Indeed, native-speaker norms of usage can sometimes give rise to misunderstandings, as we will show in the next section.

Misunderstandings in International Communication

It has been argued that traditional forms of English language teaching and assessment do not reflect the actual use of English for communication in international settings (Fang, 2017). In this section, we explore evidence from a study of interactions in English in an international setting, showing that native-like patterns of pronunciation and lexical choice do not always ensure mutual intelligibility.

Research methodology

The corpus of data consists of 10 audio-recordings collected at UBD. Each recording consists of a conversation in English between two participants, a Bruneian and a non-Bruneian, and the aim of the study is to investigate how well the latter can understand the former. There are 17 participants in the study, eight Bruneians and nine non-Bruneians, and they are identified here by their gender (F or M), followed by a two-letter code representing their country of origin. The Bruneian participants are FBr1, FBr2, FBr3, FBr4, FBr5, MBr1, MBr2 and MBr3. Four non-Bruneian participants are from China (FCh1, FCh2, FCh3 and FCh4) and there is one each from Korea (MKo), France (MFr), the Maldives (FMd), Oman (FOm) and Vietnam (FVn). At the time the recordings were made, 16 of the participants were students at UBD and one, MFr, was a visiting researcher. All participants listed English as either their second language or a foreign language, so none of them could be regarded as native English speakers, although some of the Bruneian speakers exhibit many features of standard native-speaker usage in their pronunciation and lexical choice, as will be shown in this study. The selection of the participants was based on convenience sampling. One requirement was that they were all able and willing to meet the researchers after the recording to provide feedback and assistance with the analysis. They were aware that the purpose of the study was to investigate patterns of interaction in English between Bruneian and non-Bruneian speakers in an informal context, although they did not know that it would specifically focus on instances of misunderstanding.

The recordings were made in a quiet room at UBD using a Handy H4n recorder. The researchers were not present when the recordings took place, and the participants were encouraged to discuss a range of topics, from Brunei's culture and history to other personal topics such as interests and hobbies. In total, the 10 recordings are about three hours and 39 minutes long, an average of about 22 minutes each. Table 4.2 presents a list of the recordings which are identified with the two participants involved, the first being the Bruneian and the second the non-Bruneian. Three participants took part in two separate recordings: MBr1 in MBr1 + FMd and

Table 4.2 The recordings

Recording	Duration (min:sec)
FBr1 + FMd	21:45
FBr2 + FVn	25:12
FBr3 + FCh2	22:46
FBr4 + FCh3	20:56
FBr5 + FCh4	20:27
MBr1 + FMd	21:31
MBr1 + FOm	22:29
MBr2 + FCh1	20:48
MBr3 + MFr	22:48
MBr3 + MKo	21:04
Total	3:39:26

MBr1 + FOm; MBr3 in MBr3 + MFr and MBr3 + MKo; and FMd in MBr1 + FMd and FBr1 + FMd. All others participated in just one recording.

Transcription of the recordings soon followed, and the researchers met the participants to clarify any instances of their speech that were unclear. Since the aim is to investigate how well the non-Bruneians can understand the English conversational speech of the Bruneians, the analysis involves examining instances in which the non-Bruneians failed to understand something. This was done in two ways. The researchers first looked for instances in the recordings where the non-Bruneians signalled the occurrence of a misunderstanding by asking for clarification or failing to provide a suitable response. Secondly, the researchers collected feedback from the non-Bruneian participants by playing short extracts of their recordings and asking them to transcribe what they heard. Of course, many of these extracts reflect the researchers' predictions about where a misunderstanding may have occurred, and we almost certainly overlooked some instances.

An occurrence of a misunderstanding is identified from one of three things: a clear instance of miscommunication in the recording; the participants' inaccurate transcription; or feedback from the participants reporting that they failed to understand something. We acknowledge that we cannot be sure on the basis of this kind of feedback that a misunderstanding actually occurred in all instances where the transcription of the participants is inaccurate or in their claim of not understanding something, but we believe that most of the instances do represent genuine instances of loss of intelligibility.

A total of 152 tokens of misunderstanding have been identified from the corpus. Of these 152 tokens, only 31 were signalled in the recording, so the overwhelming majority (80%) only emerged as a result of the feedback. Clearly, obtaining feedback from the participants for studies such as this is vitally important (Deterding, 2013). In fact, all the interactions generally proceeded smoothly and they show little indication of communication breakdown as speakers have a tendency to let unclear utterances pass in the hope that failure to understand a few words will not matter overall (Firth, 1996; Mortensen, 2013). Yet, at the same time, there are some words that were misunderstood.

Data analysis

Of the 152 tokens of misunderstanding, 33 seem to have been caused wholly or partly by native-like patterns of usage. In nine tokens, pronunciation seems to be a major factor in the misunderstanding, while the other 24 involve the use of English words and phrases, including idiomatic usage that non-Bruneians are not familiar with. We will first examine the nine tokens involving pronunciation and then explore the 24 lexical tokens.

Pronunciation

The nine tokens in which pronunciation is implicated are shown in Table 4.3. Tokens 1–4 involve vowels, while Tokens 5–9 involve consonants. (In the 'Context' column, the misunderstood words are shown in bold and italicized, and '?' indicates rising intonation; in the 'Heard as' column, '?' indicates the listener's inability to make a guess about the word during the feedback session.)

In Token 1, FCh1 heard *knit* as 'neat', and she explained in her feedback that she was familiar with the phrase 'close-knit' but did not understand the phrase in this utterance because of the added conjunction in *close and knit*. Of course, the insertion of *and* is the main problem, but here we focus on the pronunciation of the vowel in *knit*, as we believe it is also a factor. Note that FCh1 heard a word with a long vowel, 'neat', even though MBr2 actually pronounced *knit* with the short vowel [ɪ]. In fact, FCh1 herself often does not make a clear distinction between the long and short vowels [iː] and [ɪ]. To investigate this further, FCh1 was asked to read the sentences 'grandma likes to sew and knit' and 'she keeps the house neat and tidy', and analysis of this supplementary recording confirmed that she uses a similar close front vowel [i] for both words 'knit' and 'neat'. We can see, therefore, that the standard pronunciation of *knit* by MBr2 was misheard by FCh2 partly because of the non-standard accent of the listener.

Tokens 2, 3 and 4 involve the listener's lack of familiarity with American English pronunciation. In Tokens 2 and 3, MBr2 pronounced *leisure* and the letter Z with [iː], as [liːʒər] and [ziː], respectively, and FCh1 failed to recognize these words because she is more familiar with British English pronunciation and so would expect them to be pronounced with [e], as [leʒə] and [zed] (Wells, 2008). For Token 4, MBr2 used American pronunciation for the word *mocking* as [mɑːkɪŋ], with the vowel in the first syllable as [ɑː], and FCh1 heard 'marking' which is consistent with

Table 4.3 Tokens of misunderstanding involving native-speaker pronunciation

Token	Recording	Context	Heard as
1	MBr2 + FCh1	we try to keep it (.) *close and knit*	close and neat
2	MBr2 + FCh1	i don't have much time to do any *leisure*	?
3	MBr2 + FCh1	yeah I think world war *z* is not a bad movie	?
4	MBr2 + FCh1	sorry ah *mocking jay* which is a trilogy	marking gem
5	MBr3 + MKo	program i'm interested in? *sociolinguistic*?	for sure linguistics
6	MBr3 + MKo	erm *neurolinguistic*? And then there's one	nearer linguistics
7	FBr3 + FCh2	ah *thirteen there's thirteen* places to go to	not a good place
8	FBr3 + FCh2	next destination i think i g- i *guess* i hope so yeah	gets
9	MBr2 + FCh1	yes <spel> r t b </spel> it's ah it's in mostly at *nine*	night

[ɑː] in the first syllable in her own pronunciation of the word, because for her, *mocking* would have [ɒ].

Tokens 5 and 6 also involve American pronunciation, but in these cases it is the American accent of the listener, MKo, that caused the misunderstandings. In Token 5, MBr3 pronounced *socio-* in *sociolinguistic* with [ʃ] in the second syllable following British English pronunciation, and MKo was not familiar with use of [ʃ] in this word, as he would expect [soʊsioʊ] (Wells, 2008: 755). Similarly, in Token 6, MBr3 used [j] in the first syllable of *neurolinguistics*, following British English norms, but MKo was confused by this as he would expect the start of the word to be [nʊroʊ] following American pronunciation (Wells, 2008: 537). We can therefore conclude that, in these cases, the listener's unfamiliarity with one variety of native-speaker English pronunciation has led to a loss of intelligibility even though the pronunciation actually conforms to standard norms for that variety.

For Token 7, FBr3 pronounced the initial voiceless TH in *thirteen* as [θ], as is expected in standard varieties of English, but FCh2 failed to understand the word. Although the cause of this misunderstanding is difficult to determine, we suggest that perhaps FCh2's own avoidance of dental fricatives for the TH sounds may be a contributory factor. Jenkins (2000: 137) argues that dental fricatives are not necessary for intelligibility in ELF interactions, and studies have shown that using [t] for voiceless TH does not generally cause a problem among speakers of English in Brunei (Ishamina, 2016) and throughout Southeast Asia (Deterding & Kirkpatrick, 2006). One way or another, it seems that use of standard [θ] at the start of *thirteen* did not help in this case.

In Token 8, FCh2 heard [t] in the coda of *guess*, mishearing the word as 'gets', even though FBr3's pronunciation actually has no [t]. The cause of the misunderstanding here is uncertain, but we suggest that FCh2 was influenced by her own pronunciation patterns, as elsewhere in the recording she sometimes omitted [t] from the word-final consonant cluster [ts] such as in 'classmates' and 'its'. Given that her own realization of [ts] is variable, it seems that she sometimes hears [t] when it is not there.

In Token 9, FCh1 heard *nine* as 'night' even though the pronunciation has a clear final [n]. When she repeated the word 'nine' after obtaining clarification, she dropped the final consonant [n], pronouncing the word as [naĩ] with the vowel heavily nasalized, conforming to a tendency for speakers from China to drop a final nasal consonant, so for example 'sun' is often pronounced as [sã] (Deterding, 2006). It seems, therefore, that FCh1's own pronunciation contributed to her failure to understand *nine* by MBr2, even though the latter was perfectly standard.

The analysis above suggests that using native-speaker pronunciation does not always guarantee intelligibility in international settings. In some cases, the interlocutor's own pronunciation patterns have an impact on their perception of speech, and in these cases, use of native-speaker pronunciation does not help. There is also evidence that familiarity with only one standard variety of English, either British or American pronunciation, for example, can interfere with intelligibility, confirming that wide exposure to different varieties improves understanding (Munro *et al.*, 2006).

Lexis

This section examines the 24 tokens of misunderstanding where lexical usage is implicated. In fact, all 24 tokens are characterized by native-speaker pronunciation, which once again illustrates that imitating the speaking styles of native speakers is not necessarily helpful in international contexts.

The tokens are analyzed separately under proper nouns, words used in the education context, use of uncommon words, and finally use of unfamiliar phrases and idioms. In the analysis of some of the tokens, we investigate the frequency of the words in native speech by referring to the online Corpus of Contemporary American English (COCA) consisting of about 520 million words (COCA, 2017), as well as the British National Corpus (BNC) with about 100 million words (BNC, 2017). Here, to facilitate comparison between American and British English, we will sometimes convert the frequencies from COCA and BNC to tokens per million words (pmw), and we suggest that any word with a frequency of less than 1.0 pmw in these corpora is rather a rare word in English.

Table 4.4 shows four tokens involving proper nouns. In Token 10, FOm heard *Atlantis City* as 'Atlantic city' and in the feedback she reported that she did not know about Atlantis City or what the 'wonders of the world' were.

Table 4.4 Tokens of misunderstanding involving proper nouns

Token	Recording	Context	Heard as
10	MBr1 + FOm	the wonders of the world … the an- *atlantis city*	atlantic city
11	FBr2 + FVn	go to the museum (.) ah to see the *mona lisa*?	mona lisa
12	FBr2 + FVn	you know i learn i love *masterchef*	?
13	FBr2 + FVn	i like to watch all the food ah the *discovery channel*	real channel

Tokens 11, 12 and 13 were all misunderstood by FVn. In Token 11, although she subsequently transcribed *Mona Lisa* accurately, she stated in her feedback that she did not understand the words in the context of the utterance, and she further reported that she did not know that the Mona Lisa refers to a famous painting. In Token 12, she had not heard of the television program *Masterchef*, and in Token 13 she was not familiar with the satellite television channel *Discovery Channel*.

Table 4.5 shows nine tokens involving aspects of education. Tokens 14 and 15 both involve the metaphorical use of *dissect* to refer to analyzing

Table 4.5 Tokens of misunderstanding involving unfamiliar words used in an education context

Token	Recording	Context	Heard as
14	FBr4 + FCh3	in order to understand it we have to *dissect* it	recite
15	FBr5 + FCh4	you really really have to *dissect* the text and look at	?
16	FBr3 + FCh2	community *outreach* program? it means you help out	of which
17	MBr3 + MFr	all this erm young people the *pre-service* people	pre-service
18	FBr2 + FVn	apply to study … it's easy for you if you are *freshies*	fasy
19	MBr3 + MFr	my stress before i move on to the next *assignment*	assignment

poetry and fiction. Neither FCh3 nor FCh4 were familiar with the word even in its basic scientific context, possibly because in China students do not study science subjects in English and therefore may not be familiar with some English scientific terms. In COCA there are 511 occurrences of 'dissect' (0.98 pmw) and 50 in BNC (0.5 pmw), suggesting it is not a very common word, although at least in American English it is on the threshold of what we have suggested is a rare word.

In Token 16, FCh2 heard *outreach* as 'of which' and reported in her feedback session that she did not know *outreach*. The word seems to be quite widely used in America with 4269 occurrences in COCA (8.2 pmw), while it occurs only 120 times in BNC (1.2 pmw), so it is rather less frequent in British English.

Tokens 17 and 18 both involve words to describe the status of university students. In Token 17, MBr3 used the word *pre-service* to refer to undergraduates who have not yet started working. (In contrast, MBr3 himself was an in-service student as he had already worked for some years as a teacher.) However, MFr was not familiar with this 'pre-service' status for students. In Token 18, FBr2 referred to first-year students at the university as *freshies*, and FVn had no idea what this meant. There are just 32 occurrences of 'freshies' in COCA (0.062 pmw) and none in BNC, confirming that this is not a very common term even in America, although the full word 'freshmen' is rather more common in COCA, with 3248 occurrences (6.25 pmw) and there are 22 occurrences in BNC (0.22 pmw). The terms *pre-service* and *freshies* are commonly used at UBD, but having been at UBD for less than six months at the time of the recordings, MFr and FVn were not familiar with these terms.

In Token 19, MBr3 used the word *assignment* to refer to his schoolwork, and MFr did not understand the word used in this context until MBr3 used an alternative word 'coursework'. 'Assignment' occurs 8205 times in COCA (15.78 pmw) where it is mostly used with reference to academic work, and 1130 times in BNC (11.3 pmw) referring mostly to tasks other than schoolwork. It seems that MFr, as a European, was not familiar with *assignment* as referring to academic work.

Table 4.6 Tokens of misunderstanding involving unfamiliar words

Token	Recording	Context	Heard as
20	FBr2 + FVn	your (.) wedding *gown* or have you choose already?	?
21	FBr4 + FCh3	which black (.) tudong is it (.) like a *shawl* like this	sure
22	FBr3 + FCh2	it's like ah ah *spinning top* s- something like that	spinning cup
23	FBr3 + FCh2	i jog? and i play *squash*? ah sometimes badminton	scorsh
24	MBr2 + FCh1	so many people there it's (.) just *packed* everyday	packed
25	MBr2 + FCh1	it's kind of f- f- *starchy* a thing that ah apparently	starchi
26	MBr2 + FCh1	i see wait guangzhou is the *landlocked* area right	land lock
27	MBr1 + FMd	the tower that is defending the *nexus* you know what	?
28	FBr2 + FVn	mosque are very beautiful it's made of gold the *dome*	?
29	FBr4 + FCh3	i feel *intimidated* so i started to read english books	stimulated
30	FBr5 + FCh4	it's your opinion so you just *jot* it down and support	draw

Table 4.6 shows 11 tokens which involve unfamiliar words in contexts other than the domain of education. Both Tokens 20 and 21 involve items of clothing. In Token 20, FVn did not understand *gown* and was unable to make a guess about the word. It is a reasonably common word, with 4785 occurrences in COCA (9.20 wpm) and 770 in BNC (7.71 wpm), but FVn was not familiar with it and probably expected 'wedding dress' rather than 'wedding gown'. In Token 21, FCh3 did not understand *shawl* and transcribed 'sure' instead. 'Shawl' has 1185 occurrences in COCA (2.28 wpm) and 221 in BNC (2.21 wpm), so it is less common than 'gown', and FCh3 did not know it.

Tokens 22 and 23 involve games, and both were misunderstood by FCh2. In Token 22, she did not know *spinning top*, guessing 'spinning cup' instead. 'Spinning top' has just 37 occurrences in COCA (0.07 wpm) and 6 in BNC (0.06 wpm), so it is not surprising that FCh2 did not know it. In Token 23, she transcribed *squash* as 'scorsh', being unfamiliar with the game of squash. Although 'squash' is a common word, with 4766 occurrences in COCA (9.17 wpm) and 606 in BNC (6.06 wpm), most of the American occurrences refer to a kind of fruit, and only some of the British occurrences refer to the game, so it is not surprising that FCh2 did not know the word in this context.

Tokens 24, 25 and 26 all involve FCh1 listening to MBr2. In Token 24, MBr2 used *packed* to refer to the busy streets of the Philippines, and although FCh1 heard the word correctly, she reported that she did not understand the use of this word to refer to people. In Token 25, she did not know the word *starchy*, a word that occurs just 351 times in COCA (0.67 wpm) and 44 times in BNC (0.44 wpm), so it is not a common word. In Token 26, she did not understand *landlocked*, although she managed to guess it nearly correctly. Once again, it is not a common word, occurring just 355 times in COCA (0.68 wpm) and 31 times in BNC (0.31 wpm). However, in this case, there may be a further factor involved: as FCh1 comes from China, she would know that Guangzhou is not landlocked and is actually on a river estuary near the sea, so this may have contributed to the confusion.

In Token 27, FMd did not understand *nexus*. This word occurs 1329 times in COCA (2.56 wpm) and 118 times in BNC (1.18 wpm), but many of these occurrences refer to a brand of tablet computer, so its use to mean a connection or focal point is not very common, especially as it seems to occur mostly in computer gaming contexts.

Tokens 28, 29 and 30 all involve moderately uncommon words in English. In COCA, *dome* has 5672 occurrences (10.91 wpm), *intimidated* has 2370 occurrences (4.56 wpm), and *jot* has 1204 occurrences (2.32 wpm) if we include its inflections 'jots', 'jotted' and 'jotting'. While none of them can be regarded as rare using the 1.0 wpm threshold suggested above, at the same time they are not common words in English, and all were misunderstood.

Finally, Table 4.7 shows three tokens involving unfamiliar idiomatic phrases. In Token 31, MBr2 was telling FCh1 about a local delicacy and described it as an *acquired taste*, but FCh1 was not familiar with this phrase. There are 123 occurrences of 'acquired taste' listed in COCA (0.24 wpm) and 15 occurrences in BNC (0.15 wpm), so it is indeed a rare phrase.

In Token 32, MBr1 used the expression *funny enough* to describe the irony of his brother's profession being unrelated to his qualifications, and although FMd was able to identify the words, she did not understand them in this context. COCA lists 93 occurrences of 'funny enough' (0.16 pmw) and there are 20 instances in BNC (0.20 pmw), so it is indeed not a common phrase. (We might note here that 'funnily enough' is a little more frequent in British English, with 95 occurrences or 0.95 pmw in BNC, although this alternative phrase is not so common in America, with just 30 occurrences or 0.06 pmw in COCA.)

Finally, in Token 33, FBr2 used the idiomatic expression *for good* to explain that she had come back to Brunei permanently after studying abroad for a year. Although 'for good' is a common collocation, with 6969 occurrences in COCA, the majority of these involve other contexts, such as 'for good behavior' or 'for good drainage', and only a few involve the

Table 4.7 Tokens of misunderstanding involving unfamiliar phrases

Token	Recording	Context	Heard as
31	MBr2 + FCh1	it's quite good actually well it's an **acquired taste**	a quiet taste
32	MBr1 + FMd	but **funny enough** … his job … has less to do with	funny enough
33	FBr2 + FVn	i travel ah before i went to brunei **for good**	for good

idiomatic use of the phrase to mean permanently, and FVn was not familiar with this idiomatic usage.

Idiomatic native-speaker usage such as this can be problematic in ELF contexts. Deterding (2013) similarly showed that the use of native-speaker idioms such as 'the opium of the people' and 'great leap forward' in ELF interactions can lead to misunderstandings.

To conclude, the data analysis indicates that certain words and phrases that occur in native-speaker English can cause misunderstandings in international communication when listeners are not familiar with words such as *gown* (Token 20), *shawl* (Token 21) and *nexus* (Token 27), and idiomatic phrases such as *acquired taste* (Token 31) and *for good* (Token 33). In addition, misunderstandings can occur when usage from American English such as *freshies* (Token 18) referring to first-year students or *assignment* (Token 19) for academic work is not known by someone who is more familiar with British English.

Clearly, it is valuable for speakers of English around the world to understand words such as *shawl* and *nexus* and phrases such as *acquired taste* and *for good*, as they may encounter them when speaking with native speakers or watching American movies. However, they should be wary of using words and phrases such as these when conversing in ELF contexts, as their interlocutors may be unfamiliar with them.

Discussion

If imitating native-speaker pronunciation and using native-centric words and idioms can at times be unhelpful in achieving mutual intelligibility in international communication, then why do testing and assessment continue to be based on native-speaker standards which are highly unachievable? It has been argued that this form of assessment does not reflect the actual use of English for communicative purposes in international settings (Fang, 2017), and that assessment should reflect specific goals rather than being based on standardized large-scale tests.

Perhaps a more reasonable solution is to work towards an ELF-informed assessment, although it must be acknowledged that substantial challenges remain. For communicative effectiveness, pronunciation assessment should focus on intelligibility rather than prioritizing near native-like accents (Kang & Kermad, 2017; Sewell, 2013), but there are significant problems in determining what exactly impacts intelligibility and how we might judge whether an extract of speech would be easily understood by listeners from around the world. Perhaps it is not surprising that teachers and testers continue to make reference to widely available descriptions and reference works on native-speaker usage.

Elder and Davies (2006) have made two different proposals for establishing tests based on an ELF approach: the first suggests involving highly proficient ELF users in setting standards and including them as interlocutors in speaking exams as well as avoiding the use of native-like obscure vocabulary and figures of speech; the second proposal focuses on students fulfilling tasks such as involving interlocutors from different language backgrounds in completing a speaking assessment, and also incorporating multiple accents in listening tests. Exposure to different accents can indeed enhance understanding (Munro *et al.*, 2006), and the study discussed in this chapter provides evidence that familiarity with only one standard variety of English pronunciation and lexical usage can affect intelligibility in international communication.

Harding and McNamara (2017: 577) similarly lay a foundation for developing a construct for ELF-based assessment by suggesting that criteria for testing can be based on communicative competencies such as the ability to understand different varieties of English including a range of accents, syntactic features and discourse patterns. They also propose that, while it is important for students to produce clear pronunciation patterns that ensure a high level of intelligibility (such as those included in the Lingua Franca Core proposed by Jenkins, 2000), there are other skills that could be tested, such as the ability to negotiate meaning, to accommodate to the interlocutor's speech patterns, and to be aware of communicative breakdowns and how to repair them. Perhaps, during the testing session, assessors might pretend not to understand something and thereby see how successful the student is in explaining the problematic words or otherwise resolving the problem.

Of course, it is acknowledged that targeting specific criteria, proficiency and competencies for testing should reflect different communicative goals in specific domains. Nonetheless, one of the biggest challenges remains in gaining acceptance for the shift from traditional forms of assessment based on native-speaker standards to a more unconventional approach towards language testing. While some of the proposals outlined above might not be practical at present, one can at least suggest that students should not be penalized for deviating from native-speaker norms of usage if their speech at all times remains clear and easily understandable. It should fundamentally be acknowledged that not all patterns of native-speaker usage are helpful in international settings, and learners of English should not be required to closely mimic them.

Conclusion

In this chapter, we have shown that native-speaker usage can give rise to misunderstandings in international contexts, and that it is simply not true that strict adherence to native-speaker norms of pronunciation and lexis necessarily results in a high level of intelligibility. It is therefore unfortunate that native-speaker forms of assessment, particularly the outdated English language 'O' level, continue to be promoted in a place like Brunei, especially when so many students are failing to achieve the required grade in this examination. It seems likely, for example, that students taking the Cambridge 'O' level exam would be praised for using rare words like *nexus* or phrases like *acquired taste*, but such usage can be problematic in ELF contexts.

It would seem to be far more useful if, instead of being urged to mimic native-speaker usage, learners of English were encouraged to develop the ability to communicate effectively with people from around the world, adjusting their pronunciation where necessary (for example, by slowing down) and also by avoiding difficult words or phrases with unexpected idiomatic meanings. This kind of ELF-based pedagogy has been proposed by various scholars (Fang, 2016; Jenkins, 2007; Walker, 2010) who have argued that the ability to accommodate one's speech to the needs of one's interlocutor is an exceptionally valuable skill that could easily be promoted in the classroom. It is unfortunate that these proposals are not being adopted more widely by education authorities around the world, and it seems likely that assessment based on native-speaker norms will continue to be used for some time.

References

Bayliss, A. (2006) IELTS as a predictor for academic language performance. *Australian International Education Conference 2006*. See http://aiec.idp.com/uploads/pdf/BaylissIngram%20(Paper)%20Wed%201630%20MR5.pdf.
BNC (2017) British National Corpus. See http://corpus.byu.edu/bnc/ (accessed 7 July 2017).
COCA (2017) Corpus of Contemporary American English. See http://corpus.byu.edu/coca/ (accessed 7 July 2017).
Cotton, F. and Conrow, F. (1998) An investigation of the predictive validity of IELTS amongst a group of international students studying at the University of Tasmania. *IELTS Research Reports* 1, 72–115.
Deterding, D. (2006) The pronunciation of English by speakers from China. *English World-Wide* 27, 175–198.
Deterding, D. (2013) *Misunderstandings in English as a Lingua Franca: An Analysis of ELF Interactions in South-East Asia*. Berlin: De Gruyter.
Deterding, D. and Gardiner, I.A. (2018) New pronunciation en route to World Englishes. In O. Kang, R.I. Thomson and J.M. Murphy (eds) *The Routledge Handbook of Contemporary English Pronunciation* (pp. 218–231). New York: Routledge.
Deterding, D. and Kirkpatrick, A. (2006) Emerging South-East Asian Englishes and intelligibility. *World Englishes* 23, 391–409.
EduCo (2016) Standardized English tests predictors of academic success? *EduCo*, 21 July. See http://educoglobal.com/standardized-english-tests-predictors-of-academic-success/.
Elder, C. and Davies, A. (2006) Assessing English as a lingua franca. *Annual Review of Applied Linguistics* 26, 282–304.
Fang, F. (2016) 'Mind your local accent': Does accent training resonate to college students' English use? *Englishes in Practice* 3 (1), 1–28.
Fang, F. (2017) English as a lingua franca: Implications for pedagogy and assessment. *TEFLIN Journal* 28 (1), 57–70.
Firth, A. (1996) The discursive accomplishment of normality: On 'lingua franca' English and conversation analysis. *Journal of Pragmatics* 26, 237–259.

Gunn, G.C. (1997) *Language, Power and Ideology in Brunei Darussalam*. Athens: Ohio University Center for International Studies.

Harding, L. and McNamara, T. (2017) Language assessment: The challenge of ELF. In J. Jenkins, W. Baker and M. Dewey (eds) *The Routledge Handbook of English as a Lingua Franca* (pp. 570–582). London: Routledge.

Ishamina, A. (2016) TH in misunderstandings in Brunei English. *South East Asia: A Multidisciplinary Journal* 16, 1–7.

Ishamina, A. and Deterding, D. (2017) English medium education in a university in Brunei Darussalam: Code-switching and intelligibility. In B. Fenton-Smith, P. Humphreys and I. Walkinshaw (eds) *English Medium Instruction in Higher Education in Asia-Pacific: From Policy to Pedagogy* (pp. 281–298). Cham: Springer.

Jenkins, J. (2000) *The Phonology of English as an International Language*. Oxford: Oxford University Press.

Jenkins, J. (2007) *English as a Lingua Franca: Attitude and Identity*. Oxford: Oxford University Press.

Jones, G.M. (1996) The bilingual education policy in Brunei Darussalam. In P.W. Martin, C. Ożóg and G. Poedjosoedarmo (eds) *Language Use and Language Change in Brunei Darussalam* (pp. 123–132). Athens, OH: Ohio University Center for International Studies.

Jones, G.M. (2007) 20 Years of bilingual education: Then and now. In D. Prescott (ed.) *English in Southeast Asia: Varieties, Literacies and Literatures* (pp. 246–258). Newcastle: Cambridge Scholars.

Jones, G.M. (2012) Language planning in its historical context in Brunei Darussalam. In E. Low and Azirah Hashim (eds) *English in Southeast Asia: Features, Policy and Language Use* (pp. 175–187). Amsterdam: John Benjamins.

Kachru, B.B. (1992) Teaching World Englishes. In B.B. Kachru (ed.) *The Other Tongue: English Across Cultures* (2nd edn) (pp. 355–365). Champaign, IL: University of Illinois Press.

Kang, O. and Kermad, A. (2017) Assessment in second language pronunciation. In O. Kang, R.I. Thomson and J.M. Murphy (eds) *The Routledge Handbook of Contemporary English Pronunciation* (pp. 511–526). New York: Routledge.

Kirkpatrick, A. (2006) Which model of English: Native-speaker, nativised or lingua franca? In R. Rubdy and M. Saraceni (eds) *English in the World: Global Rules, Global Roles* (pp. 71–83). London: Continuum.

Leung, C., Lewkowicz, J. and Jenkins, J. (2016) English for academic purposes: A need for remodelling. *Englishes in Practice* 3 (3), 55–73.

Martin, P.W. and Poedjosoedarmo, G. (1996) Introduction: An overview of the language situation in Brunei Darussalam. In P.W. Martin, C. Ożóg and G. Poedjosoedarmo (eds) *Language Use and Language Change in Brunei Darussalam* (pp. 1–23). Athens, OH: Ohio University Center for International Studies.

Ministry of Education (2007) *Proposed SPN21 Curriculum: Draft*. Bandar Seri Begawan: Ministry of Education.

Ministry of Education (2009) *The National Education System for the 21st Century: SPN21*. Bandar Seri Begawan: Ministry of Education.

Mortensen, J. (2013) Notes on English used as a lingua franca as an object of study. *Journal of English as a Lingua Franca* 2 (1), 25–46.

Mundia, L. (2010) Implementation of SPN21 curriculum in Brunei Darussalam: A review of selected implications on school assessment reforms. *International Education Studies* 3 (2), 119–129.

Munro, M.J., Derwing, T.M. and Morton, S.L. (2006) The mutual intelligibility of L2 speech. *Studies in Second Language Acquisition* 28, 111–131.

Nicol, M.F. (2005) Some problems experienced by Bruneian students with the Cambridge O level English language reading comprehension paper. *South East Asia: A Multidisciplinary Journal* 5 (1/2), 47–70.

O'Sullivan, B. (2011) Language testing. In J. Simpson (ed.) *The Routledge Handbook of Applied Linguistics* (pp. 259–273). London: Routledge.

Seidlhofer, B. (2011) *Understanding English as a Lingua Franca*. Oxford: Oxford University Press.

Sewell, A. (2013) Language testing and international intelligibility: A Hong Kong case study. *Language Assessment Quarterly* 10, 423–443.

Svartvik, J. and Leech, G. (2006) *English: One Tongue, Many Voices*. Basingstoke: Palgrave Macmillan.

Tomlinson, B. (2010) Which test of English and why? In A. Kirkpatrick (ed.) *The Routledge Handbook of World Englishes* (pp. 599–616). London: Routledge.

Walker, R. (2010) *Teaching the Pronunciation of English as a Lingua Franca*. Oxford: Oxford University Press.

Wells, J.C. (2008) *Longman Pronunciation Dictionary* (3rd edn). Edinburgh: Pearson Education.

5 Global Englishes and the International Standardized English Language Proficiency Tests

James Dean Brown

This chapter begins by discussing the early literature on Global English(es) and language testing. It then briefly summarizes Brown (2014, reprinted 2015), which addressed several areas that the World Englishes community regards as problematic in language testing (linguistic norms, testing cultures, test design, testing processes and testing in various contexts), and Brown (in press), which examined how the international standardized English language proficiency tests (ISELPTs; i.e. TOEFL iBT, TOEIC and IELTS) present themselves, the definition of *English language proficiency*, the role of *persons* in testing English language proficiency, paths for changing the ISELPTs, and ways in which those alternative English language proficiency approaches can be assessed operationally. The chapter then addresses five key questions: (a) What is *English language proficiency* really? (b) Why is the so-called native-speaker standard a thing of the past? (c) What alternative models are there to the native-speaker model for English language proficiency? (d) Why is changing the ISELPTs so difficult/slow? and (e) What strategies might prove useful for effecting change in the ISELPTs?

Introduction

According to Richards and Schmidt (2010), *Global English* '(also English as an International Language, EIL)' describes:

> ... the use of English as a world language, rather than simply the language of native-speakers of English. Global English emphasizes that English is spoken as a first, second or foreign language both within and across national borders around the world, and that in many situations 'native-speaker' accents are not considered necessary or even desirable. (Richards & Schmidt, 2010: 247)

Global Englishes in the plural will be used here to acknowledge that fact that among the varieties of Global Englishes, there are *inner circle Englishes* (IC, e.g. British, American and Australian), *outer circle Englishes* (OC, e.g. Indian, Nigerian, Singaporean Englishes) and *expanding circle Englishes* (EC, e.g. in France, Japan, Colombia) (after Kachru, 1986: 121–122).

The early literature on Global Englishes and language testing

Davidson and Lowenberg (1996: 1) captured the overall issue at the nexus of language testing and Global Englishes as follows: 'The general problem can be put thus: how can English tests be best designed to accommodate varietal differences of Englishes around the world?' Elsewhere in the early literature, the effects of the *linguistic norms* used in English as a second language (ESL) and English as a foreign language (EFL) tests were discussed (Davidson, 1993; Lowenberg, 1993) and how the international standardized English language proficiency tests (ISELPTs) hold considerable power and maintain the linguistic norms because the correct answers to their test items are based on those norms (Davidson, 1993), which in turn is justified by the so-called native-speaker (NS) model (Taylor, 2006).

The early literature also dealt with the fact that *testing cultures* have developed in various countries (Davidson, 1993; Spolsky, 1993) for developing, administering and validating their testing practices (Davidson & Lowenberg, 1996). As a result, questions have arisen about: item and test bias across varieties of English (Brown, 2004); item validity and 'localized validity' for items (Davidson, 1993: 116, 2006); the meaning of testing 'linguistic norms' (Davidson & Lowenberg, 1996); the effects on test reliability of varieties of English (Davidson & Lowenberg, 1996); the relationships between test design and test use, especially with regard to English norms (Davidson, 1993; Wesolek *et al.*, 1993); the attitudes towards Englishes of learners and teachers in various contexts (Taylor, 2006); and the relationship of language tests to the actual communication needs of examinees (Clyne & Sharifian, 2008). Other authors have grappled with testing processes, for example, addressing such questions as what should be assessed, how it should be assessed and who should do the assessing (Hamp-Lyons & Zhang, 2001), as well as what input and output languages should be used and what standards should be judged (Taylor, 2002).

In addition, Chalhoub-Deville and Wigglesworth (2005: 383) criticized '... ever-increasing efforts by major language testing organizations to market their tests in countries or with populations for which they were originally not intended and/or for which appropriate research has not been carried out to justify such wide use'. Davidson (2006) further explained that:

> There is a well-established and legitimate concern that large, powerful English language tests are fundamentally disconnected from the insights

in analysis of English in the world context. These exams set linguistic norms that do not necessarily represent the rich body of English varieties spoken and used in contact situations all over the world. (Davidson, 2006: 709)

More recent contributions on Global Englishes and language testing

More recently, Brown (2014, reprinted 2015) discussed the World Englishes (WEs) issues that language testers need to include in their thinking, especially the possibility that the so-called NS norm is no longer sacred and the possible utility of IC, OC and EC Englishes perspectives for language testing. That article also discussed issues that language testers need to clarify for the WEs community, including ways in which language testing has already added to the understanding of language variation, how language testing does not entirely overlook WEs concerns, and how language testing is not just about the ISELPTs. That paper ends with seven recommendations (Brown, 2014: 16–23) which might 'make the intersection of WEs and LT [language testing] more productive' (Brown, 2014: 5).

In addition, Brown (in press) focused on three prominent ISELPTs: the *Test of English as a Foreign Language Internet Based Test* (TOEFL iBT), *Test of English as an International Language* (TOEIC) and *International English Language Testing System* (IELTS). The chapter examined the promotional materials associated with each of these tests and showed how their claims continue into their research studies on the tests. Indeed, close examination of the wording of the names of these tests revealed that they are selling themselves as tests of EFL and *international* English. Further examination of the online promotional materials for these tests showed that they all state or imply that they are testing English language proficiency (ELP). It is not uncommon for such promotional materials to oversell a product to the largest possible audience and therefore to overstate who they are designed for (in this case, the large and varied ELP audience) and what they can do (i.e. test international English). Overall, that chapter addressed six key issues: (a) how the TOEFL iBT, TOEIC and IELTS present themselves; (b) what ELP is; (c) why *persons* is important in testing ELP; (d) how we can move forward in changing the ISELPTs; (e) what some alternative approaches to ELP are; and (f) how alternative ELP approaches can be assessed operationally.

The purpose of this chapter

In this chapter, I will continue the discussion that I started in Brown (2014/2015, in press) on the ISELPTs and their relationships with Global Englishes. In the process, I will consider five new questions:

(1) What is *English language proficiency* really?
(2) Why is the so-called native-speaker standard a thing of the past?
(3) What alternative models are there to the NS model for ELP?
(4) Why is changing the ISELPTs so difficult/slow?
(5) What strategies might prove useful for effecting change in the ISELPTs?

What is *English Language Proficiency* Really?

What is a native speaker of English?

The English language that examinees encounter, and must comprehend and manipulate in the ISELPTs, is that of the native speaker (NS; see Brown, in press). Davies (2004) defined a *native speaker* as follows:

The native speaker (and this means all native speakers) may be defined in the following six ways (Davies, 1991, 2003):

(1) The native speaker acquires the L1 of which she/he is a native speaker in childhood.
(2) The native speaker has intuitions (in terms of acceptability and productiveness) about his/her idiolectal grammar.
(3) The native speaker has intuitions about those features of the standard language grammar which are distinct from his/her idiolectal grammar.
(4) The native speaker has a unique capacity to produce fluent spontaneous discourse, which exhibits pauses mainly at clause boundaries (the 'one clause at a time' facility) and which is facilitated by a huge memory stock of complete lexical items (Pawley & Syder, 1983). In both production and comprehension, the native speaker exhibits a wide range of communicative competence.
(5) The native speaker has a unique capacity to write creatively (and this includes, of course, literature at all levels from jokes to epics, metaphor to novels.
(6) The native speaker has a unique capacity to interpret and translate into the L1 of which she/he is a native speaker. Disagreements about the deployment of an individual's capacity are likely to stem from a dispute about the standard or (standard) language. (Davies, 2004: 435)

What is English language competence?

In trying to characterize the language of the target NS, various authors including Canale and Swain (1980, 1981), Bachman (1990) and Bachman and Palmer (1996) have characterized language proficiency as being made up of different competencies. For example, the Bachman (1990) model describes general organizational and pragmatic competencies and then numerous sub-competencies in each as follows:

(A) Organizational competence
    (1) Grammatical competence
        (a) Vocabulary
        (b) Morphology
        (c) Syntax
        (d) Phonology/graphemes
    (2) Textual competence
        (a) Cohesion
        (b) Rhetorical organization
(B) Pragmatic competence
    (1) Illocutionary competence
        (a) Ideational functions
        (b) Manipulative functions
        (c) Heuristic functions
        (d) Imaginative functions
    (2) Sociolinguistic competence
        (a) Sensitivity to differences in dialect or variety
        (b) Sensitivity to differences in register
        (c) Sensitivity to naturalness
        (d) Ability to interpret cultural references and figures of speech

Given the level of proficiency in English needed to master these competencies (especially those from A2 onward in the outline), I assume that these are the characteristics of native language use – but which native English, dialect, class, level of education? These are issues not tackled in such debates. Instead, the competencies are usually taken to be characteristics of the educated NS, or what has been referred to in the literature as the idealized NS, a notion that traces back to Leung *et al.* (1997: 544) who defined the *idealized native speaker* as embodying '... conventional notions of the *native speaker* of English'.

If the competencies outlined above are taken to be the 'conventional notions' characterizing the idealized NS, there must be at least 14 dimensions to be considered in testing the ELP construct – or so it is supposed by many language testers. Two key questions that remain unanswered with regard to these 14 dimensions are: (a) Which of these should test designers account for in developing ELP tests? and (b) Should separate scores be reported for each dimension of ELP? The ones chosen by-and-large for inclusion in the ISELPTs are the ones listed under A1 insofar as they are related to the reading, listening, writing and (in some cases) speaking skills. Those categories listed from A2 onward in the outline, if included at all, are largely present by accident.

What is ELP, really?

The previous two subsections described what an NS is and what the potential categories and subcategories are for ELP as they relate to the idealized NS. But I must ask if even those competencies listed in A1 are really being fully tested in the ISELPTs. As pointed out by Brown (in press):

> ... *who* we measure is also important. Let me illustrate briefly from a technical standpoint. In norm-referenced measurement like that done on the ISELPTs, *persons*[1] and their relative abilities are the main point. Indeed, testers long ago recognized that, in piloting test items, item discrimination helps us select those items that are separating high performing examinees from low performing ones.[2] Thus, while the content and difficulty of individual items is important, person abilities are at least equally important in developing ISELPTs.

In short, it does not matter if a language point is in the NS repertoire because, unless high-performing non-native speaker (NNS) examinees know that language point while low-level performers do not, that language point will not appear in an ISELPT. In other words, NNS examinees are presented with NS language material to see if they can comprehend and manipulate it. If the examinees do not know the language points involved, the items will not discriminate and therefore will be eliminated from the test. While the ISELPTs may claim to be testing the NS model of ELP, they are really testing only what the non-native speakers (NNSs) have been taught and have learned/acquired, and of that, only those language points that discriminate between high- and low-performing examinees.

Even more worrisome, because item discrimination is an indication of the degree to which an item separates the high-performing from the low-performing examinees, it is crucially important to carefully define what constitutes performing high and low. If high-performing is defined as answering correctly in response to Midwest North American NS Englishes[3] (whether written or oral) and low-performing is defined as answering incorrectly, the ISELPT scale will only discriminate between those examinees who are or are not able to deal with a narrow range of materials in North American Englishes.

Thus the items that remain in the ISELPTs have never really been a sample of the idealized NS language, but rather they are only those items that survive because they distinguish between high-performing and low-performing NNS examinees of a particular type when confronted with English language materials of a specific kind. And, strangely enough, it is those items that serve as the basis for the scores that are then interpreted as representing the ELP construct around the world.

Why is the So-called Native-speaker Standard a Thing of the Past?

In this section, I will distinguish between language material issues and person issues in discussing why I believe the idealized NS is a thing of the past in ELP testing. Recall that the ISELPTs are created based on a subset of idealized NS language materials, and then those items that survive the piloting process are the ones that discriminate between high- and low-performing NNS examinees (persons).

Language material issues

The 'curious position' of native speakers

As Davies (2004) pointed out:

> the concept of native speaker occupies a curious position in applied linguistics. On the one hand, it is widely used as a benchmark for knowledge of a language (and as such attracts opposition because it excludes those who are not native speakers), and as a criterion for employment; on the other hand a definition of the native speaker is elusive. (Davies, 2004: 431)

I would contend that Davies' 'concept of native speaker' describes *persons* who are NSs, and that the 'benchmark for knowledge of a language', more commonly referred to as ELP, represents how idealized NS English materials of one sort or another discriminate between high- and low-performing NNSs of a specific type. Thus, the 'concept of native speaker' and the 'benchmark for knowledge of a language' are completely different things.

The NS ELP standard is still inadequately defined

Recall that the ELP proficiency model described above (after Bachman, 1990; Bachman & Palmer, 1996; Canale & Swain, 1980, 1981) contained 14 separate dimensions. But what exactly is meant by each of the 14 dimensions? For example, taking just the first one, what does *vocabulary* (A.1.a.) mean? Are collocations included? Phrasal verbs? Idioms? Swear words? And are both passive and active knowledge included for each case? Is all of that meant to be in speaking only? Or in reading, writing and listening too? And perhaps more germane to this chapter, whose vocabulary? Idealized NSs (whatever that is)? A real-life sample of educated NSs? Ordinary or average NSs? Of which English(es)? Should the list include the vocabulary necessary to communicate locally in English? Globally? To communicate with IC, OC and EC speakers of English? In short, what does vocabulary mean and encompass?

Similar questions should also be addressed for each of the other 13 dimensions of the ELP proficiency model described above. That is why I say that NS ELP is still inadequately defined.

NS English is many things

In addition, the so-called NS standard itself, even if it could be clearly defined, ranges considerably across geographical locations. There are many different types of NSs ranging across Englishes, dialects of those Englishes, social classes and other variables. Educated IC NSs of English from the UK and US have enough trouble understanding one another without throwing in London's Cockney and Boston's Southie dialects. Also consider all the dialects of English around the world from North America, the Caribbean, Austronesia, Africa, south Asia, southeast Asia and Europe. Which of these is not an NS? In addition, consider the variety of NS or near-NS teachers that EFL students may be exposed to during their studies, all of whom represent examples of various IC, OC and EC Englishes. Thus, English is many things.

NS proficiency is a moving target

We often forget that NS proficiency is not a single 'baseline' or standard that all NSs reach, but rather it ranges enormously. For example, the SAT *verbal* test scores for NSs range from 200 to 800 which is a wide spread of abilities indeed and, for the most part, even that range only represents the spread of abilities among North Americans with ambitions to go on to college or university. Even at the so-called highest levels of society, Americans range widely in proficiency, for example, from G.W. Bush and Donald Trump to Bill Clinton and Barack Obama levels. Consider additionally what the ranges of abilities must be for all Americans at all educational levels, not to mention the ranges in the task types that various NSs can perform with English. In other words, the NS standard is not a thing, not a 'baseline', but rather is a wide range or moving target.

Person issues

In Brown (in press) I suggested that test developers should zero in on the variation that arises from differences among persons when those persons are confronted with ISELPT items, and that therefore it is important to examine the actual examinees (the persons) and their needs. I concluded, '… that the variation that occurs naturally among the persons learning and using English has more to do with multiple Englishes (and multiple dimensions) than with the variance that occurs when persons encounter some idealized NS Standard English'.

The NS standard is an impossible dream

Even if we could define the idealized NS standard, that standard cannot be reached by the vast majority of EFL students around the world in the few hundreds of hours of English that most EFL students get in junior and high school, and even their EC bilingual teachers, who do study English for many thousands of hours, would rarely call themselves native speakers. Thus, the

NS standard (whatever that is) is an impossible dream for most EFL students, one that is not attainable. In fact, the very idea of an NS standard as a goal sets most students of EFL up for a massive sense of failure.

The NS standard isn't even desirable

Perhaps, more importantly, the profession needs to ask itself why an L2 speaker of English would ever want to be an NS of English. It is the height of arrogance to even propose that EFL students should abandon or supplement their identities as NSs of Chinese or Spanish by becoming NSs of English. Why is it not good enough to be EC Chinese speakers of English or EC Spanish speakers of English?

Communicating with native speakers is not the only possibility

From another angle, the field has traditionally thought in terms of helping NNSs of English listen to and speak with NSs of English (or read native text and write to NSs) in possible combinations as follows: NS–NNS and NNS–NS. However, this simplistic view of how NNSs communicate in English has overlooked one other very important combination, NNS–NNS, which it turns out is quite common and much more complex than it at first appears to be (Levis, 2005). Moreover, Table 5.1 shows the possible combinations of speakers/writers and listeners/readers of IC, OC and EC Englishes. Notice that only the two squares that are in bold italics (i.e. *IC–EC* and *EC–IC*) are truly NS–NNS and NNS–NS in the traditional sense. Several other possible combinations present themselves: the OC–EC and EC–OC combinations involve NNSs communicating with OC speakers/writers and listeners/readers, not to mention the EC–EC interactions which involve NNSs communicating with NNSs. Naturally, given the fluid nature of communication, these distinctions are somewhat arbitrary and artificial.

The NS standard is not what students will encounter/need

After taking the ISELPTs required to gain admission to universities in the US, UK, Canada, New Zealand or Australia, it turns out that students will not need to communicate with idealized NSs at all. Instead, such students will find themselves surrounded in most university settings by a bewildering variety of IC, OC and EC Englishes and dialects from around the

Table 5.1 World Englishes speaker/writer and listener/reader matrix

	Inner circle listener/reader (IC)	Outer circle listener/reader (OC)	Expanding circle listener/reader (EC)
Inner circle speaker/writer	IC–IC	IC–OC	*IC–EC*
Outer circle speaker/writer	OC–IC	OC–OC	OC–EC
Expanding circle speaker/writer	*EC–IC*	EC–OC	EC–EC

Source: Adapted from Levis (2005: 373).

nation and world, few of which resemble anything like the idealized NS standard that they were tested on. What those students need, then, is the ability and flexibility to understand a variety of Englishes as well as to make themselves intelligible to that same wide range of speakers of Englishes.

What Alternative Models Are There to the NS Model for ELP?

If not the NS model, then what? Language testers often act as though the NS model is the only option. However, Brown (in press) offers a number of different alternatives to the NS model that should perhaps be taken seriously. To understand these alternative models for ELP, it is first necessary to understand why people learn English and how a Global English standard might be a first step to replacing the idealized NS standard. This section will then finish with a discussion of six alternative top-down, language-materials focused approaches to ELP, and eight bottom-up, persons-focused approaches.

Why do people learn English?

Brown (2012: 149) made several points worth considering in thinking about testing and Global Englishes, especially about why people study English. Most of those reasons fall into two categories: global or local reasons. Traditionally, *global reasons* for learning English focus on the usefulness of English, arguing that English is:

(1) the principal means of communicating globally;
(2) one way to foster internationalism or globalism;
(3) important for gaining entry into higher education;
(4) the primary language for accessing global information.

Such lofty goals for learning English are often cited by governments and educational institutions. In contrast, *local reasons* for learning English tend to focus on what people actually do with English locally:

(1) communicating locally with compatriots who speak other mother tongues;
(2) working locally with foreign tourists;
(3) gaining advantage over other local people in business dealings;
(4) speaking with friends or family members who speak English;
(5) acquiring the prestige locally of speaking English.

What makes these two different sets of reasons for learning English important to the discussion in this chapter is the fact that those people who are most likely to take the ISELPTs are learners who have predominantly global purposes for learning English. Brown (2012) argues that most other people (i.e. the vast majority of EFL learners) need English for local purposes or maybe just to meet the English requirements in their schools or work situations.

Could a Global English standard replace the NS model?

McKay and Brown (2015) propose what they call a *Global English Standard* (GES), which:

- is based on the second definition of *standard* discussed above which focuses on the system of English, rather than on some idealized NS;
- recognizes that there is a system of English that is taught across the globe to NSs (regardless of which English or dialect they speak, or their social standing or educational level) and to so-called non-native speakers alike;
- emphasizes the idea that capital-G English Grammar (especially the written grammar) is fairly homogeneous across all Englishes, dialects and learners;
- acknowledges the importance of a centre or common system around the world for English that will maximize effective communication – especially in certain formal genres of written English;
- sidesteps the sense (implicit in the idealized NS standard) that NSs own English and its standard, instead promoting the idea that GES, by definition, is owned by all speakers of English;
- can easily coexist with various Englishes and dialects around the world, whenever and wherever it is needed, including local EILs everywhere (McKay & Brown, 2015: xv).

GES sidesteps many of the problems raised by the idealized NS standard, and indeed would address the needs of people in that relatively small group of students who actually have global reasons for learning English, such as immigrating or studying abroad, and therefore end up taking the ISELPTs.

Alternative models for ELP

Brown (in press) proposes a number of alternative approaches for defining ELP, some of which are top-down, language-materials focused approaches (meaning that they focus on the English language itself in one way or another and how the candidates match up to that language), whereas others are bottom-up, persons-focused approaches (meaning that they look at what people can do with the language in one or the other and measure differences in the abilities of people as they exist in the real world).

The *six top-down, language-materials focused approaches* to defining the ELP construct are:

(1) *The traditional approach* claims to measure levels of NS standard English competence, or ELP, based on the idealized NS by discriminating between examinees who comprehend and manipulate specific types of NS language materials effectively or poorly. This is the approach that is currently in wide use.

(2) *Truth-in-advertising approach* would be the same as (1) but, instead of claiming to measure overall ELP, this approach would openly acknowledge that the test measures the ability to comprehend and manipulate materials in one particular English and for one purpose. For instance, if the TOEFL defined itself as measuring the levels of proficiency in general North American English (whatever that is) for academic purposes, that would provide a sort of truth-in-advertising.
(3) *Multiple WEs approach* would measure competence in multiple Global or World Englishes including at least IC and OC WEs by discriminating between examinees who comprehend and manipulate IC and OC WEs language materials effectively or poorly.
(4) *English as a lingua franca (ELF) approach* would measure levels of ELF competence by discriminating between examinees who comprehend and manipulate ELF language materials effectively or poorly.
(5) *Global Standard English (GES) approach* would measure levels of competence in some well-defined GES by discriminating between examinees who comprehend and manipulate GES language materials – perhaps from a variety of WEs as in (3) – effectively or poorly.
(6) *Functional English(es) approach* would measure levels of competence to function in a variety of English(es), perhaps by discriminating between examinees who function effectively or poorly vis-à-vis a variety of WEs language materials.

The *eight bottom-up, persons-focused approaches* to defining the ELP construct are:

(1) *Effective communicator approach* would measure levels of ability to communicate in a variety of WEs by focusing on whatever discriminates between examinees who communicate effectively in a variety of WEs from those who do so poorly.
(2) *Scope of proficiency approach* would assess the examinees' abilities to be locally effective, nationally effective or internationally effective in shuttling between WEs, by focusing on whatever discriminates between examinees who can be characterized as only able to communicate locally from those who can do so nationally and those who can be internationally effective in shuttling between a variety of WEs.
(3) *Scale of range approach* would measure the examinees' range of types and topics and ability to produce utterances/sentences in Englishes by focusing on whatever discriminates between examinees who can only deal with a few types of discourse and topics with a few utterances/sentences from those who can deal with many.
(4) *Intelligibility approach* would measure the examinees' abilities to make themselves understood by assessing how easy it is for speakers of various (or appropriate) WEs to understand the examinee and

thereby discriminating between examinees who can make themselves understood well and those who do so poorly.
(5) *Resourcefulness approach* would measure how linguistically resourceful the examinees are by assessing their resourcefulness in communicating by discriminating between those examinees that use few linguistic and paralinguistic resources and those who use many.
(6) *Symbolic competence approach* would measure the examinees' levels of symbolic competence by focusing on their multilingual abilities by discriminating between those examinees who use few multilingual resources (e.g. code-switching) and those who use many in communicating.
(7) *Intercultural communication skills* approach would measure the examinees' abilities to communicate internationally by discriminating between those examinees with little cultural knowledge that helps them communicate from those who have a great deal.
(8) *Performative ability approach* would measure the examinees' versatility to do things with English by discriminating those who can accomplish few tasks in English from those who can accomplish many.

Why is Changing the ISELPTs so Difficult/Slow?

Why are the ISELPTs so difficult/slow to change? Actual change can occur in the nature of the ISELPTs. I witnessed such change as a participant in the TOEFL 2000 project, during which the constructs underlying the TOEFL were dramatically changed, and such change can occur again. However, because of the large number of stakeholder groups involved, the process is slow, like turning a large ship.

Consider just the seven main groups of stakeholders that directly influence the ISELPTs: *the profession* (i.e. the researchers and theoreticians in the field); *testing organizations* (the organizations that develop, administer, score and validate the ISELPTs); *language testing researchers* (usually university professors who tend towards validity purism); *language testers at the organizations* (language testers immersed in the practical and organizational issues of test development and validation); *decision makers* (admissions or hiring officers at various universities and companies, respectively); *examinees* (those taking the tests); and *English language teachers* (those impacted by the fact that some of their students want to 'prepare' for the ISELPTs).

Naturally, there may also be other stakeholder groups like politicians, publishers and the public, depending on the context. Nonetheless, I witnessed the seven stakeholder groups (described in the previous paragraph) interacting and reacting in the TOEFL 2000 project in a slow collective evolution of our collective view of what ELP validity is. So change is possible. However, since the responsibility for change does involve all seven groups, the profession (including those concerned with Global English issues) must be patient with the fact that they are only one-seventh of the equation. As Elder and Harding (2008: 34.8) pointed out, 'we are not always in a position to dictate policy. And, Taylor (2006) cautioned that we must be wary of dismissing stakeholders' views as uniformly unenlightened'.

What Strategies Might Prove Useful for Effecting Change in the ISELPTs?

Stop-the-misuse-of-ISELPT-scores strategy

The validity of the ISELPTs is always a central concern. Unfortunately, many people seem to have the misconception that there is some ultimate, perfect, true construct that we are trying to test and that validity is somehow a constant. I have learned the hard way that test validity is not a truth nor is it constant. I have also learned that *tests* are not valid or invalid. Instead, the *scores* derived from tests can be studied in terms of how valid they are for certain uses or purposes in specific contexts at particular times. This suggests that the validity of the ISELPTs might be movable, that is, that validity might vary at different times in history (as discussed in the previous section), as well as in different contexts (e.g. certain ISELPT score uses that might arguably be valid in the United States might be very difficult to defend in the UK, Korea and Saudi Arabia). Thus, complaints about misuses of test scores often arise – complaints that may well be justified.

One strategy that many stakeholder groups can agree on and even act on immediately is to stop the misuse of the current ISELPT scores. Unfortunately, decision makers have been known to use the ISELPT scores in a number of inappropriate ways. For example, I have seen instances of administrators not understanding the purpose or scope of ISELPT scores, not knowing the importance of the standard error of measurement in interpreting cut-points, or just generally misusing scores. As a result, I have little faith in the ability or willingness of decision makers to always act professionally. To be fair, these people are generally overworked and understaffed and, worse yet, under-trained with regard to using test scores to make sound decisions.

Thus, while I certainly agree with Davidson's (1994) idea that test developers should be held accountable by test users, I also believe that test developers (and perhaps the entire language teaching profession) should hold test users to account, especially in instances where the entire testing purpose has been twisted beyond any conceivable recognition (as in the case described by Childs, 1995, of using TOEIC scores to investigate achievement gains over a mere 53 hours of instruction).

What I am advocating is that we monitor the test users and decision makers around us to make sure they do not misuse the ISELPTs by using them for placement purposes, diagnostic testing, progress testing, achievement testing or for grading. Any such misuses should be exposed as Childs (1995) did, and stopped.

Research-evidence strategy

Another useful strategy would be to continue producing *research evidence* describing the various Englishes and dialects around the world and documenting the characteristics of WEs, ELFs and EILs wherever they appear. Other research should examine the degree to which multidimensional models of ELP describe reality as well as their importance in language teaching and learning. Increasing support for the multidimensional nature of ELP (in some or all of the dimensions described in this chapter) will as a side consequence undermine and diminish the so-called validity of the unidimensional model of idealized NS English. If such evidence were to be presented in conference papers, in organized colloquia or even at conferences specifically established to grapple with these issues, the ISELPT organizations would gradually have to pay attention. The point here is that evidence of the full nature of ELP needs to be understood and presented in a variety of ways in numerous venues.

Change-what-students-are-learning strategy

One rather difficult way to modify what appears in the ISELPTs is to *change what students are learning* in their classrooms. When they are taught some form of prescriptive grammar based on the myth of the idealized NS model, then items based on those notions in the ISELPTs are more likely to discriminate and therefore will survive piloting processes and end up in the tests. However, if the majority of students around the world were taught GES, WEs, ELF or EIL, gradually the piloting procedures involved in developing the ISELPTs would end up selecting items not directly related to idealized NS English, but rather to what the high-performing students know but the low-performing ones do not.

Eliminate-the-test-preparation-industry strategy

This strategy would require changing the test preparation industry along with the notions that they perpetuate (i.e. that examinees can *learn the test* and thereby substantially raise their scores on the ISELPTs). This huge worldwide industry publishes books and offers training courses to prepare for these tests – mostly based on idealized NS English and with zero empirical evidence that they work. If this sounds like a scam, perhaps it is. But as long as there is profit to be made by these companies, I have little hope that they will change, except perhaps because of pressure from shifting markets, as discussed next.

Market-based strategies

One market-based strategy would be for a group of like-minded scholars to independently build tests of GES and/or WEs that include combinations of Global Englishes using approaches that reflect bottom-up understandings of how persons differ in ELP. Such a test would then need to compete for market share not only in terms of examinees but also in terms of score users' willingness to use the new test for decision making.

Alternatively, a group of like-minded scholars could propose such a test to an existing ISELPT organization and join with them in building it. In either case, the idea would be to build a better mousetrap – in this case, perhaps a test that would actually deserve to be called the *Test of English as an* **International** *Language*.

One last market-based strategy would apply Davidson's (1994) idea of test user responsibility, which he described as follows: 'I contend that a major impetus for change in the testing companies must be its users. They are the buyers, and the factory will not be motivated to change its product unless the buyers demand something new, something better' (Davidson, 1994: 384). I would go even further and suggest that test users and the profession more generally demand something new of the ISELPT organizations. If the pressure is sufficient over time, the organizations will respond. Importantly, if they respond, so will the test preparation industry and, of course, the teaching and learning of English around the world.

Written guidelines strategy

This last strategy involves creating *written guidelines* as proposed by Davidson (1993):

> Ultimately, a language testing standards 'movement' may result in some sort of set of written guidelines endorsed by many professional organizations. It is important that such a document be informed by many interest areas within the general field of language teaching and applied linguistics. One such interest area is that represented by the phenomenon of English varieties. (Davidson, 1993: 113)

Since Davidson wrote that, the 2000 *International Language Testing Association (ILTA) Code of Ethics* (available at 'Code of Ethics for ILTA', https://www.iltaonline.com/page/CodeofEthics) has provided some professional support which could be used to promote changes:

Principle 1
Language testers shall have respect for the humanity and dignity of each of their test takers. They shall provide them with the best possible professional consideration and shall respect all persons' needs, values and cultures in the provision of their language testing service.
…

Annotation
- Language testers shall not discriminate against nor exploit their test takers on grounds of age, gender, race, ethnicity, sexual orientation, language background, creed, political affiliations or religion, *nor knowingly impose their own values* (for example social, spiritual, political and ideological), to the extent that they are aware of them. (Code of Ethics for ILTA, pdf version, p. 2, emphasis added, https://www.iltaonline.com/page/CodeofEthics)

So far, this Principle and the accompanying Annotation have been missed opportunities to stop the imposition of idealized NS English. Another missed opportunity is represented by the fact that the 2007 *ILTA Guidelines for Practice* (available at 'Guidelines for Practice', https://www.iltaonline.com/page/ITLAGuidelinesforPra) is of little help with regard to the issues discussed in this chapter. However, it is possible that one day such a document could help to greatly change views of ELP around the world.

Conclusion

To sum up, after briefly discussing the literature on Global English(es) and language testing, this chapter examined Brown (2014, reprinted 2015), which addressed several areas the WEs community regards as problematic in language testing (linguistic norms, testing cultures, test design, testing processes and testing in various contexts), as well as Brown (in press), which examined how the ISELPTs (i.e. the TOEFL iBT, TOEIC and IELTS) present themselves, the definition of *English language proficiency*, the role of *persons* in testing ELP, paths for changing the ISELPTs (including 13 alternative approaches to defining the ELP), and ways in which those alternative ELP approaches can be assessed operationally. The chapter continued by exploring the relationships between Global Englishes and ELP as it is represented by the ISELPTs by addressing five questions: (a) What is *English language proficiency*, really (including what an NS of English is, what English language competence is, and what ELP really is)? (b) Why is the so-called NS standard a thing of the past, including language materials issues (like the 'curious position' of NSs, how the NS ELP standard is inadequately defined, how NS English is many things, and how NS proficiency is a moving target) and persons issues (like how the NS standard is an impossible dream, how the NS standard is not even desirable, and how communicating with NSs is not the only possibility)? (c) What alternative models are there to the NS model for ELP (based on why people learn English and replacing the NS model with a global English standard, and describing six top-down, language-materials focused approaches and eight bottom-up, persons-focused approaches)? (d) Why is changing the ISELPTs so difficult/slow? and (e) What strategies for change might prove useful for effecting change?

If some or all of the strategies suggested above (i.e. the stop-the-misuse-of ISELPT-scores strategy, research-evidence strategy, change-what-the-students-are-learning strategy, eliminate-the-test-preparation-industry strategy, market-based strategies and written-guidelines strategy) were applied by EFL/ESL teachers, researchers and administrators around the world, the large ISELPTs and the language testers associated with them would have to pay attention. That in turn could: (a) lead to the incorporation of the notions of Global Englishes into the important decisions being made with these tests; (b) improve the validity of the test scores; and (c) increase their ethical use. Perhaps more importantly, such strategies would eventually lead to improvements in the impact of the ISELPTs on EFL/ESL teaching and learning processes around the world.

Similarly, local practitioners who are responsible for designing local or national English tests owe it to their students to free themselves from the trap imposed by the so-called NS standard, so they can draw on the notions discussed in this chapter to meet the needs of the students they serve. This may simply mean designing English tests based on local English materials and standards appropriate in their particular contexts, or may mean adopting a new definition of ELP more appropriate to the WEs, EIL and ELF uses for which their students most likely need English.

Notes

(1) Note that the word *persons* is used in a unique way in measurement circles to denote this important aspect of assessment. Please bear with me.
(2) Because today the ISELPTs may be revised using item response theory (IRT), it is worth mentioning that similar item creation, piloting and selection processes go on when using IRT. However, instead of item discrimination, item fit is used to select those items that survive into the final versions of the test.
(3) Note that North American English is referred to as North American Englishes here because of the number and variety of dialects, some of which are difficult for other NSs to understand (e.g. the Down-East dialect in Maine).

References

Bachman, L.F. (1990) *Fundamental Considerations in Language Testing*. Oxford: Oxford University Press.
Bachman, L.F. and Palmer, A.S. (1996) *Language Testing in Practice*. Oxford: Oxford University Press.
Brown, J.D. (2004) What do we mean by bias, Englishes, Englishes in testing, and English language proficiency? *World Englishes* 23, 317–319.
Brown, J.D. (2012) EIL curriculum development. In L. Alsagoff, S. McKay, G.W. Hu and W.A. Renandya (eds) *Principles and Practices for Teaching English as an International Language* (pp. 147–167). London: Routledge.
Brown, J.D. (2014) The future of World Englishes in language testing. *Language Assessment Quarterly* 11 (1), 5–26.
Brown, J.D. (2015) The future of world Englishes in language testing. In A. Kunnan (ed.) *Language Testing and Assessment: Critical Concepts in Linguistics* (pp. 358–386). London: Routledge. Reprinted with permission from Brown (2014).

Brown, J.D. (in press) World Englishes and international standardized English proficiency tests. In C. Nelson and Z.G. Proshina (eds) *The Handbook of World Englishes* (2nd edn). Malden, MA: Wiley-Blackwell.

Canale, M. and Swain, M. (1980) Theoretical bases of communicative approaches to second language teaching and testing. *Applied Linguistics* 1, 1–47.

Canale, M. and Swain, M. (1981) A theoretical framework for communicative competence. In A.S. Palmer, P.J.M. Groot and G.A. Trosper (eds) *The Construct Validation of Tests of Communicative Competence* (pp. 31–36). Washington, DC: TESOL.

Chalhoub-Deville, M. and Wigglesworth, G. (2005) Researcher report: Rater judgment and English language speaking proficiency. *World Englishes* 24, 383–391.

Childs, M. (1995) Good and bad uses of TOEIC by Japanese companies. In J.D. Brown and S.O. Yamashita (eds) *Language Testing in Japan* (pp. 66–75). Tokyo: Japan Association for Language Teaching.

Clyne, M. and Sharifian, F. (2008) English as an international language: Challenges and possibilities. *Australian Review of Applied Linguistics* (International Forum on English as an International Language, Special forum issue edited by F. Sharifian and M. Clyne) 31 (3), 28.1–28.16.

Davidson, F. (1993) Testing English across cultures: Summary and comments. *World Englishes* 12 (1), 113–125.

Davidson, F. (1994) The interlanguage metaphor and language assessment. *World Englishes* 13, 377–386.

Davidson, F. (2006) World Englishes and test construction. In B. Kachru, Y. Kachru and C. Nelson (eds) *The Handbook of World Englishes* (pp. 709–717). Malden, MA: Wiley-Blackwell.

Davidson, F. and Lowenberg, P. (1996) Language testing and World Englishes: A proposed research agenda. Paper presented at the *3rd Conference of the International Association of World Englishes*, Honolulu, HI.

Davies, A. (1991) *The Native Speaker in Applied Linguistics*. Edinburgh: Edinburgh University Press.

Davies, A. (2003) *The Native Speaker: Myth and Reality*. Clevedon: Multilingual Matters.

Davies, A. (2004) The native speaker in applied linguistics. In A. Davies and C. Elder (eds) *The Handbook of Applied Linguistics* (pp. 431–450). Oxford: Blackwell.

Elder, C. and Harding, L. (2008) Language testing and English as an international language: Constraints and contributions. *Australian Review of Applied Linguistics* 31 (3), 34.1–34.11.

Hamp-Lyons, L. and Zhang, B. (2001) World Englishes: Issues in and from academic writing assessment. In J. Flowerdew and M. Peacock (eds) *English for Academic Purposes: Research Perspectives* (pp. 101–116). Cambridge: Cambridge University Press.

Kachru, B.B. (1986) The power and politics of English. *World Englishes* 5 (2/3), 121–140.

Leung, C., Harris, R. and Rampton, B. (1997) The idealised native speaker, reified ethnicities, and classroom realities. *TESOL Quarterly* 31, 543–560.

Levis, J.M. (2005) Changing contexts and shifting paradigms in pronunciation teaching. *TESOL Quarterly* 39, 369–377.

Lowenberg, P.H. (1993) Issues of validity in tests of English as a world language: Whose standards? *World Englishes* 12 (1), 95–106.

McKay, S.L. and Brown, J.D. (2015) *Teaching and Assessing EIL in Local Contexts Around the World*. New York: Routledge.

Pawley, A. and Syder, F.H. (1983) Two puzzles for linguistic theory: Nativelike selection and nativelike fluency. In J.C. Richards and R. Schmidt (eds) *Language and Communication* (pp. 191–226). Harlow: Longman.

Richards, J.C. and Schmidt, R. (2010) *Longman Dictionary of Language Teaching and Applied Linguistics* (4th edn). Harlow: Pearson.
Spolsky, B. (1993) Testing across cultures: An historical perspective. *World Englishes* 12 (1), 87–93.
Taylor, L. (2002) Assessing learners' English: But whose/which English(es)? *University of Cambridge ESOL Examinations Research Notes* 10, 18–20.
Taylor, L. (2006) The changing landscape of English: Implications for language assessment. *ELT Journal* 60 (1), 51–60.
Wesolek, C., Graney, J. and Stueve, J. (1993) The Philippine Refugee Processing Center: A case study. *World Englishes* 12 (1), 107–112.

6 Looking through the Eyes of Global Englishes: Enhancing English Language Teaching in Multicultural Classrooms

Maria Luz Elena N. Canilao

English has many flavors, but there are many teachers who forget this reality because the language curriculum and the school culture dictate that they merely focus on what is regarded as Standard English. They favor native-speaker norms and enforce the English-only policy in the classroom. For them, the concept of Global Englishes is threatening. Instead of seeing its power to facilitate learning, they question and resist it. For other teachers who acknowledge the potential of Global Englishes, it poses a dilemma because they are uncertain about advocating it, not wanting to go against established English language teaching approaches. This chapter describes English language teaching in the Philippines and discusses the challenges that 10 PhD students face in adopting Global Englishes in their teaching contexts as revealed in a focus group discussion. It unveils the cultural and linguistic divides that exist in tertiary multicultural classrooms in various regions in the country. Possible steps and practical options that may be taken in espousing Global Englishes to promote diversity and equality are offered. Principles that may be considered in producing lessons to enhance students' intercultural awareness and competence are presented. The chapter shows how spaces for alternative perspectives and innovative practices may be created in English language teaching.

Introduction

Looking through the eyes of Global Englishes (GE) entails a critical examination of my own journey with the English language and the dilemmas of fellow teachers in meeting their students' needs and society's expectations. The accounts in this chapter illustrate the intricacies of English language teaching (ELT) in postcolonial settings such as the Philippines and show the gains and pains of adopting GE as a pedagogical paradigm to guide educators and scholars in their search for new policies and practices that may improve ELT in multicultural classrooms. In qualitative research, investigators may reveal where they are coming from to show how their background and experiences help shape their analysis (Cresswell, 2013, 2014). Thus I frame this chapter with themes that present my own specific encounters and eureka moments in relation to the historical backdrop of ELT in the Philippines, the GE framework and related concepts and studies, and my main findings and conclusions. These personal themes demonstrate how I shifted from a monolingual position to a GE perspective in ELT and disclose the complex process and factors that are involved. I speak as an English language learner, teacher, trainer, researcher, and supporter of GE. This structure is designed to invite and inspire readers to evaluate their own attitudes, beliefs and habits and see how GE may be considered as an alternative track in their particular contexts.

Reflections of a Non-native English Speaking Learner: The Primacy of Standard English

I will begin this section by sharing my experiences as a non-native English speaking (NNES) learner in a Quezon City private school in the 1970s and 1980s. Situated in Metro Manila (also currently referred to as the National Capital Region), Quezon City is a major urban center where major government offices, universities and business establishments are located. It was in this setting that I first discovered the supremacy of English in the academic domain in the Philippines. I was in a kindergarten classroom that was composed of big tables with distinct colors. The blue table was at the center while the purple table where I was assigned to stay was at the periphery. One day, I mingled with my classmates at the blue table, but my teacher told me to go back to the purple table. I observed the children at the blue table and realized that all of them were eloquent English speakers. It could have been pure coincidence that they were asked to stay in the middle, but whatever it was, I felt bad that I could not join them because I did not speak the way they did. The classroom setup was a microcosm of center and periphery ELT contexts that are separated by the privileging of the former and the exclusion of the latter (Canagarajah, 1999).

Since my linguistic awakening in kindergarten, I had embraced what most Filipinos perceive as Standard English (SE) which school authorities prescribed. SE may refer to any English variety that is considered legitimate by academics, professional writers and other influential groups in a particular country, and it is usually based on British English (BrE) and American English (AmE) (Rubdy & Saraceni, 2006; Tupas, 2006). Philippine English (PhE), patterned after AmE, for instance, is considered acceptable by the education sector in the Philippines (Bautista, 2000). Thus in this work I refer to SE mainly as the AmE or PhE variety which is favored in academe and other domains (e.g. government, business) in the country.

In grade school and high school I had to follow the English Only Policy (EOP) to avoid being fined for using Tagalog[1] and other languages in classes that were taught in English. This gave me the compulsion to learn and use English, but it gave me the impression that all other languages were inferior to English. Thus my enthusiasm for Kapampangan,[2] my first language (L1), faded. The EOP dates back to the 1900s when American colonizers replaced the Spanish conquerors who had ruled the Philippines for about 300 years (Mindo, 2008; Cruz, 2010). Free education was offered by the Americans, and for practical and ideological purposes English was used as the sole medium of instruction (Bernardo, 2008) and the 'Americanization' of Filipino students began (Mindo, 2008: 163). Seen as a language of opportunity and embraced by many Filipinos, English became a symbol of privilege as the EOP was duplicated in many upper-class homes (Brigham & Castillo, 1999).

A language policy twist happened from the 1930s to the 1960s when the regional languages were acknowledged in basic education because of the nationalist movement in the country (Mindo, 2008). Local experiments (e.g. Cena, 1958) also proved that students performed better when the vernacular was used as a medium of instruction (Bernardo, 2008; Brigham & Castillo, 1999). However, English, which was regarded as an international language, would regain its dominant place through the Bilingual Education Policy (BEP) (Brigham & Castillo, 1999). The 1974 BEP mandated English as the main medium of instruction together with Pilipino[3] to develop the competence of learners in these languages (Bernardo, 2008; Cruz, 2010). The 1987 BEP which followed recognized English and Filipino[4] as the primary languages of instruction, and regional languages as auxiliary mediums of instruction (Cruz, 2010; Nolasco, 2008).

I conquered SE in grade school in the same institution and my efforts were rewarded in high school when I was placed in the honors class. Classes were heterogeneous at the elementary level, but the high school scheme mirrored the linguistic classification in my kindergarten class. As a graduating student, I realized the benefits of having access to SE. University entrance exams used SE and measured SE language skills which gave me an advantage. Moreover, in college most professors required SE in academic requirements. I understood the power of SE even more when I joined the workforce because employers preferred applicants who were proficient in it. After graduation in the late 1980s, I worked as a copywriter and account executive in marketing and publication companies that welcomed SE-trained graduates from top universities.

Being educated in this type of system unmasked one aspect of reality in the Philippines I could not escape. Having access to SE may be quite empowering in terms of academic attainment and career advancement, but the lack of it may mean stagnation and stigmatization. SE was my passport to scholastic success as an NNES student and professional progress as an NNES graduate. However, in the process of acquiring it, I lost the opportunity to unearth the wealth of my mother tongue and my own culture. The conflict between SE and other languages is an issue that teachers in multicultural teaching contexts need to confront seriously.

Realizations of an ELT Explorer: The Wonders of Global Englishes

In the 1990s, I decided to teach English at an exclusive high school in Quezon City. Teaching the way I had been taught and following the school culture in my workplace, I leaned towards SE and implemented the EOP in my English classes. When I talked to my students inside and outside the classroom I used formal English most of the time. When I started teaching English at the tertiary level in the early 2000s, I kept to this practice, thinking it was the best way to help students enhance their communication skills. However, one day a Filipino undergraduate student heard me chatting in informal Tagalog with a fellow teacher in the workroom. He confronted me and asked in shock and disbelief, 'Ma'am, *marunong kang mag-Tagalog?* [you know how to speak in Tagalog]?' That made me pause and think about the possible negative statement I was making against the use of other languages through my monolingual language practice in the classroom.

The EOP instils in the minds of teachers and learners that English is a pure and prime language that cannot be stained by other languages. It also presumes that language learning is impeded by the use of different languages in the classroom. A closer look at it, though, would bear out that English is the epitome of a hybrid language shaped by its contact with other languages (Canagarajah, 2013). Studies have also shown the advantages of employing the students' L1 and code-switching in fostering language learning in bilingual and multilingual classrooms (Martin, 2014; Tollefson, 2007). Despite these realities, the EOP has remained prominent in various schools in the Philippines (Gallego & Zubiri, 2011; Smolicz *et al.*, 2001). This colonial remnant promotes cultural models that regard English as the superior language and the language of education. Cultural models are assumptions that are passed on through social interaction and different media, and they may compete, evolve and change over time (Gee, 1999).

Conflicting cultural models in the field of education were pronounced in the Philippines in the 2000s when some policymakers supported

Executive Order (EO) No. 210 strengthening the use of English as a medium of instruction at the primary levels of education (Mindo, 2008). EO 210 was initiated to address the burgeoning business process outsourcing (BPO) industry which needed Filipino call center agents who were highly proficient in English (Llanto, 2008). However, mother tongue based multilingual education (MTBMLE) advocates fought hard to revive the use of the L1 as a medium of instruction in basic education. MTBMLE supporters won the battle in 2009 when the Department of Education (DepEd) defied EO 210 and institutionalized the MTBMLE Policy through DepEd Order No. 74 (Nolasco, 2010). This new policy was officially recognized by the succeeding administration with the Enhanced Basic Education Act of 2013 establishing the K-12 Program in the nation (Congress of the Philippines, 2013). Cultural models promoting the mother tongue as a language of literacy were revived as a result. Studies (e.g. Burton, 2013; Paulson Stone, 2012), nevertheless, reveal that some teachers and parents contested it, not wanting to deprive children of accessing English, the language used for standardized tests and the perceived language of achievement.

At that point I was a PhD student who began to be immersed in alternative views that acknowledged other Englishes that have emerged as a result of colonization and globalization. I was introduced to the World Englishes (WE) perspective and Kachru's Three Circles model. Inner circle countries (e.g. UK, US) use English as a native language (ENL), while outer circle countries (e.g. India, the Philippines) consider English as a second language (ESL) and expanding circle (e.g. China, Thailand) countries learn English as a foreign language (EFL) for international communication (Kachru, 2005; Svartvik & Leech, 2006). Furthermore, I was enlightened by the idea of linguistic imperialism (Phillipson, 1992) which divulges the dominance of English in powerful domains of society and the prevalence of linguicism. Critical pedagogy (CP) serves to overcome linguistic imperialism in ELT by tackling the rift between the center ('native English communities') and periphery ('non-native communities') contexts and viewing learning as personal, situated and cultural (Canagarajah, 1999: 4). Likewise, English as an international language (EIL) proponents aim to promote linguistic equality, emphasizing the need for students to appreciate their own culture and other varieties of English.

From a CP and EIL angle, the learners' culture should be taken into account in choosing teaching approaches, norms and materials. The inclusion of cultural content is fundamental because it 'provides students with the opportunity to learn more about their own culture and to acquire ... English to explain their own culture to others ...' (McKay, 2004: 19–20). Developing students' intercultural awareness and competence is essential, especially that they live in a global world (Lee, 2012). I have taught English language courses to university students and adult learners and ELT courses to graduate students from different regions of the Philippines and various continents of the world. Teaching students from the Basque Country, Brazil, Cambodia, Canada, China, Ivory Coast, Japan, Myanmar, Nepal, Nigeria, South Korea, Russia, Senegal, Taiwan, Thailand, Tibet, Timor, Vietnam and the United States has made me realize the importance of incorporating lessons that would enable them to appreciate their own culture and other people's customs.

The English as a lingua franca (ELF) position also helped me understand how non-native speakers (NNSs) and native speakers (NSs) of English expressed their ideas in the classroom. ELF is employed by speakers from various linguistic backgrounds, and it includes interactions that may involve both NNSs and NSs (Jenkins, 2012). Seidlhofer (2006) and Jenkins (2007) draw attention to the importance of examining how NNSs communicate with one another using English, the language they share. It describes how NNSs interact with one another using their linguistic resources including their L1 and other languages in their repertoire and engage in code-switching to show their cultural identity, express affinity and make their statements intelligible to achieve their communication purposes. ELF also includes NSs who go through the same process and who may need to acquire ELF as they intermingle with language users from diverse contexts (Jenkins, 2012).

Moreover, my knowledge of translanguaging and translingual practice – two related concepts that advocate the use of linguistic assets in multilingual classrooms – has enabled me to develop activities that make use of students' first or home languages in understanding texts and developing compositions in English. Translanguaging (García, 2009) may involve the use of code-switching and translation as pedagogical and cognitive tools to help multilingual students grasp notions, while translingual practice (Canagarajah, 2006, 2013) highlights the hybridity and fluidity of languages, the multimodality of communication, the process of emerging norms and the negotiation of meaning between speakers from different cultural backgrounds. Unlike the monolingual orientation that highlights the mastery of rules patterned after NS models, the translingual position encourages the use of the L1 and C1 (first culture) in ELT because languages are not seen as clashing forces but as complementary elements that enrich one another (Canagarajah, 2006, 2013). Thus the latter emphasizes the importance of providing spaces for learners to assert their linguistic and cultural identities through practices such as code-meshing that enable them to intersperse L1 expressions and their local varieties of English in compositions (Canagarajah, 2013; Canagarajah & Wurr, 2011).

GE encompasses these distinct positions, specifically WE, ELF and EIL, and opposes the imposition of monolingual standards in ELT (Galloway & Rose, 2014, 2015; Jenkins, 2015; Murata & Jenkins, 2009). This counter-paradigm promotes the linguistic and cultural diversity that is necessary in empowering students in multicultural settings. It also reflects Canagarajah's (2013) translingual standpoint. GE highlights the importance of exposing students to English varieties and ELF interactions and equipping them with strategies that may enable them to communicate effectively with speakers from various regions (Galloway & Rose, 2015). GE emphasizes the need for learners to realize that Englishes are not limited to SE such as BrE or AmE. Teachers have to take a balanced approach in ELT and expose learners to other English varieties and modify assessment practices that are solely anchored in SE patterns (Farrell & Martin, 2009; Mukminatien, 2012; Tomlinson, 2006).

My dissertation on multilingualism helped me digest GE principles further and review my language beliefs and classroom policies such as the EOP. The autonomy that I enjoyed in my teaching context, the flexibility of our English language syllabi designed to develop students' communication skills, and the convictions I shared with many university colleagues enabled me to improve my teaching practices and design creative lessons through the eyes of GE. In my undergraduate language classes, for example, students are allowed to use any term from their linguistic repertoire to explain concepts during class discussions. Topics on English varieties and cultural diversity are incorporated into my lessons. Grammar activities include the analysis of texts to show them how rules vary across cultures. Code-meshing in composition is also encouraged and multimodal tasks are provided. However, students do expect to learn SE in order to survive in an academic world that demands that they follow SE norms. Some learners also prefer traditional teacher-centered methods because of their cultural upbringing. Thus I come up with a balance of unstructured speaking and writing lessons that enable them to express themselves fearlessly and structured ones that require them to apply SE conventions conscientiously.

Satisfied with my attempts, I started to present my GE innovations in the ELT workshops I facilitated. I often encountered resistance from teacher participants who were ideologically attached to monolingual traditions. I also noticed that some teachers disregarded their local varieties of English. For example, in one workshop a teacher participant from the southern part of the Philippines used the term 'regional defect' to describe their local accent in English. This attitude suggests Filipino society's high regard for NS norms which is common in other Asian countries such as China (Fang, 2016), Thailand (Jindapitak & Boonsuk, 2018) and Vietnam (Ton & Pham, 2010). According to Kachru (1992), there is a need for NNSs to accept their local variety of English and 'develop an identity with the local model of English without feeling that it is a "deficient" model' (Kachru, 1992: 67–68). McKay (2006) also argues that monolingual programs espousing NS norms should be replaced by an EIL curriculum which local educators in multilingual settings may own and develop according to their specific teaching contexts and students' needs. Kirkpatrick (2010) proposes an ELF multilingual model that recognizes local varieties of English as possible benchmarks in Association of Southeast Asian Nations (ASEAN) countries such as the Philippines.

Nonetheless, Jenkins (2012) observes that, while ELF use has become widespread among speakers in different settings, ENL standards stressing accuracy continue to dominate the areas of ELT assessment and materials development. In the Philippines there is little room given for other local varieties of English and alternative teaching approaches to be recognized in many schools (Karami & Zamanian, 2015). Local English college textbooks in the country seldom introduce WE and ELF notions to enhance students' sociolinguistic awareness and skills that are vital in communicating across cultures. Thus teacher education needs to include WE and ELF perspectives to raise the awareness of English teachers and equip them with skills in developing materials that will enhance their students' ability to recognize Englishes that are currently used in today's world (Vettorel, 2015).

Tupas (2006) points out that many English language teachers in the Philippines have a predicament when it comes to choosing the specific model of English to teach. While they are aware of local varieties of English their students use in their classes, utilize code-switching as a pedagogical tool, believe in localizing or Filipinizing instructional materials and understand the importance of recognizing learners' linguistic and cultural identities, they are inclined to favor SE for practical and instrumental purposes, given the global and local demand for graduates who are proficient in SE. In addition, it is important to acknowledge the existence of unequal Englishes, a concept which underscores 'the unequal ways and situations in which Englishes are arranged, configured, and contested' (Tupas & Rubdy, 2015: 3). Therefore, while GE is a promising option in ELT, it may be difficult in postcolonial settings such as the Philippines to integrate it because of educational structures that breed unequal Englishes. To shed light on these complexities, I conducted a study to look at the realities of teaching multicultural classes in the Philippines. It focused on these questions:

- What challenges do English language and literature graduate students in the Philippines face in exploring alternative ELT paradigms in multilingual classrooms?
- How does their exposure to GE help form the way they look at their ELT policies and practices in their teaching contexts?

Discoveries of a Language Researcher: The Gap between Englishes

This qualitative study involved a PhD research class consisting of 12 students majoring in English language and literature at a private university in Metro Manila. Ten of them (nine female and one male graduate students) agreed to participate in the study. This particular graduate class was chosen because they have experiences teaching English in multicultural classrooms, and they come from different Philippine regions. They were also taught basic and related GE concepts in their PhD courses. Ethical procedures were followed in conducting the study. Consent forms were obtained from the participating institution and participants.

In conducting the study, I employed a face-to-face focus group interview with the participants and used an open-ended question or prompt to draw out their views (Cresswell, 2014). The 10 participants were asked to describe the challenges of teaching English to multilingual students in relation to SE and GE in a focus group discussion (FGD). The FGD was conducted after their PhD research class, their common time, in their classroom. Each participant had one turn in relaying his/her account and views, and no time limit was given. The session ran for about two hours. Based on the audio-recording of the FGD, their responses were coded according to the main themes that surfaced from their narratives. Narratives are usually employed in qualitative studies because they are effective tools for reflecting on classroom practices and uncovering teachers' perspectives (Clandinin & Connelly, 2000; Johnson, 2006). This section presents the main findings.

Linguistic, cultural and socio-economic divisions exist in multicultural classrooms in different regions of the Philippines

Participant 1 (P1) teaches speech to students at a tertiary institution in Nueva Vizcaya, an agricultural province of Cagayan Valley in Region II in Northern Luzon. It is predominantly composed of Ilocano and Tagalog migrants and local residents including Ifugaos and Igorots (Nueva Vizcaya Government, 2015). P1's classes include students from different provinces in their region. Her main concern as a speech teacher is the distinct regional accents of students belonging to the minority groups. Because the majority groups have a tendency to look down on these accents, the minority groups usually keep quiet and avoid reciting in class. While P1 focuses on communication and intelligibility, she is also expected to teach pronunciation based on Standard American English (SAE). They have a speech lab to exercise students' speaking skills. The models and materials they use promote SAE norms. She encourages her students to listen to SAE models but she does not force them to modify their accents according to SAE.

> P1: Sometimes ... their classmates who come from majority groups ... they laugh at their classmates who have strong regional accents ... My problem there is ... to correct or not to correct that? But of course, we know that these are regional variations ... but they should be made aware of American sounds ...

Participant 2 (P2) shares similar experiences. She works at a university in Iligan City, an urban center of Region X in Northern Mindanao. The majority of residents are Roman Catholic, and the other groups include Higaonons and Maranao (Iligan Government, 2012). In P2's classes composed of minority groups, the ones who do well are from affluent homes while those who have academic challenges are from financially struggling families. Knowing that their classmates are from the high-income class, students from the low-income class tend to be shy and remain passive in class. When the minority groups are in a class primarily composed of the majority group, the former feel isolated and remain silent. When students in P2's classes speak their own English variety it is common for their classmates to laugh at them. These students do not mind as long as their classmates belong to the same cultural group.

Participant 3 (P3) also encounters these linguistic and cultural hierarchies that divide students in multicultural classes. P3 teaches university students in Pampanga, an agricultural province in the heart of Region III in Central Luzon. The primary language spoken in this area is Pampango or Kapampangan (Provincial Government of Pampanga, 2017). Most of the students are locals of the province and from nearby areas such as Tarlac and Metro Manila. There are also students recruited from south-central Mindanao for the university's varsity teams. In many instances, because of their unique accent, students from Mindanao are mocked by their classmates. While they usually do not react to it negatively, P3 cites an instance when a student felt very offended because of successive teasing and decided not to speak in their class anymore.

Participant 4 (P4) has parallel experiences. She teaches speech and literature classes at a private university in Cebu, a highly developed province in the Central Visayas Region or Region VII. The main language spoken by the residents is Cebuano and English is commonly used in commerce and education in this area (Cebu Provincial Government, 2019). She also observes that that there are some students who laugh at themselves because they are not fluent in English and they feel uncomfortable with their English.

Participant 5 (P5) echoes the same observation. He teaches at a university in Davao, a province in the southeastern part of Mindanao in Region XI. Davao City, its capital, is an urbanized commercial hub. It is composed mainly of Cebuanos, Bisaya and Davaweños (Davao City, 2011). He conveys that in areas such as the central part of Mindanao, the minority groups are ridiculed by the majority groups because of their accent and thus the former refrain from using English.

While teachers may be aware of GE, they may be constrained by institutional policies and programs, instructional materials, stakeholders' expectations, and senior colleagues, administrators and trainers who have a strong monolingual stance

P1's account described previously indicates that she leans towards GE but she is inhibited by the speech program that prioritizes SAE. In the case of P2, SAE models are also used. Her students, especially the ones from the minority groups, find it difficult to imitate the prescribed American accent and, like P1, she does not impose it on them. Her biggest difficulty is making her lessons relevant to her students because of the prescribed materials.

> **P2**: My problem is that especially since we've discussed ... World Englishes, our materials are really highly technical and *parang* devoid *siya* [it seems devoid] of context especially cultural context *ng* [of] Mindanao. It's really difficult for them to interact with the pieces and the selections that we have in our workbooks ... especially for speech ... We follow the American Standard of English.

P3 also teaches SAE and admits implementing the EOP in her language classes specifically when it comes to writing because of her senior colleagues' influence. The university considers the call center industry a promising option for their graduates, and thus the oral communication course focuses on the mastery of SAE pronunciation. P3 does not think it is a good idea because it limits the options of their students.

> **P3**: The problem is that since we are ... trained or we are told that students should use English when you ask something in English, they should answer completely in English. But then again, when you read the students' answers, they are actually correct. It's just that they do not know the term ... in English. And sometimes ... I give ... *nakakahiya* [it's embarrassing] ... deductions when they use another language ... I'm not really strict with the language they use. It's just with the exam *kasi nga* [because] our ADMIN [administrators] would always say that we should train our students to be proficient in the Standard American English ... Now, I realize that's wrong.

In the same way, SAE is favored in the private university where P4 teaches speech classes. Most of the students come from their province and nearby regions and others come from foreign countries. Their clientele, particularly Asian students, expect to be taught SAE and therefore the oral communication program uses SAE models and materials. According to P4, these students want to learn AmE because 'they have been told that the American English is the kind of English that will take them to places'. Their parents send them to this university for this purpose. Thus the school provides well-maintained speech labs where teachers and students are expected to follow SAE norms, imitate the prescribed American accent and use American idioms. Additionally, students are given an accent training program and teachers conduct one-on-one sessions with them, so the students' enunciation is enhanced.

When she did her demonstration as a teacher applicant, P4 was asked to model SAE because this ability is one of the gauges for selecting English teachers. Her senior colleagues, considered the 'pillars' of their English Department and schooled in monolingual practices, rate junior teachers according to how well they model SAE and underscore the importance of grammar according to SAE, especially in language and writing classes. Her fellow teachers are not familiar with GE principles, but P4 is aware that her multicultural classroom may be a perfect 'site for translingual practices'. However, she cannot allow such practices in her speech classes, considering the stakeholders' expectations, the syllabus, the departmental ELT policies and the criteria for teacher evaluation.

> P4: What has been ingrained *sa mga utak namin* [in our minds] as teachers is to give the clients what they are asking for and it's usually Standard American English ...

Similarly, P5 points out that their senior colleagues and administrators are the 'gatekeepers of the English language' in their school. He was told that 'code-switching is a wrong practice'. He said that taking PhD courses made him realize that there are other Englishes, but WE is a 'foreign term' in their teaching context. He believes that teachers should be taught WE. Their current focus in teaching English is 'more on the form than the function of English'. Participant 6 (P6) teaches English at the same university where P5 works. She talks about a senior English teacher who emphasizes the importance of grammar and gives deductions for errors. P6 states, '*Galit na galit siya sa* grammar *ng* students [This teacher is infuriated by the students' grammar]'. Participant 7 (P7), a colleague of P5 and P6, mentions that the EOP is followed in their English language classes as well, specifically in their AB English Program.

In her first years of teaching, Participant 8 (P8) also implemented the EOP because she was told by her instructor that code-switching is a bad practice in the English classroom. P8 teaches tertiary level students at Sultan Kudarat, an agricultural province in the southwestern part of Mindanao in Region XII. The area is composed mainly of Ilonggo, Maguindanaoan and Ilocano locals (Sultan Kudarat, 2010, 2017). She recalls that one of her former instructors told her that 'it's a mortal sin ... to use Filipino and English in one sentence'. However, she allowed code-switching later on because her students found it hard to understand the lessons. There is no formal training on WE for teachers in their university, but after having been taught WE in her PhD courses, she realized that while AmE forms are followed, teachers in her context actually use and promote PhE varieties.

Participant 9 (P9) has the same teaching context as P8. She is involved with an English proficiency program supported by an inner circle agency to improve students' English language skills needed in the workplace. Speech labs are used for this program, and they are considered 'English only zones'. Their materials also promote SE. She recalls how her NS trainer gave her 'a minus point' because of her regional accent in their training session when she conducted a teaching demonstration. After being exposed to WE, P9 realized that it is 'not a disadvantage to have a regional accent'. She also sees the potential of the English proficiency program in making students aware of WE because sample dialogues include exchanges between NNS and NS speakers. She believes that SE is still necessary, but she is thinking of using WE principles in teaching English and exercising 'academic freedom'.

Participant 10 (P10), on the other hand, narrates what she did as a gatekeeper herself. She has taught English at a university in Manila. The capital of the Philippines, Manila is one of the biggest cities in the country and it ranks first among the world's most densely populated cities. It is composed of Tagalogs and migrants from different regions of the country (World Population Review, 2017). She shares her previous experience as an English department head at an international school in China. Coming from various provinces in the Philippines, Filipino teachers used local varieties of English in teaching students of different nationalities. There were students who complained about their NNES teachers, suggesting their preference for NES instructors. Thus P10 trained the Filipino teachers to use 'Manila English' which she considered accurate because it mirrored AmE. After taking her PhD courses she saw her attitude as form of linguicism. Prior to her work in China, she also taught at an international school in Metro Manila. In a post-FGD email interview, P10 was asked to elaborate on her decision to use Manila English as the standard in teaching English.

> P10: Manila English sounded more neutral than ... provincial Englishes. In international schools/contexts, regional accents are discouraged/discriminated. Manila English also sounded closer to American English or 'sosyal' [classy] English. Maybe I got this perspective because I studied in Manila for my undergrad onwards.

Englishes are designated different spaces in multicultural ELT settings in the Philippines

P4 acknowledges that her students use their local English versions outside the classroom, but these varieties are forgotten once they step into their speech classes. There are students who complain about the switching to AmE in their speech classes because 'they have their own English' which they use at home, with peers and on social media. According to P4, some students say that '... *Masyadong OA [Overacting]*. [It's too exaggerated.] I don't feel comfortable speaking that way.'

> P4: When they [students] enter the speech classroom, they're entering another space and it's like a make-believe space wherein ... you have to speak like someone else ...

In her literature classes, P4 allows code-switching and uses her local English accent. Thus she switches her identity and language depending on what class she teaches. P4 also observes that her fellow English teachers feel bad when their graduates end up becoming call center agents when their program actually equips them with skills that are ideal for the BPO industry. P4's teaching context shows how difficult it is to find room to incorporate GE principles in her speech classes with all the institutional and practical factors she has to take into account.

P3 also allows code-switching in her literature classes, especially in discussions. However, when it comes to language classes the EOP is strictly enforced. P5 uses and allows code-switching in his literature classes as well because his former teacher told him that in a literature class what should be taught is literature, not language. Thus P5 uses translations and explanations in Bisaya, the local language, when discussing concepts. Even as a student, he used code-switching by adding local expressions at the end of his English statements despite the EOP prescribed by his teachers. Moreover, the EOP is also usually enforced particularly among AB English majors in their context. Like the other research participants, P9 also mentions that there are certain expectations that English majors have to meet especially with the use of SE.

According to P7, their students use basic 'survival English' and they find it difficult to grasp literary texts written in English. The EOP is followed only in English classes composed of AB English majors and the only place of English is in the English classroom, especially in theses and oral presentations. The common language spoken in their teaching context is Bisaya, the local language. The use of English is associated with students who study at elite private institutions in their province. She states: 'If you come from my school known as a school of poor students, if you speak English … you will be [an] outcast.'

The responses show that participants have a heightened awareness of GE principles and reveal their conscious resistance to current monolingual practices in their teaching contexts. It is important to note that the FGD was done in the participants' PhD classroom with their classmates who were exposed to the same ELT perspectives. Thus they spoke as graduate students who wore the lens of GE in presenting their views. Being away from their teaching contexts also enabled them to talk about their experiences openly and critically. As graduate students, therefore, they are free to wear the lens of GE, but it is evident that some of them may have to take it off as soon as they step back into their ELT classrooms because of their teaching conditions that require them to promote SE norms exclusively. This double life is a complication that most teachers have to endure in ELT, and it is not that easy to solve.

Insights of a Global Englishes Supporter: The Link between Englishes

In this borderless digital age, new language modes have emerged and communication among speakers from distinct backgrounds have become more common. GE as a pedagogical paradigm includes a wide range of perspectives that are useful in helping learners in today's times connect with other people more effectively and appropriately. Nevertheless, my research discoveries show the wide gap between Englishes and build a strong case for GE which may link them together. The rejection of regional accents is a sign of unequal Englishes that are embedded in multicultural classrooms. The minority groups are silenced and disempowered because their Englishes do not mirror the SE that is accepted by the majority groups. The United Nations Educational, Scientific, and Cultural Organization (UNESCO, 2003: 33) views 'language as an essential component of inter-cultural education in order to encourage understanding between different population groups and ensure respect for fundamental rights' and enjoins institutions to support its bid for eradicating all forms of discrimination, including linguicism, at all levels of education. GE is one way of promoting linguistic and cultural diversity and equality in ELT and it is a vital option that teachers may take to facilitate learning in the classroom.

However, adopting GE is not easy if you are constantly monitored by authorities who are SE stalwarts and your teaching career is dependent on their evaluation. It is not easy if your syllabus prescribes the sole teaching of SE and if you do not have the materials and the training to design GE lessons. It is not easy if language policymakers and materials designers are unaware of GE. It is not easy if monolingual policies and practices such as the EOP remain entrenched in educational structures. As my research discoveries reveal, there are many hindrances to the application of GE in multicultural classrooms that are confined in monolingual spheres in the Philippines. The findings show why teachers may refrain from applying GE principles in some teaching contexts that expect them to model and promote SE standards exclusively. Inclusion of GE in their lessons may mean a poor rating or it may even cost them their jobs. Despite these obstacles, possible steps may be taken to turn them into opportunities to promote GE in ELT. The solution has to involve various layers of society and it has to be twofold: change has to come both from the top and from the bottom tiers of educational organizations.

One measure is to reorient policymakers, administrators, educators and other stakeholders who have been deeply immersed in monolingual beliefs and practices and inspire them to follow the mandate of UNESCO through various fora. Gatekeepers themselves are pressured by social, institutional and professional demands as P10's narrative suggests and, whether they are aware of GE or not, they may be as intimidated as teachers whose employment may be on the line if they deviate from prescribed ELT practices. Hence, while gatekeepers may hold positions of power, they may not have enough power or will to influence change in the academic domain because of the expectations they need to fulfil and/or because of their views shaped by hardcore and inflexible

SE dogmas. Thus local and global education organizations and institutions have to come together, review their own ELT perspectives and practices vis-à-vis UNESCO's principles, decide on a collective effort to promote diversity and equality, and create a campaign to enhance the public's awareness about linguistic rights that have to be respected in all domains of society.

Furthermore, it is imperative that materials developers incorporate topics and tasks that teach the value of diversity in ELT programs. As indicated in a previous section, scholars (Farrell & Martin, 2009; Jenkins, 2012; Karami & Zamanian, 2015; Mukminatien, 2012; Tomlinson, 2006) have already observed that WE and ELF concepts are excluded from local English college textbooks. Also, language lessons and ELT materials development and evaluation continue to privilege accuracy based on SE standards. The participants have voiced this need; thus GE principles have to be taken into account in reviewing and producing English language courses. Materials developers play a vital role in providing teachers with a compass for creating innovative lessons. Hence they need to design instructional tools including textbooks and audio-visual aids carefully to ensure that no type of discrimination is fostered nor any social group marginalized. Forms of ELT assessment must not be limited to the mere evaluation of SE proficiency but must be expanded. For instance, instruments (e.g. rubrics for assessing oral communication and writing skills) may be adjusted to acknowledge other English varieties and modes of expression (e.g. use of gestures in oral communication; use of symbols, fonts or images in presenting written output in laid-out pages or PowerPoint slides).

Another crucial step is the review and improvement of teacher education programs. Courses on GE that may broaden the worldview of teachers have to be integrated. Teachers have to be trained in addressing possible linguistic inequalities that may arise in their multicultural classrooms and developing students' cultural awareness and intercultural competence. I echo Vettorel's (2015) call for exposing English teachers to WE and ELF views and aiding them with tools that may help them form lessons that enhance students' linguistic awareness. Students should be taught explicitly to treat other people who belong to different cultural, linguistic and socio-economic groups with genuine respect. They should be educated about the power of language so that they become agents of equality rather than agents of discrimination.

As the findings reveal, SAE currently dominates the ELT domain and other local varieties of English and local languages are limited to spaces such as literature classes. In rigid teaching contexts where monolingual paradigms are prominent, teachers may add activities that raise the awareness of students about GE. Models illustrating other English varieties may be incorporated. Discussions about the differences between SE taught in the classroom and the local English varieties used by the students may be fused in language lessons to make students realize that English has many flavors. In composition classes, personal writing activities that focus on content rather than form and structure patterned after NS norms may be provided. Some participants have seen the possibilities of applying GE in their contexts, and this may be a good starting point. Teachers may also include activities and allot sessions that will allow students to 'speak freely' and use their local English varieties and other languages in settings where EOP is enforced. Code-switching and code-meshing may be applied to enable students to use words and expressions from their linguistic repertoire. For example, they can talk and write about their unique regional dishes and cultural beliefs, practices and rituals. Such topics and activities entail the use of local expressions, and through these exercises students may realize that languages work together and not against each other. I have done these activities in my classes, and I have witnessed how the use of different languages enhances ELT in my own teaching context as described below:

> Languages are not necessarily at war with each other; they complement each other in communication. Therefore, we have to reconsider the dominant understanding that one language detrimentally 'interferes' with the learning and use of another. The influences of one language on the other can be creative, enabling, and offer possibilities for voice. (Canagarajah, 2013: 6)

These are just a few basic ideas but they may help create ripples of change at the classroom level. Further research has to be done involving learners and teachers in multicultural classrooms to investigate the impact of structures such as the imposition of the EOP and monolingual standards in English language classes. Scholars may continue pursuing studies on how GE principles are applied successfully in terms of ELT policies, practices and assessment. Shifting to a GE pedagogical paradigm does not have to be done in one giant leap, especially in postcolonial settings such as the Philippines. Being a product of EOP, I practiced EOP, and I understand why it is difficult for those who defend ENL standards to embrace GE principles. It is possible to reach a middle ground by providing spaces for both SE and other Englishes in ELT which may benefit learners. As I have experienced, it takes small steps to achieve ELT improvements by looking through the eyes of GE. My ELT journey continues, and I still have a lot to explore. Small steps may pave the way for other teachers, administrators, materials developers, scholars and policy makers who may want to take alternative routes in finding answers to current ELT challenges. These small steps may lead to more paths towards educational innovations that lower cultural, linguistic and socio-economic walls and foster diversity, equality and unity in multicultural classrooms.

Notes

(1) In 1940, Tagalog, the regional language of Filipinos from Southern Luzon, was proclaimed as the national language because it was considered as the most developed local language (Brigham & Castillo, 1999). Later on, the name of the national language was changed to Pilipino, which is based on Tagalog, and then to Filipino (Cruz, 2010). Thus, Tagalog, Pilipino and Filipino are synonymous. Tagalog is a popular lingua franca in Metro Manila.
(2) Kapampangan is the regional language of Filipinos from Pampanga, located in Central Luzon.
(3) See Footnote (1).
(4) Filipino may refer to the national and official language in the Philippines and 'it may also refer to the citizens and nationals of the Philippines' (Canilao, 2018: 139).

References

Bautista, M. (2000) *Defining Standard Philippine English: Its Status and Grammatical Features*. Manila: De La Salle University Press.
Bernardo, A.B. (2008) English in Philippine education: Solution or problem? In K. Bolton and L. Bautista (eds) *Philippine English: Linguistic and Literary Perspectives* (pp. 29–48). Hong Kong: Hong Kong University Press.
Brigham, S. and Castillo, E. (1999) Language policy for education in the Philippines. Technical Background Paper No. 6. Philippines Education for the 21st Century – the 1998 Philippines Education Sector Study. Manila: Asia Development Bank and World Bank.
Burton, L.A. (2013) Mother tongue-based multilingual education in the Philippines: Studying top-down policy implementation from the bottom up. Doctoral dissertation, University of Minnesota.
Canagarajah, S. (1999) *Resisting Linguistic Imperialism in English Teaching*. Oxford: Oxford University Press.
Canagarajah, S. (2006) An interview with Suresh Canagarajah by Rani Rubdy. In R. Rubdy and M. Saraceni (eds) *English in the World: Global Rules, Global Roles* (pp. 100–211). London: Continuum.
Canagarajah, A.S. (2013) *Translingual Practice: Global Englishes and Cosmopolitan Relations*. New York: Routledge.
Canagarajah, A.S. and Wurr, A.J. (2011) Multilingual communication and language acquisition: New research directions. *Reading Matrix: An International Online Journal* 11 (1), 1–15.
Canilao, M.L.E. (2018). English in the teaching of mathematics: Policies, realities, and opportunities. In I.P. Martin (ed.) *Reconceptualizing English Education in a Multilingual Society* (pp. 137–161). Singapore: Springer Nature Singaore.
Cebu Provincial Government (2019). *Facts and Figures*. See https://www.cebu.gov.ph/about-cebu/facts-and-figures/.
Cena, D. (1958) The local dialects as the medium of instruction in the primary grades. *Philippine Studies* 6 (1), 115–120.
Clandinin, D.J. and Connelly, F.M. (2000) *Narrative Inquiry: Experience and Story in Qualitative Research*. San Francisco, CA: Jossey-Bass.
Congress of the Philippines (2013) Republic Act No. 10533. *Official Gazette*. Manila: Office of the President of the Philippines. See https://www.officialgazette.gov.ph/2013/05/15/republic-act-no-10533/.
Creswell, J.W. (2013) *Qualitative Inquiry and Research Design: Choosing among Five Approaches* (3rd edn). Thousand Oaks, CA: Sage.
Creswell, J.W. (2014) *Research Design: Qualitative, Quantitative and Mixed Methods Approaches* (4th edn). Thousand Oaks, CA: Sage.

Cruz, I. (2010) Mother tongue education. In R. Nolasco, F. Datar and A. Azurin (eds) *Starting Where the Children Are* (pp. 48–51). Quezon City: 170 + Talaytayan MLE.

Davao City (2011) *Profile*. See http://www.davaocity.gov.ph/davao/.

Fang, F. (2016) Investigating attitudes towards English accents from an ELF framework. *Asian Journal of Applied Linguistics* 3 (1), 68–80.

Farrell, T. and Martin, S. (2009) To teach Standard English or World Englishes? A balanced approach to instruction. *English Teaching Forum* 2, 2–7.

Gallego, M.K.S. and Zubiri, L.A.M. (2011) MTBMLE in the Philippines: Perceptions, attitudes, and outlook. In A. Shafaei (ed.) *Frontiers of Language and Teaching, Vol. 2. Proceedings of the 2011 International Online Language Conference (IOLC 2011)* (pp. 405–414). Boca Raton, FL: Brown Walker Press.

Galloway, N. and Rose, H. (2014) Using listening journals to raise awareness of Global Englishes in ELT. *ELT Journal* 68, 386–396.

Galloway, N. and Rose, H. (2015) *Introducing Global Englishes*. Abingdon: Routledge.

García, O. (2009) Education, multilingualism and translanguaging in the 21st century. In A.K. Mohanty, M. Panda, R. Phillipson and T. Skutnabb-Kangas (eds) *Multilingual Education for Social Justice: Globalising the Local* (pp. 140–158). New Delhi: Orient BlackSwan.

Gee, J.P. (1999) *An Introduction to Discourse Analysis: Theory and Method*. London: Routledge.

Iligan Government (2012) *About Iligan*. See http://www.iligan.gov.ph/about-iligan/.

Jenkins, J. (2007) *English as a Lingua Franca: Attitude and Identity*. Oxford: Oxford University Press.

Jenkins, J. (2012) English as a lingua franca from the classroom to the classroom. *ELT Journal* 66, 486–494.

Jenkins, J. (2015) *Global Englishes: A Resource Book for Students* (3rd edn). London: Routledge.

Jindapitak, N. and Boonsuk, Y. (2018) Authoritative discourse in a locally-published ELT textbook in Thailand. *Indonesian Journal of Applied Linguistics* 8 (2), 193–204.

Johnson, K.E. (2006) The sociocultural turn and its challenges for second language teacher education. *TESOL Quarterly* 40 (1), 235–235.

Kachru, B. (1992) Teaching world Englishes. In B. Kachru (ed.) *The Other Tongue: English Across Cultures* (2nd edn) (pp. 355–365). Champaign, IL: University of Illinois Press.

Kachru, B. (2005) *Asian Englishes: Beyond the Canon*. Hong Kong: Hong Kong University Press.

Karami, S. and Zamanian, M. (2015) A review of English teaching practices in the Philippines. *Journal of Language Sciences & Linguistics* 3, 145–151.

Kirkpatrick, A. (2010) *English as a Lingua Franca in ASEAN: A Multilingual Model*. Hong Kong: Hong Kong University Press.

Lee, K. (2012) Teaching intercultural English learning/teaching in world Englishes: Some classroom activities in South Korea. *English Teaching: Practice and Critique* 11 (4), 190–205.

Llanto, J. (2008) Legislators push English as medium of instruction. *Newsbreak*, 9 June. See https://news.abs-cbn.com/special-report/06/09/08/legislators-push-english-medium-instruction.

Martin, I. (2014) Commentary. Codeswitching in universities in Singapore and the Philippines. In R. Barnard and J. McLellan (eds) *Codeswitching in University English-Medium Classes: Asian Perspectives* (pp. 174–185). New York: Multilingual Matters.

McKay, S. (2004) Teaching English as an international language: The role of culture in Asian contexts. *Journal of Asia TEFL* 1 (1), 1–22.

McKay, S. (2006) EIL curriculum development. In R. Rubdy and M. Saraceni (eds) *English in the World: Global Rules, Global Roles* (pp. 114–129). London: Continuum.

Mindo, D. (2008) English language teaching, curriculum innovations and implementation strategies: Philippine experience. In Y.H. Choi and B. Spolsky (eds) *ELT Curriculum Innovation and Implementation in Asia* (pp. 161–189). Asia TEFL. Seoul: edKLC.

Mukminatien, N. (2012) Accommodating World Englishes in developing EFL learners' oral communication. *TEFLIN Journal* 23 (2), 222–232.

Murata, K. and Jenkins, J. (eds) (2009) *Global Englishes in Asian Contexts: Current and Future Debates*. Basingstoke: Palgrave Macmillan.

Nolasco, R.M. (2008) The prospects of multilingual education and literacy in the Philippines. In A. Bernardo (ed.) *The Paradox of Philippine Education and Education Reform: Social Sciences Perspectives* (pp. 133–145). Quezon City: Social Science Council.

Nolasco, R. (2010) Fixing education through language. In R. Nolasco, F. Datar and A. Azurin (eds) *Starting Where the Children Are* (pp. 85–87). Quezon City: 170 + Talaytayan MLE.

Nueva Vizcaya Government (2015) *Provincial Profile*. See https://nuevavizcaya.gov.ph/provincial-profile/10/.

Paulson Stone, R. (2012) A professional development program for the mother tongue-based teacher: Addressing teacher perceptions and attitudes towards MTBMLE. Doctoral dissertation, University of Massachusetts Amherst. See http://scholarworks.umass.edu/open_access_dissertations/592.

Phillipson, R. (1992) *Linguistic Imperialism*. Oxford: Oxford University Press.

Provincial Government of Pampanga (2017) *Profile*. See http://www.pampanga.gov.ph/.

Rubdy, R. and Saraceni, M. (2006) Introduction. In R. Rubdy and M. Saraceni (eds) *English in the World: Global Rules, Global Roles* (pp. 5–16). London: Continuum.

Seidlhofer, B. (2006) English as a lingua franca in the expanding circle: What it isn't. In R. Rubdy and M. Saraceni (eds) *English in the World: Global Rules, Global Roles* (pp. 40–50). London: Continuum.

Smolicz, J., Nical, I. and Secombe, M. (2001) English as the medium of instruction for science and its effects on the languages of the Philippines. In U. Ammon (ed.) *The Dominance of English as a Language of Science* (pp. 205–226). Berlin: De Gruyter Mouton.

Sultan Kudarat (2010) *Socio-economic Profile: Sultan Kudarat Province*. See http://sultankudaratprovince.gov.ph/wp-content/uploads/2012/08/SEP-2010_Sultan-Kudarat-Province.pdf.

Sultan Kudarat (2017) *General Information*. See http://sultankudaratprovince.gov.ph/category/general-information/.

Svartvik, J. and Leech, G. (2006) *English: One Tongue, Many Voices*. New York: Palgrave Macmillan.

Tollefson, J.W. (2007) Ideology, language varieties, and ELT. In J. Cummins and C. Davison (eds) *International Handbook of English Language Teaching* (pp. 25–36). New York: Springer.

Tomlinson, B. (2006) A multi-dimensional approach to teaching English for the world. In R. Rubdy and M. Saraceni (eds) *English in the World: Global Rules, Global Roles* (pp. 130–150). London: Continuum.

Ton, N.H. and Pham, H.H. (2010) Vietnamese teachers' and students' perceptions of Global English. *Language Education in Asia* 1 (1), 48–61.

Tupas, T. (2006) Standard Englishes, pedagogical paradigms, and conditions of (im)possibility. In R. Rubdy and M. Saraceni (eds) *English in the World: Global Rules, Global Roles* (pp. 169–185). London: Continuum.

Tupas, R. and Rubdy, R. (2015) Introduction: From world Englishes to unequal Englishes. In R. Tupas (ed.) *Unequal Englishes: The Politics of Englishes Today* (pp. 1–17). New York: Palgrave Macmillan.

UNESCO (2003) *Education in a Multilingual World*. Paris: UN Educational, Scientific, and Cultural Organization.

Vettorel, P. (2015) World Englishes and English as a lingua franca: Implications for teacher education and ELT. *Iperstoria – Testi Letterature Linguaggi* 6, 229–244.

World Population Review (2017) *Manila Population 2017*. See http://worldpopulationreview.com/world-cities/manila-population/.

7 Contextualizing Teaching English as a Local/Global Language: A Bottom-up Sociolinguistic Investigation

Jim Chan

The emergence of new English varieties in recent decades has focused scholarly attention on new perspectives on teaching English as an international language. As non-native speakers of English are now the overwhelming majority in international communication, Global Englishes scholars have advocated that English language targets in contemporary education should be redefined so as to cater for second language learners' future language needs. This chapter discusses the possibility of establishing appropriate English language teaching goals for a specific sociolinguistic setting, as exemplified by a bottom-up investigation in Hong Kong. It draws on findings derived from a large-scale research project investigating Hong Kong's current English language teaching curricula, assessments and classroom practices and the relevant stakeholders' (i.e. professionals, students and teachers) English use experience and attitudes towards English language learning. These empirical findings can inform pedagogical recommendations in three main dimensions, namely: (1) recognizing and benchmarking the localized learning target; (2) contextualizing English learning activities; and (3) shifting the pedagogical foci in English curricula and assessments in English language teaching. The chapter concludes by highlighting the values of a bottom-up approach to investigating contextual language needs and, subsequently, establishing learning targets that are most relevant to L2 learners in individual societies.

Introduction

One major consequence of the emergence of new Englishes in the era of globalization is their changing functions and forms in increasingly multilingual communities. English no longer belongs solely to native speakers (NSs) situated in the inner circle; it also belongs to any NSs or non-native speakers (NNSs) who learn or use it for a wide range of purposes in diverse social contexts. Thus communication using English (or also involving other languages) has become more complex, dynamic and fluid, and NS linguistic forms may be less important for effective communication (Baker, 2015; Canagarajah, 2013; Jenkins, 2015; Jenkins *et al.*, 2011). These changes have challenged traditional learning and teaching goals and practices in English language teaching (ELT), which are mainly guided by NS norms and learning and teaching principles. As NNSs are now the overwhelming majority in international communication (Seidlhofer, 2011), scholars have advocated that English language targets in contemporary education should be redefined to cater to second language (L2) learners' future language needs in local and international settings (Canagarajah, 2013; Kirkpatrick, 2007a, 2011, 2014).

Central to this redefinition of L2 language learning goals, as informed by groundbreaking World Englishes (WE) and English as a lingua franca (ELF) research, is a pluricentric view of English, which emphasizes equality, preservation of one's cultural identity and mutual respect among speakers of different English varieties while ensuring or enhancing mutual understanding (Jenkins *et al.*, 2011; Kachru & Nelson, 2006; Kirkpatrick, 2007a; Seidlhofer, 2009). From this perspective, it is argued that ELT pedagogies and practices should be reoriented to achieve such language goals by focusing on communicative competence in local/international contexts (rather than linguistic forms) (Canagarajah, 2013, 2017), adopting a localized teaching model (Kirkpatrick, 2007a, 2011; Murphy, 2014), maintaining mutual intelligibility (Jenkins, 2000; Nelson, 2011; Sewell, 2016), raising learners' awareness of local/global language use and culture and language variation (Baker, 2012, 2015; Byram, 2012; Walker, 2010) and promoting their own cultural identity (Kirkpatrick, 2007a; Phillipson, 2009).

As these core principles in redefining language goals have emerged from empirical research in multilingual contexts mainly in the outer (and expanding) circle (Kachru & Nelson, 2006) and international contexts such as continental Europe (Seidlhofer, 2011) and ASEAN (Kirkpatrick, 2010), it is crucial to examine whether and how these proposals and the corresponding findings can be applied to and implemented in English language education in a specific sociolinguistic setting. It is the purpose of this chapter to discuss the possibility of establishing appropriate localized ELT goals with the exemplification of a bottom-up investigation in Hong Kong from a sociolinguistic perspective. This chapter draws on findings derived from a large-scale research project investigating an array of contextual issues in Hong Kong, including: the contexts of language use; the interlocutors involved; challenges in international communication; attitudes towards local and inner circle English varieties and English language learning; and current ELT curricula, assessments and classroom practices. By aligning theories on teaching English as an international language (or ELF) with specific sociolinguistic settings and existing practices, the chapter discusses the pedagogical implications and highlights the values of a bottom-up approach to investigating contextualized language needs and, subsequently, establishing learning targets that are most relevant to L2 learners in individual societies.

An Overview of the Research Project

This research project investigated the (dis)connection of the sociolinguistic reality and ELT practices in Hong Kong and established appropriate English learning goals for local L2 students. More specifically, it explored three main issues: (1) the use of spoken English in Hong Kong's sociolinguistic environment; (2) major stakeholders' attitudes towards English varieties and English learning; and (3) current practices in English language education. It adopted a mixed-methods approach that enabled the triangulation of quantitative and qualitative data. The quantitative methods included a structured questionnaire survey and the verbal guise technique[1] (VGT), whereas the qualitative methods consisted of semi-structured focus groups/individual interviews, document analysis and a school case study.[2]

Table 7.1 presents an overview of the various research methods adopted in the large-scale project and the samples and participants

Table 7.1 Overview of research methods and samples/participants

Qualitative method	Quantitative method	Samples/participants
Document analysis		• Textbooks (two publishers) • ELT curricula • Public examination papers
School case study		• School documents • Classroom observations + audio-recording of teachers' speech • Interviews (teachers and students)
Focus group and individual interviews		• Junior secondary students ($n = 75$) • Senior secondary students ($n = 46$) • Professionals ($n = 18$) • Teachers ($n = 16$)
	Questionnaire survey	• University students ($n = 141$) • Teachers ($n = 132$) • Professionals ($n = 131$) • Band 1 students[a] ($n = 447$) • Band 2 students ($n = 406$) • Band 3 students ($n = 458$)
	Verbal guise test	• Junior secondary students ($n = 164$) • Senior secondary students ($n = 89$) • Full-time university students ($n = 133$) • Professionals ($n = 102$)

Note: [a]Students in Hong Kong are classified into Bands 1–3 (Band 1: higher academic attainments; Band 3: lower academic attainments) according to the three-band scale when they advance to secondary education.

involved. The interviews and questionnaire were used to uncover the use of spoken English by and language attitudes of students (of different academic levels), teachers (using English to teach ELT and content-area subjects) and professionals (in various disciplines), all of whom contribute to the real use and long-term development of English in Hong Kong. In addition, the VGT was used to elicit the participants' familiarity with and underlying perceptions of diverse English varieties (e.g. Hong Kong English, British English, American English). The teaching and learning practices of English were examined by means of document analyses of two sets of junior and senior secondary commercial English textbooks, the secondary English language education curricula and public examination papers and a school case study, which involved analysis of school documents, lesson observations, phonological analysis of teachers' classroom speech and interviews with students and teachers. The following sections discuss the key findings derived from these methods with respect to the aforementioned three dimensions and their implications for devising localized L2 English learning goals.

Use of Spoken English in Hong Kong: Contexts and Challenges

A key argument for education reform in the era of globalization, as informed by WE and ELF research, is the prominence of L2 speakers (or NNSs) rather than NSs in English communication in most outer circle (e.g. India, Singapore) and international contexts (e.g. continental Europe, ASEAN) (Kirkpatrick, 2010; Seidlhofer, 2009, 2011). Much of the early empirical research in this area has described linguistic features (e.g. phonology, lexis/lexico-grammar, pragmatics), mainly in interactions among L2 speakers and especially in business (e.g. Charles, 2007; Ehrenreich, 2010; Evans, 2014) and academic settings (e.g. Björkman, 2013; Jenkins, 2014; Mauranen, 2012; Smit, 2010). These important findings have contributed to our understanding of the changing nature of English, which has become more dynamic and fluid in multilingual settings (Baker, 2015; Jenkins, 2015; Jenkins *et al.*, 2011) and has informed pedagogies for teaching English as an international language. It is therefore pertinent to evaluate how these empirical findings and pedagogical recommendations are applicable to the Hong Kong context from a sociolinguistic perspective.

The use of English in Hong Kong shares features in both outer and expanding circle contexts. Like many former British colonies (e.g. Singapore, India), English has been Hong Kong's key medium for written communication in the government, legislation, law courts and education, and the role of written English has remained important since Hong Kong's return to Chinese sovereignty in 1997 (Evans, 2010; Lai, 2012). Nevertheless, as the majority of Hong Kong residents speak Cantonese as their first language (over 90%), English is less used as a tool for intra-ethnic communication (as in many outer circle countries such as Singapore, Nigeria and the Philippines); indeed, it is more used as a tool for international communication. This use of spoken English resembles that in the expanding circle and perhaps most international contexts, presumably mainly involving L2 English speakers of different cultural and linguistic backgrounds. Empirical studies conducted in Hong Kong have revealed that English is often spoken in business and academic discourses, especially in formal situations such as meetings, interviews, presentations, seminars and conferences (Evans, 2010, 2011, 2013).

Although the English speaking situation in Hong Kong apparently aligns with those found in ELF contexts (e.g. in the VOICE, ACE and ELFA corpora; see Kirkpatrick, 2010; Mauranen, 2012; Seidlhofer, 2011, respectively), the survey findings in this study seem to suggest that most participants (involving secondary and university students, professionals and teachers) were exposed more to NS than NNS accents in the media such as TV channels and films, probably owing to the US/UK dominance of the mass media and entertainment industry (Chan, 2017). There was, however, a lack of consensus in their responses as to whether they encountered more NSs or NNSs at work or study and on the internet (Chan, 2017). These findings were confirmed by the participants in the interviews, particularly the professionals, many of whom reported that they encountered both NSs and NNSs in their daily English communication depending on their occupational natures (Chan, 2018a). Their interlocutors in the workplace were from a variety of inner (e.g. Britain, Australia, Canada), outer (e.g. Hong Kong, India/Pakistan, Singapore, the Philippines) and expanding (e.g. Japan, mainland China, Taiwan) circle territories (Chan, 2018a). One possible reason for their frequent encountering of NSs was Hong Kong's status as an international city since the colonial period and its tight connection with traditionally strong economic markets (e.g. in North America, Britain) (Evans, 2014). In addition, a significant number of Hong Kong citizens have immigrated to inner circle countries (e.g. Australia, Canada) in the past few decades (especially before 1997) and have returned to Hong Kong recently because of the economic opportunities in East Asia (Ley, 2013). The second generation of these Hong Kong people is likely to comprise NSs or bilingual individuals (i.e. highly proficient in both English and Cantonese). From this perspective, an English learning and teaching goal neglecting the presence of (a considerable proportion of) NSs in English communication in Hong Kong may not be entirely appropriate.

Interestingly, regardless of the interviewed professionals' differing occupational disciplines (e.g. commerce, business, government, education, social work), they shared a range of similar challenges and observations in their daily English communication (Chan, 2018a).

- Accent variation was a major source of problems in communication, but it depended on specific varieties of accents (e.g. Indian). Hong Kong English pronunciation was reported to seldom cause intelligibility problems.
- Cultural differences often caused communication problems.
- Telephone conversation tended to be more difficult than face-to-face interactions due to the absence of visual clues in communication.
- Communication problems occurred in both NS–NNS and NNS–NNS interactions, especially when the interlocutors lacked awareness of international/intercultural communication. The communication strategies adopted in NS–NNS and NNS–NNS interactions were different.
- Some Hong Kong people were relatively weak at and less confident in listening to and speaking English because this was less of a focus in their prior English training.
- The English proficiency of the speakers (e.g. choice of vocabulary, fluency) played an important role in mutual understanding, but grammatical correctness was less important in everyday (especially NNS–NNS) communication.
- Communication problems could be addressed by using written clues (or drawing), speaking slowly, asking for repetition and clarification, using simple English, mutual accommodation and advanced technology.
- The ability to understand an L2 accent could be enhanced by accumulated experience.

In contrast, the interviewed students and teachers showed little knowledge and awareness of real-life English use and the potential challenges in international communication, due largely to their limited experience of English use outside the classroom and, more importantly, the overemphasis on language form and academic English at school. These factors might have led to their (mis)conceptions of English use outside school (Chan, 2018b). For instance, although the students considered being intelligible as crucial for English communication, many of them regarded NSs as their potential future interlocutors in their first impressions. Similarly, the teachers had some experience communicating with NSs in daily life, but they apparently had little experience with communication in international contexts involving a wide range of NNSs. Most of them regarded NS English as the authoritative guide, particularly in terms of grammar and pronunciation (and NS culture) (see also Tsui & Bunton, 2000).

These findings echo the literature on the complex nature of international English communication, which involves a high degree of uncertainty and possibility (e.g. Baker, 2015; Canagarajah, 2017) (yet students and teachers showed little awareness in this regard). They also highlight the need to reconsider English learning goals and teaching approaches that could better prepare learners for their future English use. Essentially, these revised learning targets should offer greater flexibility to learners in their language choice and emphasize mutual collaboration to achieve certain communicative purposes.

Attitudes Towards English Varieties and English Learning

In addition to a needs analysis that uncovers the English-using practices in local and international contexts, another vital parameter determining the choice of localized English learning targets is local people's attitudes towards the vernacular vis-à-vis NS English varieties and their perceptions of English learning. In this respect, attitudinal studies worldwide have revealed two main findings: (1) L2 speakers'/learners' adherence to NS standards due to their perceived high status; and (2) their desire to express their local cultural identities using their own English varieties (Ahn, 2015; Cavallaro & Ng, 2009; Edwards, 2015; Jenkins, 2007; McKenzie, 2010; Sasayama, 2013; Wang, 2015).

In the present study, Hong Kong people's language attitudes were investigated by means of both direct (i.e. questionnaire and interview) and indirect (i.e. VGT) measures. In alignment with the literature (e.g. Edwards, 2015; Jenkins, 2007; McKenzie, 2010), the survey results revealed prominent NS Anglophone-centric attitudes among most of the participants, who perceived NS pronunciations as a legitimate variety and a standard and NSs as the owners of English. They also showed a tendency to associate this NS standard with high education, a high English proficiency, wealth and better careers (see Chan, 2017, for the complete questionnaire findings). Hong Kong English (HKE) accents were generally regarded as 'errors' that needed to be corrected and not a teaching model, although many also believed that speaking like an NS was less important than maintaining mutual understanding (Chan, 2017). In terms of accent and identity, the findings showed that Hong Kong people tended not to desire to retain features of their own English variety, although they did not have a strong feeling if others could tell their identity based on their accent. It was also found that the more educated the students in the local education system were (e.g. university students rather than junior secondary students), the more prominent their Anglophone-centric attitudes (especially towards Received Pronunciation, RP) and the greater their negativity towards local (or other NNS) English varieties. This was probably due to an implicit (or even explicit) focus on NS targets in the local English language curricula (see the following discussion).

The interview data confirmed the students', teachers' and professionals' aspirations to NS standards when they were asked to explain their choice of English learning targets (Chan, 2018b). Five recurring themes emerged in the interview data: (1) the high status of NS English; (2) the (un)attainability of English targets; (3) practical needs in communication; (4) perceptions of the local English variety (i.e. HKE); and (5) requirements in assessments. While the majority of the professionals and students recognized the unquestionably high social status and pragmatic values of NS English, many underlined the lack of attainability of an NS target in Hong Kong's Cantonese speaking environment. In terms of intelligibility, HKE was deemed to be 'acceptable' (and unavoidable), as it could be understood by most foreign listeners according to the professionals' experience. However, although many attitudinal studies highlighted local people's desires to preserve their local cultural identities using their own English varieties in international/intranational communication (see Cavallaro & Ng, 2009; Jenkins, 2007; Sasayama, 2013), this theme was found to be less salient or even unmentioned in the interview data. Instead, the notion of HKE was stigmatized by the participants, who often associated it with the Cantonese-translated English expressions and L1-influenced 'mistakes' or 'errors', which differed significantly from the typical HKE features documented in the literature, especially in terms of vocabulary (Benson, 2000; Cummings & Wolf, 2011; Evans, 2015) and pronunciation (see Chan, 2014b; Deterding *et al.*, 2008; Hung, 2000; Setter *et al.*, 2010; Sewell & Chan, 2010).

Furthermore, although the teachers acknowledged the importance of ensuring mutual understanding in communication, their expectations for students' English learning tended to be confined to the perceived NS-oriented assessment criteria of high-stakes public examinations. The findings illustrated a hierarchical attitude in Hong Kong people's English learning targets in the descending order of an NS target, an educated local target (e.g. qualified English teachers' English variety) and an intelligibility-oriented target (see Kirkpatrick, 2007a; Murphy, 2014; Sewell, 2016). Being able to maintain mutual understanding was considered the basic criterion in English language learning and teaching.

In addition to the direct measures (questionnaire and interviews) eliciting the participants' overt language attitudes, the indirect VGT evaluated their underlying (or covert) awareness of and attitudes towards English varieties as complementary findings (see Chan, 2013, 2016b). The participants (including professionals, university students and secondary students) were asked to listen to the speech samples of speakers of seven English varieties from the inner (Britain, America, Australia), outer (Hong Kong, India, the Philippines) and expanding (China) circles in the VGT and to complete an elicitation task examining their awareness of English varieties, perception of English varieties in the dimensions of status and solidarity, and choice of English varieties in various local formal (e.g. being a teaching model, news broadcast, job interviews, business meetings) and less formal English speaking contexts (e.g. directing NS visitors, classroom discussion, chatting with NNS friends).

The results generally complemented findings from previous VGT studies (e.g. Bolton & Kwok, 1990; Zhang, 2013) that many Hong Kong people were capable of identifying the local HKE accent. However, our findings further suggest that most of the participants were able to distinguish between NS and NNS accents based on the speakers' speech features. Many of them believed that their pronunciation was closer to the British and American pronunciation than to the HKE pronunciation and that all of the NS pronunciations were more intelligible than any of the NNS pronunciations.[3] Moreover, the VGT findings revealed that the participants rated NS accents higher than NNS accents in terms of status and solidarity. These results imply that Hong Kong people may not regard HKE as a symbol of solidarity, unlike the case of other outer circle countries such as Singapore, where Singaporean English has been widely used by residents for everyday social purposes (Cavallaro & Ng, 2009).

Another crucial discovery of the VGT related to participants' contextual variation in their choice of English varieties in English speaking situations with different levels of formality (e.g. formal versus informal) and interactional patterns (e.g. monologue versus dialogue). The findings reveal an emerging attitudinal pattern in their choice in which the participants had less adverse reactions to NNS accents in less formal and more interactive situations (e.g. directing NS visitors, classroom discussion, chatting with NNS friends). It was also found that the more educated the students in the local context were, the more prominent their Anglophone-centric attitudes (especially towards RP) and the greater their negativity towards the local (or other NNS) accents. This finding is consistent with findings from the questionnaire survey and interviews. Despite the overall Anglophone-centric attitudes of Hong Kong people, the additional factor (i.e. situation differences) affecting their attitudes towards English varieties and learning may have significant implications for designs of the teaching and learning of English as an international language (see the following).

Current Practices in English Language Education

While the preceding two sections discuss the sociolinguistic reality of how (spoken) English is being used in Hong Kong and the major stakeholders' awareness and attitudes towards English varieties and learning/teaching, it is important to critically evaluate the current practices in English language education in order to offer recommendations. Our investigation comprised two main components: the teaching and assessment foci in the ELT curricula; and assessments, commercially published textbooks (Chan, 2014a) and classroom teaching and modelling (Chan, 2014b).

The document analysis suggested that elements of cultural issues and values were indeed incorporated in the secondary ELT curriculum and textbooks, but the school-exit public examination (which was mainly based on the senior secondary curriculum) mainly focused on the English language and its usage. Probably influenced by WE research, ELT textbooks are locally contextualized: themes and tasks are designed to be rooted in Hong Kong students' perspectives. However, the textbook design has a relatively narrow scope, as it focuses on NS pronunciation (particularly RP) and local and NS cultures but does not account for the realities of international communication involving people of diverse NNS and NS backgrounds and their corresponding cultures and English varieties (Chan, 2014a).

As for the description of a learning target, although the ELT curricula claim to aim for communicative competence, there is a lack of clarity regarding which pedagogical ideologies the curricula conform to. For instance, in the speaking paper of the Hong Kong Diploma of Secondary Education Examination (HKDSE) (i.e. the high-stakes school-exit public examination for university admission), the assessment descriptors for Level 7 (highest) suggest that candidates should pronounce 'all sounds/sound clusters and words clearly and accurately' (HKEAA, 2012: 160), but the notion of pronunciation accuracy is not clearly defined. This is likely to be left to the interpretation of the examiners, who are often practising local teachers. It is therefore uncertain whether features of the local English variety or other varieties are regarded as 'mistakes' or 'errors' and subsequently penalized during public assessments regardless of whether they are intelligible in international communication.

In the listening examination, one breakthrough in the task design is the inclusion of a small proportion of local HKE speakers, even though the majority have an NS accent. The assessment guide for the listening paper suggests that one of the aims of the listening assessment is to examine candidates' ability to 'understand speakers with a range of accents and language varieties in speech delivered at a moderate pace' (CDC, 2007: 49), although there is no specification of which kinds of accent should be involved. However, in the rather conventional design of the ELT textbooks, typical HKE phonological features are stigmatized (or regarded as 'errors') in the speaking tasks, and their listening tasks fail to fulfil the curricula's suggestion of exposing students to various English accents (Chan, 2014a). More specifically, there is a clear disjunction among the language-using situations (e.g. international settings), the identity of speakers (mainly NNSs, especially local students/teachers) and their accents (i.e. mainly RP) in the audio-recordings in the listening textbooks.

Notwithstanding this prominence of NS pronunciation in the ELT textbooks, our school case study indicated that the major source of English exposure in the classroom was local teachers' English pronunciation (>70% of classroom time over a week) rather than the generally perceived NS models (see Chan, 2014b). Under the medium-of-instruction policy in Hong Kong, these local teachers may include both ELT teachers and content-area teachers who teach academic subjects (e.g. mathematics, science) in English. The pronunciations of six teachers in the classroom setting were recorded for further phonological analysis to identify features of dictionary and non-dictionary (or HKE) English. The data revealed relatively higher proportions of HKE consonant and vowel features in the subject teachers' speech than in the ELT teachers', but numerous HKE features were shared by all of the teachers. The findings suggest that these forms of HKE are already practising pronunciation models, as teachers are presumably the students' role models in the school context. Although subject teachers may not teach English pronunciation explicitly due to their key concerns being on subject matters, students may subconsciously model parts of their pronunciation on them, especially for some content-specific vocabulary and language that only appear in the subjects. As illustrated in Table 7.2, the features of the teachers' HKE pronunciation were identified, quantified and aligned according to their prominence in the data.

In the interviews, the ELT teachers shared their pedagogical foci of pronunciation teaching, which revealed that they tended to emphasize the dictionary NS standard at the word level more than at the suprasegmental level (e.g. intonation, stress) (see Chan, 2018b). Furthermore, they were inclined to associate the concept of accent with suprasegmental rather than segmental pronunciation, and they believed that learners did not necessarily need to conform to the former. At both levels, however, students were in fact modelling the pronunciation of the ELT teachers, who inevitably spoke some degree of HKE (cf. Table 7.2). Another intriguing finding from the interviews is that the content area teachers contributed extensively to the teaching of word-level pronunciation when they taught an academic subject in the medium of English because they were aware that being able to pronounce a word was essential for the students to memorize its spelling, especially in the examination. On a relatively small scale, the phonological analysis not only revealed pronunciation models practised in the classroom, but also provided a foundation for the further development of localized targets/teaching models in the local ELT curriculum. This is discussed as follows.

The Bottom-up Investigation and Pedagogical Implications

The previous sections have reported some of the key findings of a bottom-up sociolinguistic (and partly linguistic) investigation, revealing the (dis)connection between real-life language needs and the design and practice of current English language education. The contextual information gathered is valuable and perhaps necessary for establishing more appropriate English learning targets and offering pedagogical recommendations for English language education in specific sociolinguistic contexts.

Table 7.2 Prominence of HKE vowels and consonants in teachers' speech

Feature	Examples from speech	Frequency of occurrences in the data (%)
Vowels		
Substitution of /æ/ with /e/	'c<u>a</u>n', 'h<u>a</u>m', 'th<u>a</u>nk'	90.9
Substitution of /aɪ/ and /aʊ/ with /ʌɪ/ and /ʌʊ/, respectively	'ab<u>ou</u>t' /ʌʊ/, 'wr<u>i</u>te' /ʌɪ/, 'l<u>i</u>ke' /ʌɪ/	89.8
Reduction of /aʊ/ to /ɑ/	'd<u>ow</u>n' /ɑŋ/, 'pron<u>oun</u>' /ɑŋ/, 'c<u>ou</u>ntable' /ɑŋ/	88.9
Reduction of /eɪ/ to /ɪ/ or /e/	't<u>a</u>ke' /ɪ/, 'str<u>ai</u>ght' /ɪ/, 'r<u>ai</u>n' /ɪŋ/, 'ch<u>a</u>nge' /ɪŋ/, 'ag<u>ai</u>n' /e/	58.5
Non-reduced vowels	'atm<u>o</u>sphere' /oʊ/, 'dam<u>a</u>ge' /eɪ/, 'c<u>o</u>ncern' /ɒ/, '<u>a</u>way' /ɑ/	28.4
Pronunciation of /ə/ in 'the'	'th<u>e</u>'	15.4
Mergers of /ɪ/ and /i/	'n<u>ee</u>d', 'f<u>ee</u>ling', 's<u>ea</u>soning'	9.7
Consonants		
Hidden /k/ in coda	'effe<u>c</u>ts', 'si<u>x</u>', 'ne<u>x</u>t'	100.0
Substitution of final /dʒ/ with /tʃ/	'pa<u>ge</u>', 'dama<u>ge</u>', 'chan<u>ge</u>'	100.0
Deletion of /l/ preceded by a vowel	'wi<u>ll</u>' /u/, 'e<u>ls</u>e' /u/, 'spe<u>l</u>t' /u/	98.3
Substitution of /z/ with /s/	'<u>z</u>ebra', 'rea<u>s</u>on', 'plea<u>s</u>e'	98.0
Substitution of /ð/ with /d/	'<u>th</u>is', 'fur<u>th</u>ermore', 'toge<u>th</u>er'	91.8
Variation or deletion of final /d/	'a<u>dd</u>' (unreleased), 'wor<u>d</u>' (unreleased), 'oxi<u>d</u>e' (deleted), 'clou<u>d</u>' (deleted), 'goo<u>d</u>' /ʔ/, 'coul<u>d</u>' /ʔ/, 'min<u>d</u>' /n/, 'kin<u>ds</u>' /ns/	91.0
Substitution of /v/ with /w/ or /f/	'<u>v</u>alue' /w/, '<u>v</u>ehicle' /w/, 'co<u>v</u>er' /f/, 'e<u>v</u>ery' /f/, 'gi<u>v</u>e' /f/	79.5
Variation or deletion of final /t/	'i<u>t</u>' (unreleased), 'le<u>t</u>' (unreleased), 'wri<u>t</u>e' (deleted), 'ou<u>t</u>' (deleted), 'no<u>t</u>' /ʔ/, 'pu<u>t</u>' /ʔ/, 'polluta<u>nts</u>' /ns/, 'jus<u>t</u>' /s/	71.6
Variation or deletion of final /k/	'li<u>k</u>e' /ʔ/, 'tal<u>k</u>' /ʔ/, 'as<u>k</u>' (deleted), 'thin<u>k</u>' (deleted)	69.9
Substitution of /θ/ with /f/	'<u>th</u>ing', 'any<u>th</u>ing', 'wi<u>th</u>'	21.6
Simplification of initial consonant cluster	'ch<u>l</u>orine' (deleted), 'p<u>r</u>oblem' (deleted), '<u>bl</u>ack' /br/, '<u>pr</u>oblem' /p'/, '<u>tr</u>y' /tʃ/, 'ni<u>tr</u>ogen' /tʃ/	17.2

Source: Adapted from Chan (2014b).

The following explains how specific pedagogical recommendations could be derived from the contextual findings in three main areas: (1) recognizing and benchmarking the localized (educated) pronunciation target; (2) contextualizing English learning activities; and (3) shifting the pedagogical foci in English curricula and assessments. Many of these recommendations are likely to be equally applicable to other similar contexts, subject to adjustments according to specific sociolinguistic environments.

Recognizing and benchmarking the localized pronunciation target

In his proposal of benchmarking an intelligibility-oriented teaching model, Kirkpatrick (2007b) suggests that the local educated form of English (modelled by successful multilingual ELT teachers) should be identified, described and codified with reference to intelligibility findings (e.g. Jenkins's Lingua Franca Core, 2000). He argues that this benchmark is more appropriate and attainable than an exonormative NS standard in multilingual settings and that it enhances both teachers' and learners' self-confidence and self-esteem, hence promoting their own local cultural identities (Kirkpatrick, 2007a). Nevertheless, while this long-term goal of adopting a localized model or target is seemingly practical and beneficial, Hong Kong people's generally negative attitudes towards HKE and adherence to NS norms (as shown in our findings) make the implementation difficult, although Kirkpatrick anticipates a gradual shift in social acceptance upon the codification and standardization of the localized English variety (Kirkpatrick, 2007a).

In this respect, a relatively milder suggestion or possibly an intermediate step to Kirkpatrick's proposal could be what Sewell (2016) calls a 'feature-based approach', which orients pronunciation teaching and modelling 'towards the intelligibility principle rather than the nativeness principle' regardless of whether 'nativeness' is seen as residing in 'native-speaker models' or in 'local nativised ones', which in his view are 'too restrictive' (Sewell, 2016: 98). This approach prioritizes local pronunciation features that would enhance or hinder international intelligibility and make them foci in English teaching. From this perspective, the alignment of HKE pronunciation features in the present study according to their prominence in the teachers' speech may serve as an initial step, and they could be further compared with the intelligibility findings to identify any pedagogical foci. Nevertheless, as our sociolinguistic findings suggest that both NSs and NNSs are present in local English speaking settings, there seems to be a need to also consider intelligibility studies of a greater variety of listeners. The inclusion of such prioritized features in the local curriculum and assessment may increase the recognition of the local English variety and hopefully initiate attitudinal change among the general public in the long term. One advantage of this teaching pedagogy is hence its shifted attention towards specific pronunciation features to give learners greater flexibility in their choice of pronunciation target as long as it is internationally intelligible (see Sewell, 2016).

Contextualizing English learning activities

The present study identified misalignments between real-life English use and English language education in the Hong Kong context. In the ELT curricula, assessments and teaching materials, there is a clear discrepancy between the limited NS accents adopted in the audio materials (i.e. mainly RP) and the large variety of NS and NNS pronunciations people may encounter in their daily-life English communication. The design of only including NS pronunciations in the examinations and ELT textbooks is contrary to the vital role NNSs play in international settings (Seidlhofer, 2011). This may lead to two main drawbacks. First, the overemphasis on NS accents (and particularly RP) in ELT may fail to equip learners with the ability to address the major sources of communication problems in Hong Kong or any other international contexts, as reported in the interview data (e.g. accent variation and cultural differences). Secondly, the rather inauthentic English speaking tasks do not reflect learners' future English use and may be misleading. The limited focus on NS English in the ELT curricula and materials may risk (re)producing learners who lack awareness of language variation in international communication but continue to adhere to NS correctness. According to our findings, many secondary school students instantly associated their potential interlocutors in English communication with NS foreigners, and the majority of the participants were found to have Anglophone-centric attitudes. In contrast, HKE was stigmatized or generally regarded as second class (or 'mistakes'/'errors'). This orientation towards NS standards and negativity towards the HKE (or other NNS) pronunciations were evidently more prominent among students at higher levels in the local education system. The current curricula, assessments and teaching materials apparently do not offer learners a real choice of their own English learning target but may reinforce NS correctness, as they are not informed of the genuine role of English.

One principle to address the aforementioned disadvantages in contemporary English education is to present learners with the sociolinguistic reality in the local/international setting based on the relevant sociolinguistic findings. In practice, it is possible that the design of speaking/listening tasks takes into account real-world English use situations (e.g. international communication), the corresponding speakers' identity (i.e. NSs versus NNSs) and their accents and cultures to raise students' awareness of authentic English use. As the VGT findings suggest that Hong Kong people have fewer reservations about the use of NNS accents in more casual and interactive English speaking situations, stakeholders (including education officials) may feel more accepting of the incorporation of these accents in (semi-)authentic listening tasks. In addition, this task design is compatible with the adoption of task-based language teaching advocated in most contemporary ELT syllabi worldwide by considering specific English speaking contexts and purposes.

Shifting the pedagogical foci in English curricula and assessments

Although the local ELT curricula claim to place strong emphasis on communicative competence, its implementation in examinations and ELT textbooks is still (implicitly) guided by an NS standard. Training from this perspective may offer little assistance to students, who are likely to encounter problems such as accent variation, telephoning and cultural differences in their future use of English (as revealed in the professionals' responses). Given the time constraints in any ELT syllabi, it seems more efficient and effective to equip students with the ability to cope with these contextual challenges in English communication, which in the Hong Kong context involves considerable numbers of NSs and NNSs. According to our findings, some focal areas in teaching spoken English include appropriate use of vocabulary, speech fluency, communication and accommodation skills, and understanding the cultures and accents of people from different nationalities.

Given that English use in one's future life is unpredictable and may depend on occupation, it should be stressed that an English learning target should remain a personal choice of individuals as long as they are able to communicate with the interlocutors. The participants' choices might have been subject to factors such as the status and pragmatic values of the language goal, its intelligibility and perceived attainability with reference to their own learning ability and style. Subsequently, in assessments, the requirement of highlighting intelligibility rather than an NS standard should be explicated, as in daily ELT teaching. As most of the participants perceived the HKE pronunciation as less of a problem in international settings, phonological features that cause communication problems could be emphasized in examinations and teaching. In current practice, teachers have only vague ideas of how to teach and examine suprasegmental features and usually only require students to imitate their stresses and intonations. Upon further investigation of the intelligibility of HKE with reference to both NS and NNS listeners, English teachers should be informed, probably in their teaching education, about how they should teach and evaluate pronunciation based on intelligibility findings, be aware of the global use of English, and understand the core principle that students can choose their own pronunciation targets on the condition that they are able to communicate with English speakers of different linguistic and cultural backgrounds.

Conclusion

Using Hong Kong as an example case, this chapter has underscored the importance of investigating local language needs and developing the learning tasks and goals that are most relevant to L2 learners in specific social settings. This bottom-up sociolinguistic investigation reveals areas of disconnection between language use and attitudes among major stakeholders (e.g. students, teachers, professionals) in the local context and current ELT practices. This local sociolinguistic information can in turn align with existing global findings (e.g. the ELF literature) so as to inform pedagogical recommendations. First, as local English teachers are already using existing teaching models in the classroom, it is suggested that these endonormative models be recognized and benchmarked as one of the learning alternatives in the English language curriculum. Such benchmarking processes should also consider the issue of intelligibility, which in the Hong Kong context involves both NS and NNS listeners. Secondly, English learning activities should be developed on the basis of a detailed needs analysis. For instance, as accent variation and telephoning were reported to be major challenges facing HKE speakers, communicative tasks can be designed by incorporating the locally relevant English accents in the corresponding English speaking situations. Thirdly, the pedagogical foci in English curricula and assessments should be on communicative proficiency in international English use rather than on native correctness. Given the high complexity and uncertainty in global communication, some focal areas in teaching spoken English, as revealed in our findings, include appropriate use of vocabulary, speech fluency, communication and accommodation skills, and understanding the cultures and accents of NSs and NNSs. By aligning both global and local sociolinguistic (and linguistic) findings, it is hoped that ELT curricula, assessment and instructional materials can be better developed to cater for students' future English needs in individual societies.

Notes

(1) The verbal guise technique is one of the most frequently adopted indirect approaches to investigating people's underlying language attitudes. In our VGT task, the participants listened to the same content-neutral text read and recorded by seven speakers of specific English varieties and rated each of the speakers on a Likert scale. The findings were used to complement those derived from the interviews and questionnaire, where the participants' language attitudes were elicited by their responses to direct questions.
(2) It should be noted that parts of the findings derived from the questionnaire (Chan, 2017), interviews (Chan, 2016a, 2018a, 2018b), VGT (Chan, 2013, 2016b), document analysis (Chan, 2014a) and phonological analysis of teachers' speech (Chan, 2014b) have been reported in individual papers with specific foci. The purpose of this chapter, however, is to provide a holistic picture of this research project and offer pedagogical recommendations concerning the L2 English learning goals by drawing together the key sociolinguistic (and some linguistic) findings.
(3) It is noted that the participants only indicated their perception/impression of whether they understood the speakers' English in the VGT task rather their true ability to recognize and understand each word in the speech samples (see Chan, 2013, 2016b).

References

Ahn, H. (2015) Awareness of and attitudes to Asian Englishes: A study of English teachers in South Korea. *Asian Englishes* 17, 132–151.

Baker, W. (2012) From cultural awareness to intercultural awareness: Culture in ELT. *ELT Journal* 66 (1), 62–70.

Baker, W. (2015) Culture and complexity through English as a lingua franca: Rethinking competences and pedagogy in ELT. *Journal of English as a Lingua Franca* 4 (1), 9–30.

Benson, P. (2000) Hong Kong words: Variation and context. *World Englishes* 19, 373–380.

Björkman, B. (2013) *English as an Academic Lingua Franca: An Investigation of Form and Communicative Effectiveness*. Germany: Walter de Gruyter.

Bolton, K. and Kwok, H. (1990) The dynamics of the Hong Kong accent: Social identity and sociolinguistic description. *Journal of Asian Pacific Communication* 1 (1), 147–172.

Byram, M.S. (2012) Language awareness and (critical) cultural awareness – relationships, comparisons and contrasts. *Language Awareness* 21 (1–2), 5–13.

Canagarajah, A.S. (2013) Redefining proficiency in global English. In N.T. Zacharias and C. Manara (eds) *Contextualizing the Pedagogy of English as an International Language: Issues and Tensions* (pp. 2–11). Newcastle upon Tyne: Cambridge Scholars.

Canagarajah, A.S. (2017) A competence for negotiating diversity and unpredictability in global contact zones. In A. De Fina, J. Wegner and D. Ikizoglu (eds) *Diversity and Super-diversity: Sociocultural Linguistic Perspectives* (pp. 65–79). Washington, DC: Georgetown University Press.

Cavallaro, F. and Ng, B.C. (2009) Between status and solidarity in Singapore. *World Englishes* 28, 143–159.

CDC (Curriculum Development Council) (2007) *English Language Education Key Learning Area: English Language Curriculum and Assessment Guide (Secondary 4–6)*. Hong Kong: Hong Kong Government Printer.

Chan, J.Y.H. (2013) Contextual variation and Hong Kong English. *World Englishes* 32 (1), 54–74.

Chan, J.Y.H. (2014a) An evaluation of the pronunciation target in Hong Kong's ELT curriculum and materials: Influences from WE and ELF? *Journal of English as a Lingua Franca* 3 (1), 143–168.

Chan, J.Y.H. (2014b) Exposure to accents and pronunciation modelling: A case study of a secondary school in Hong Kong. *International Journal of Applied Linguistics* 24 (3), 390–415.

Chan, J. Y. H. (2016a) Contextualising a pedagogical model in English-language education: The case of Hong Kong. World Englishes 35 (3), 372–395.

Chan, J.Y.H. (2016b) A multi-perspective investigation of attitudes towards English accents in Hong Kong: Implications for pronunciation teaching. *TESOL Quarterly* 50, 285–313.

Chan, J.Y.H. (2017) Stakeholders' perceptions of language variation, English language teaching and language use: The case of Hong Kong. *Journal of Multilingual and Multicultural Development* 38 (1), 2–18.

Chan, J.Y.H. (2018a) Contexts, problems and solutions in international communication in Hong Kong: Insights for teaching English as a lingua franca. *Journal of Asia TEFL* 15, 257–275.

Chan, J.Y.H. (2018b) The choice of English pronunciation goals: Different views, experiences and concerns of students, teachers and professionals in Hong Kong. *Asian Englishes*. Advance online publication. doi:10.1080/13488678.2018.1482436

Charles, M. (2007) Language matters in global communication. *Journal of Business Communication* 44, 260–282.

Cummings, P.J. and Wolf, H.G. (2011) *A Dictionary of Hong Kong English: Words from the Fragrant Harbor*. Hong Kong: Hong Kong University Press.

Deterding, D.H., Wong, J. and Kirkpatrick, A. (2008) The pronunciation of Hong Kong English. *English World-Wide* 29, 148–175.

Edwards, J.G.H. (2015) Hong Kong English: Attitudes, identity, and use. *Asian Englishes* 17, 184–208.

Ehrenreich, S. (2010) English as a business lingua franca in a German multinational corporation. *Journal of Business Communication* 47, 408–431.

Evans, S. (2010) Language in transitional Hong Kong: Perspectives from the public and private sectors. *Journal of Multilingual and Multicultural Development* 31, 347–363.

Evans, S. (2011) Hong Kong English and the professional world. *World Englishes* 30, 293–316.

Evans, S. (2013) Perspectives on the use of English as a business lingua franca in Hong Kong. *Journal of Business Communication* 50, 227–252.

Evans, S. (2014) Teaching business correspondence: Lessons from the globalised workplace. *Asian Journal of Applied Linguistics* 1 (2), 102–120.

Evans, S. (2015) Word-formation in Hong Kong English: Diachronic and synchronic perspectives. *Asian Englishes* 17, 116–131.

HKEAA (Hong Kong Examinations and Assessment Authority) (2012) *Hong Kong Diploma of Secondary Education Examination (English Language): Examination Report and Question Papers*. Hong Kong: Hong Kong Government Printer.

Hung, T.T.N. (2000) Towards a phonology of Hong Kong English. *World Englishes* 19, 337–356.

Jenkins, J. (2000) *The Phonology of English as an International Language: New Models, New Norms, New Goals*. Oxford: Oxford University Press.

Jenkins, J. (2007) *English as a Lingua Franca: Attitude and Identity*. Oxford: Oxford University Press.

Jenkins, J. (2014) *English as a Lingua Franca in the International University: The Politics of Academic English Language Policy*. Abingdon: Routledge.

Jenkins, J. (2015) Repositioning English and multilingualism in English as a lingua franca. *English in Practice* 2, 49–85.

Jenkins, J., Cogo, A. and Dewey, M. (2011) Review of developments in research into English as a lingua franca. *Language Teaching* 44, 281–315.

Kachru, Y. and Nelson, C.L. (2006) *World Englishes in Asian contexts*. Hong Kong: Hong Kong University Press.

Kirkpatrick, A. (2007a) *English in Southeast Asia: Literacies, Literatures and Varieties*. Newcastle: Cambridge Scholars.

Kirkpatrick, A. (2007b) Setting attainable and appropriate English language targets in multilingual settings: A case for Hong Kong. *International Journal of Applied Linguistics* 17, 376–391.

Kirkpatrick, A. (2010) *English as a Lingua Franca in ASEAN: A Multilingual Model*. Hong Kong: Hong Kong University Press.

Kirkpatrick, A. (2011) English as an Asian lingua franca and the multilingual model of ELT. *Language Teaching* 44, 212–224.

Kirkpatrick, A. (2014). Teaching English in Asia in non-Anglo cultural contexts: Principles of the 'Lingua Franca Approach'. In R. Marlina and R.A. Giri (eds) *The Pedagogy of English as an International Language: Perspectives from Scholars, Teachers, and Students* (pp. 23–34). Cham: Springer.

Lai, M.L. (2012) The linguistic landscape of Hong Kong after the change of sovereignty. *International Journal of Multilingualism* 9, 1–22.

Ley, D. (2013) Does transnationalism trump immigrant integration? Evidence from Canada's links with East Asia. *Journal of Ethnic and Migration Studies* 39, 921–938.

Mauranen, A. (2012) *Exploring ELF: Academic English Shaped by Non-native Speakers.* Cambridge: Cambridge University Press.

McKenzie, R.M. (2010) *The Social Psychology of English as a Global Language: Attitudes, Awareness and Identity in the Japanese Context.* Heidelberg: Springer.

Murphy, J.M. (2014) Intelligible, comprehensible, non-native models in ESL/EFL pronunciation teaching. *System* 42, 258–269.

Nelson, C.L. (2011) *Intelligibility in World Englishes: Theory and Application.* New York: Routledge.

Phillipson, R. (2009) *Linguistic Imperialism Continued.* Hyderabad: Orient Blackswan Private.

Sasayama, S. (2013) Japanese college students' attitudes towards Japan English and American English. *Journal of Multilingual and Multicultural Development* 34, 264–278.

Seidlhofer, B. (2009) Common ground and different realities: World Englishes and English as a lingua franca. *World Englishes* 28 (2), 236–245.

Seidlhofer, B. (2011) *Understanding English as a Lingua Franca.* Oxford: Oxford University Press.

Setter, J., Wong, C.S.P. and Chan, B.H.S. (2010) *Hong Kong English.* Edinburgh: Edinburgh University Press.

Sewell, A. (2016) *English Pronunciation Models in a Globalized World: Accent, Acceptability and Hong Kong English.* Abingdon and New York: Routledge.

Sewell, A. and Chan, J. (2010) Patterns of variation in the consonantal phonology of Hong Kong English. *English World-Wide* 31, 138–161.

Smit, U. (2010) *English as a Lingua Franca in Higher Education: A Longitudinal Study of Classroom Discourse.* New York: Mouton de Gruyter.

Tsui, A. B. M. and Bunton, D. (2000) The discourse and attitudes of English language teachers in Hong Kong. *World Englishes* 19 (3), 287–303.

Walker, R. (2010) *Teaching the Pronunciation of English as a Lingua Franca.* Oxford: Oxford University Press.

Wang, W. (2015) Teaching English as an international language in China: Investigating university teachers' and students' attitudes towards China English. *System* 53 (1), 60–72.

Zhang, Q. (2013) The attitudes of Hong Kong students towards Hong Kong English and Mandarin-accented English. *English Today* 29 (2), 9–16.

8 From Learners to Users: Reframing a Japanese University Curriculum towards a 'World Englishes Enterprise'-Informed English as a Medium of Instruction Model

James D'Angelo

This chapter first provides an explication of the 'WE enterprise' – an umbrella term used to describe the interrelated pluricentric paradigms of World Englishes, English as an international language and English as a lingua franca. It then proceeds to elaborate on ways in which these paradigms can better inform – and help to critically reframe – the field of English language education, especially with regard to the rapid growth of English as a medium of instruction programs around the globe. The chapter then considers the case of the Chukyo University Department of World Englishes, and efforts there to increase and make more effective use of English as a medium of instruction classes in which Japanese students are mixed with exchange students from various contexts. Various obstacles and challenges are discussed, including the resistance of the Japanese faculty to teach in English, how to deal with the disparate proficiency range among the Japanese students, and differences in the classroom culture of Japan and other countries. The chapter concludes with an extensive list of suggestions to help facilitate more effective implementation of English as a medium of instruction at the university curriculum and classroom level, as it is the clear trend for the future.

Introduction

Pluralistic approaches to English and English language pedagogy have become more widely known and researched since the emergence of the Kachruvian World Englishes (WE) model in the mid-1980s. WE paved the way to critically challenging a native-speakerist view of English, and subsequently the paradigms of English as an international language (EIL)[1] and English as a lingua franca (ELF) have led the way in showing concrete ways in which a more realistic view of the global use, and multilingual users, of English can inform language curriculum and pedagogy. And in fact, the application of these theories goes well beyond language study, to higher education in general. Especially important, in the growing field of ELF (D'Angelo, 2017), is the view that university students who study English in countries where English is not a native or official/second language should be viewed as *users* of English rather than *learners* (Mauranen, 2012). This argument is evidenced by the increasing globalization of universities worldwide, many of these in expanding circle contexts such as Austria, Finland, Italy, Korea and Japan, where students are not studying English per se but are studying various academic disciplines *in* English, and lecturers from those contexts are also conducting their classes primarily in English. These universities are of course still offering many courses in the local mother tongue, but have also made a commitment to being part of the global competition to attract the best minds, and to offer a broad range of coursework in the global lingua franca, English.

This chapter will investigate the type of curriculum and classroom changes needed to prepare expanding circle students to enter such globally minded universities on exchange, and also how to meet the needs of exchange students who enter our universities, through offering strong content-oriented programs via English as a medium of instruction (EMI). To achieve such a reframing of curricular policy, a critical assessment of the outdated but still dominant paradigms of ELT (EFL, native-speakerism, the communicative method, etc.) is necessary to increase awareness of what is needed to reform education in Asia and beyond to come into alignment with the reality of GE.

Background

In this chapter the main focus is not mainly on actual English language education itself, especially regarding the early acquisition of English proficiency. Rather, it is on how what I term the 'WE enterprise' (Bolton, 2005, 2012; D'Angelo, 2015b) – in which EIL and ELF are viewed as related paradigms under the WE umbrella – has helped us critically reframe views on the use of language in many contexts and domains, and how this can be applied to global higher education in the English medium or EMI.

To summarize the main contributions of the WE enterprise (hereafter WEE) in challenging more established constructs, it is still very helpful to look at Kachru's 'six myths' regarding English (D'Angelo, 2012: 291–292; Kachru, 2005: 16–18):

- *Myth 1: The native speaker idealization myth.* The native speaker (usually a white middle-class American) is the only expert of the correct variety.
- *Myth 2: The native versus non-native speaker interaction myth.* Most expanding circle speakers learn English in order to interact with, and are most likely to encounter, inner circle idealized native speakers.
- *Myth 3: The culture identity (or monoculture) myth.* English is closely connected to British or American culture, and thus those cultures must be studied as an integral part of learning English.
- *Myth 4: The exocentric norm myth.* The model of 'correctness' comes from an inner circle variety. It denies the rich creativity of Japanese or other expanding circle English in the process of adaptation to the local context (Kachru, 2003).
- *Myth 5: The interlanguage myth.* Non-inner circle varieties are somehow deficient/substandard varieties, falling short of native speaker proficiency.
- *Myth 6: The Cassandra myth.* The 'Balkanization' of English as it spreads around the world spells the impending doom of the language.

While these myths were explained by Braj Kachru from the perspective of the WE paradigm, much of ELF and EIL research echoes the same potential fallacies in traditional, native speaker (NS)-dominated approaches to ELT and SLA: what Canagarajah refers to as 'West-based' or 'Center-based' ELT (Canagarajah, 2000). For in the EMI-based international university, the majority of interlocutors will not be native speakers (NSs), a native model of English will not be stressed (Kalocsai, 2014), and students and professors from many different non-native cultural backgrounds will be together using a form of highly 'Educated English' – a type of acrolectal English which shows sophistication and high international intelligibility, but still shows the distinctness of a user's local context (Bamgbose, 1982; D'Angelo, 2015b; Kachru, 2003). In such an increasingly common global context, the depth of one's knowledge and preparedness in the field of study, as well as negotiation, accommodation and meta-cultural competence (Sharifian, 2009) skills will be much more important than native-like pronunciation and grammatical accuracy based on NS norms.

To further strengthen this argument, well-known WE scholar S.N. Sridhar eloquently listed a dozen accomplishments of the WE paradigm at the 2010 IAWE Conference in Vancouver (Sridhar, 2010). This was in response to Bolton's summary of Phillipson's latest attack on WE in his newest book at the time, *Linguistic Imperialism Revisited* (Phillipson, 2010). D'Angelo (2010) provides a list of such accomplishments:

- WE looks at the sociolinguistic reality of English based on descriptive rather than prescriptive linguistics/grammar.
- Non-native speakers (NNSs) outnumber NSs, so NSs can no longer claim 'ownership' of 'standard English'.
- Where English has some official role in various domains of society, codifiable, endonormative local standards develop (see Schneider, 2007).
- Because English is 'equidistant' from all other local languages, such as in West Africa or India, it provides a neutral[2] language that all groups can use. While remnants of anticolonial feeling still exist vis-à-vis attitudes towards English, English would still be a more 'neutral' choice in India than choosing Hindi as the official language (a point also made in Nihalani, 2002).
- The well-documented outer circle varieties are now widely recognized as 'legitimate'.
- The L1 or substrate language is seen as an asset, rather than a source of 'interference'. English-knowing bi/multilinguals have a language 'repertoire' to draw on and employment of code-mixing and code-switching is a linguistic resource/strategy.
- The culture/ethos of IVEs is not inner circle, but shows the color of the local context.
- Thanks to intelligibility studies, 'Tower of Babel' or 'Cassandra' fears that speakers of different IVEs will not be mutually comprehensible are unproven. Acrolectal or mesolectal speakers of local varieties succeed in international interactions.
- The *educated* local variety becomes the model, and is also taught by non-native locals.
- The 'Kachru ethos' (Bolton, 2005) shows inclusivity/fellowship for all users of English.
- WE proves the value of systemic/functional grammar in which language changes to fit its actual uses and users.
- WE has shown that via bi-/multilingualism, English is not a 'killer language'[3] (see Mufwene in D'Angelo, 2004).

Again here (as with Kachru's myths), where Sridhar was primarily outlining his claims with reference to postcolonial outer circle varieties, the references to global sociolinguistic reality, NNSs outnumbering NSs, the value of L1 and other languages as an asset for plurilingual users, cultural relativity, the importance of an 'educated' English, the importance of a functional view of language, and the general attitude of 'inclusivity' towards all users of English are crucial points in an EIL- or ELF-informed view of language. Hence the usefulness of the 'WEE' concept in which these paradigms are viewed as closely related and supportive of one another, is clear. While Kachru himself stressed to Mufwene some time before the 2004 IAWE Conference at Syracuse University that 'WE is not dependent on English being a global language' (D'Angelo, 2004: 31), in today's increasingly globalized world, English may in fact claim global status, as seen in the title of this volume.

In the next section I will first investigate the endeavors made in my own context, the Department of World Englishes (DWE) at Chukyo University in Nagoya, Japan, to prepare our students to deal with and succeed in a global context. The section following that will then look at Chukyo and other universities in Japan and their effort to attract more international EMI students.

Preparing 'Globalized' Japanese Students

In the following subsection, various features of the curriculum of the DWE will be outlined and looked at from a realistic, critical perspective – demonstrating the success and failures we have experienced as well as the difficulties of implementing a new type of curriculum. It is interesting to note that WE research prior to the re-emergence of EIL and development of ELF rarely looked at higher education,[4] since in outer circle contexts such as Singapore, India, East Africa, the Philippines, etc., it was assumed that higher education all takes place in English, and students from the outer circle were quite capable of studying in inner circle contexts as well. Thus there were few WE studies that looked at how to prepare expanding circle students to succeed in the context of greater mobility in higher education fostered by the ease of border crossing in the European Union, as well as the overall globalization of higher education. Yet thanks especially to work in ELF, many new insights can be gained into this phenomenon today (Bjorkman, 2014; Jenkins, 2014; Mauranen, 2012; Vettorel, 2014).

The Department of World Englishes: Theoretical foundation

The DWE offers the most extensive English and EMI coursework at Chukyo. The college was founded in 2002, replacing the former Department of English Language and Literature. Dean Sanzo Sakai had participated in several summer programs at the East/West Center in Hawaii which were offered to Japanese and other Asian academics in the 1970s and 1980s under the direction of Larry E. Smith. Smith's early work on EIL and his collaboration with Braj Kachru in the development of the WE paradigm was of great influence in Japan, and Sakai was joined by other scholars such as Takao Suzuki, Nobuyuki Honna and Nobuyuki Hino, for whom EIL and WE concepts provided a convincing alternative to the native-speakerism outlook then (and in many cases still today) prevalent in Japan. Sakai shared academic exchange with Honna, who also founded the Japanese Association for World Englishes (JAFAE) in 1997 which provides a common forum where WE-aware local scholars could exchange ideas and interact with like-minded scholars in Singapore, Malaysia, China, Hong Kong, Thailand, the Philippines, Eastern Russia and Indonesia.

Sakai hence took the opportunity in 2002 to form a College of World Englishes at Chukyo. In order to get off on the right foot, WE scholar and phonologist Paroo Nihalani, formerly of the National University of Singapore,[5] spent one year with us at the DWE as a visiting scholar, and through his influence hosted a Workshop in 2003 at which Braj and Yamuna Kachru came and gave papers, along with Takao Suzuki (1978), Honna (2008) and other leading scholars.[6] Braj Kachru was thrilled to witness the foundation of a College of World Englishes, something which he himself could not establish at the University of Illinois. Through the liaison with these important EIL/WE scholars, our faculty became keenly aware of the shortcomings of native-speakerism, and the weakness of the dominant *Eikaiwa* (English conversation) model in Japan, based on Western influenced TESOL and the communicative method. Thanks to the input of these scholars, we were able to envision EMI-based coursework as being the best way to develop what WE researchers viewed as a more practical/desirable goal of ELT: rather than native-like proficiency/'fluency', our goal became to develop 'Educated Japanese English' – the type of English that would be more effective in international business and academic settings. As a result, we developed a content-based stream which included classes such as Workshop, second and third year seminars in English, 'Language and Culture' and 'Language Variation', as well as electives in 'New Management Trends' and 'Global Economic Trends'.

The program also includes four skills classes in oral communication, presentation, communicative writing and reading, but our overall focus is different, and the emergence of the field of ELF has helped further recognize the needs of our students and begin to develop a curriculum to meet those needs. One of the fundamental differences in such an approach is to place less emphasis on grammatical accuracy and error correction, and more emphasis on developing students' communication strategies, negotiation and accommodation skills, familiarity with English varieties, and the ability to discuss wider topics with some degree of intellectual depth. We attempt to do this in as many classes as possible, although in actuality many of the part-time non-Japanese faculty who teach the skills classes do not have adequate training in the implications of WEE for English pedagogy (D'Angelo, 2012, 2015b). The author is currently the only full-time faculty member in his major, with a WE/EIL/ELF theoretical stance; this makes it difficult to implement WEE across the curriculum, which would be the ideal situation, as recommended in Dogancy-Aktuna and Hardman (2008).

In addition, there is a certain lack of critical thinking capabilities and intellectual curiosity in Japanese students from those tiers of universities below the very top ranks (D'Angelo, 2002; McVeigh, 2002). This is, however, a complex issue, since the part-time teachers who prepare students for their first and second year presentations in our annual Group Research Convention, for example, allow the students to choose their own topics, which tend to be rather trite issues in wider society, with very similar topics being chosen every year, such as Fair Trade chocolate, recycling, Japanese '*Omotenashi*' hospitality, smartphone and SNS addiction, overwork in Japan, Japanese robots and Japanese washlet toilets. The topics are not in and of themselves non-academic, but the students tend to approach them from a very experiential, non-critical stance. The teachers themselves are in the majority of cases not active researchers, and hence are not able or inclined to help the students structure their group presentations with use of good academic sources and referencing, a literature review, or methodology and data analysis. One notable exception was one adjunct teacher who held a full-time position at a Japanese university and who was an active researcher in the field of pragmatics. Again, we must be careful not to overgeneralize, but this is mentioned to give some idea of the obstacles faced in Japan.

Specifics of EMI in the Department of World Englishes

Within the context of WEE, it is important for an expanding circle context such as Japan to consider the overall needs of its institutions as well as the needs of its students. At DWE, the majority of our students wish to use English in their future careers, and Chukyo itself wishes to expand its number of international students, as stated in official documents and documents from the university's 'Next 10' Committee which is looking closely at initiatives needed to keep us competitive over the next decade. This kind of planning can to some extent be done at the university's administrative level, but also requires an enlightened faculty who see the benefits of content-based coursework. Even within the DWE there are Japanese faculty members who are resistant to overemphasizing English, since many students will also be required to be very proficient in Japanese reading and writing in their futures. As a result, of the 124 credits needed to graduate, 44 must still be taken within the School of Liberal Arts, whose offerings are exclusively in Japanese. In addition, among the DWE's elective classes, those taught by Japanese professors are predominantly in Japanese (D'Angelo, 2012).

For our own DWE majors, the following classes are offered in English:

- 21 required one-credit classes in English skills (oral communication, reading, presentation, writing, etc.);
- the required Singapore seminar and 15-day study tour;

- Introduction to World Englishes class (with some Japanese language scaffolding);
- second year seminars on either England, the USA, the Philippines, France or Zambia (non-inner circle contexts are the result of being able to employ part-time teachers from those countries);
- certain elective classes: these include New Management Trends, Global Economic Trends, Language and Culture, Language Variation;
- one out of five of the third/fourth year seminar classes (those taught by non-Japanese faculty);
- elective in Early English Education (taught by a Japanese professor interested in EMI).

DWE students make significant progress in their Test of English for International Communication (TOEIC) scores between the first and third year, with average scores rising from 540 to 620 in the second year, and to 695 in the third year. Usually several students score over 900, and as many as 20 of the DWE's 96 students per class-year exceed 800 on the TOIEC. Unfortunately, there are also a significant number of lower level students (roughly 20%) who remain mired with TOEIC scores in the 400s and 500s even into their third year of university. Of special concern is the low level of reading scores as compared with those on the listening section. I have recently requested the full-time faculty member in our major, of which the author is the chair, to investigate the cause of the lower reading scores, through qualitative interviews with students and an assessment of the reading curriculum. One potential reason is the native orientation of these standardized tests, which may handicap those students who have not already had exposure to inner circle contexts and speakers. Another possible cause may be that the reading curriculum currently stresses the concept of 'extensive reading', a very popular method among NS practitioners, which may promote fluency and automaticity but does not prepare students for doing academic work at an overseas university. I also posit that one reason that NS practitioners are so enamored of extensive reading is that it can help promote a more natural feel for use of articles and prepositions, which is valued in the NS view of accuracy (D'Angelo, 2015b). A student of the DWE who went on one-year overseas study at the University of Tampere in Finland, in English-medium content classes in management and intercultural studies, expressed that the reading program through the first three semesters had left him sorely underprepared for the lectures and reading materials he encountered there. He sent a specific request in a long email to the author that the reading and first year seminar programs be more heavily laden with actual content-based work from major areas in the humanities (Nishii, 2015).

For overseas study, where the Test of English as a Foreign Language (TOEFL) is the measuring stick, in the year 2015, 48 students at Chukyo who desired to go on one-year overseas study scored over 500 on the paper-based TOEFL. Of these, 42 were from the DWE, while three were from the Department of British and American Cultural Studies, two were from International Liberal Arts and one was from the Psychology Department. While not all our students wish to spend a year overseas, the data reveal that roughly one-third of DWE students have it within their reach to do an EMI, content-based year abroad. If semester abroad students are factored in, in this upcoming Fall 2017, since our recent reorganization of the DWE into three majors, for the author's 'World Englishes Career Major' a remarkable 35 out of 62 second year students will be going on either semester or one-year study abroad, leaving fewer than half their counterparts still in Japan!

While not all of our students are capable of competently handling the material and expectations in an overseas EMI program, the numbers indicate that a large percentage of them *are*, which is impressive for a school such as Chukyo, and indicates that more and more Japanese students may reach such a level in coming years. Yet it is mainly those majoring in English who can do this, whereas in a European university, those majoring in management, computer science or environmental sciences may also be able to do so (Kalocsai, 2014). The other two new majors within our department also offer a similar proportion of EMI classes, and almost as high a percentage of second year students who will go abroad. One drawback which the numbers do not reveal is the extent to which our students may be able to participate effectively in classroom discussions in the global classroom, as explained below.

In my own third year seminar class in Fall 2016, there were 11 American exchange students and 10 Japanese students. The desks were set up in two rectangular horseshoes, and the Japanese students were stunned by the degree to which the Americans openly debated with one another across the rectangle, and actually began laughing at how outspoken the Americans were. They had never seen anything like this in all their years of school. Murata and Iino (2014) support this observation in their experiences at Waseda University, where in the School of International Liberal Studies (SILS), which is fully EMI with a high percentage of foreign students, the Japanese students – who are among the most highly proficient English students in Japan – also are shocked at the outspokenness of their international classmates. The Japanese, who were very confident upon being accepted onto the program, go through a period of culture shock and gravitate towards the fringes of the classrooms, rarely speaking out. It is only *after* they have spent the mandatory sophomore year overseas and then return that they begin to feel comfortable speaking out and expressing themselves in front of their international peers. Thus for Japanese students in general, this is a hurdle which must be overcome if they are truly to participate in international discussions.

Attracting high level international students

At Chukyo, the lack of true EMI classes can pose problems for developing a high level of academic English among our own DWE students, and also limits the number of EMI offerings to students from overseas. Table 8.1 lists the full range of coursework available to international students at Chukyo. The contents are mainly in the area of cultural studies, which may receive credit at the students' home universities, provided they are humanities majors. A program such as the Waseda SILS would have much more extensive offerings in EMI.

The list is rather short, considering that approximately 20 international exchange students are in attendance at Chukyo every semester. This does not include the 120 Chinese students who are also at Chukyo, enrolled in normal degree programs in departments such as economics, management, policy, law and sports science. The majority of the 20 international students are those majoring in Japanese, who have Japanese as a minor or are double majors. Since 2016, however, Chukyo has also accepted students who have no prior education in Japanese, and such students may choose to study beginning Japanese or can be exempted from taking Japanese classes. Of these 20 non-Chinese international students, only a handful have the level of Japanese proficiency to take content lectures from other faculties in Japanese (or some which are 'English assisted' – where the course is mainly taught in Japanese, but the faculty member is willing to provide some English scaffolding to the foreign students). In addition, many of the classes listed in Table 8.1 are taught by foreign part-time teachers who hold a masters' degree but do not have a doctorate. In addition, the Japanese students in these elective classes are of mixed proficiency, so the teacher is unable to use difficult reading materials. Whereas for a humanities class in the inner or outer circle it would be common for students to have to read 20–40 pages of a textbook (or several textbooks) per week, in Japan the reading might consist of only two pages. And even at this reduced level, the lower half of the Japanese students in the DWE would complain that it is way over their heads in terms of academic vocabulary, phrasing and sentence structure. For this reason, in my own doctoral work (D'Angelo, 2015b), I recommended that a special 'honors' track be created within the DWE, and that only those students be allowed to register for those classes open to the international students. Through such a measure, the international students would have a higher rate of satisfaction, and would be more likely to recommend Chukyo to their classmates back at their home institution.

A crucial limit to the number of content classes from various disciplines offered in English is the lack of willingness of many tenured Japanese professors to teach in English. This tendency was confirmed in a comprehensive study of the faculty at the University of Hiroshima, an Imperial national university, which is part of the Japanese Ministry of

Table 8.1 Chukyo University classes for overseas exchange students

Course Name	Professors	Credits	Semester
American Literature A	ARMSTRONG	2	Spring
Introduction to American Studies	ARMSTRONG	2	Spring
Introduction to Canadian Cultural Studies I	ARMSTRONG	2	Spring/Fall
Women's History	BOULANGER	2	Fall
World's Fairs in North America (Seminar)	BOULANGER	2	Spring/Fall
Introduction to Sports and Society II (Seminar)	BOULANGER	2	Spring
Canadian Women's History (Seminar)	BOULANGER	2	Spring
Language Variation	D'ANGELO	2	Fall
Language and Culture	D'ANGELO	2	Spring
Global Economic Trends	D'ANGELO	2	Fall
New Management Trends	D'ANGELO	2	Spring
British Social History	KRUSE	2	Spring
British Studies	KRUSE	2	Fall
USA abroad I (Seminar)	MORRISON	2	Spring/Fall
Philippine Culture and Current Issues I, II	PALISADA	2	Spring/Fall
Intro. to Studies in the English Speaking World	PICCOLO	2	Spring
Studies in the English Speaking World	PICCOLO	2	Fall
Literatures of the English Speaking World	PICCOLO	2	Fall
Introduction to Irish Studies I, II (Seminar)	PICCOLO	2	Spring/Fall
American Social History	WACHOLTZ	2	Spring
American Studies	WACHOLTZ	2	Fall
Current Topics I, II	YASUDA	2	Spring/Fall
Intercultural Communication I, II	HARRIS	2	Spring/Fall
International Business (Project Research A)	KAWABATA	2	Spring
Introduction to Business Management I	KRAUS	2	Spring
Media and Global Society	MIYATA	2	Spring
Canadian Literary and Cultural Studies	ARMSTRONG	2	Spring

Education's 'Global 30' program, whereby it attempts to promote universities to offer entire majors in the arts and sciences in English (Sponseller, 2015). Although the professors were much more comfortable writing papers in English for international journals, and also to a large extent presenting their work at international conferences, they hesitated to use EMI in their own classes.

If, however, Chukyo were to attract 50 or 100 international students expecting to study various disciplines in English at a sophisticated academic level, rather than the current level of just 20, it would be necessary to offer a broader range of coursework for them. To do this, a strong figure at the top, such as the university President or the Interdepartmental Dean's Committee, would need to commit to each department providing a certain range of classwork in English. Chukyo currently has 12 departments, with each department broken into two or three sub-majors. If a commitment could be obtained from each sub-major to offer three classes in English, one could add as many as 100 new content-based classes. The Japanese professors would need to be shown relevant data, such as those gained in the Netherlands, which demonstrate that although some international students complain about the intelligibility of their professors, for the majority of students the professors' content knowledge in the field is more important than the accuracy or pronunciation of their English (Lehtonen et al., 1999).

Sarah Kaur Gill (Gill, 2004) outlined the importance of this issue at the 2004 JACET Conference in Nagoya. She stressed that if Malaysian universities are to compete, they must consider the challenge from places such as the Netherlands, where the majority of higher education is conducted in English. Quoting Wachter et al. (2008), she mentioned that 'A university may lose out on attractiveness, if not endanger its existence, if the students opt to stay away as a reaction to an internationalization deficit' (Gill, 2004).

According to Gill, at the University of Maastricht (also in Holland) as much as 50% of their student body is made up of international students. While this is the case in one or two specialized programs in Japan, for a second-tier level university such as Chukyo – currently ranked 113th out of 710 universities – it would not be a possibility (UniRank). But on a smaller scale, in certain classes advertised to international students, there could be a significant percentage of them in class. In such a case, the Japanese students would be challenged to put themselves forward in classroom discussions, and would have to handle a larger amount of academic reading. To be able to create this kind of setting in Japan, rather than just for those students who are able to qualify for one-year overseas study, a two-track program is suggested (see D'Angelo, 2015b). For those students who study in content programs overseas, the minimum standard is 500 on the paper-based TOEFL test and in many cases is as high as 550. This standard could be slightly relaxed, to perhaps above 470 on the TOEFL or above 720 on the TOEIC test. By creating a kind of honors program within the DWE, the Chukyo students who have the potential and interest would be pushed harder to become effective ELF 'users', and the international students would be more satisfied. One very intelligent exchange student from the USA – who was in his second semester at Chukyo – was overheard in the author's own Intercultural Communication class saying to a newly arrived exchange student, 'Whatever class you take here will be an ESL class'. He was alluding to the essential fact that even for content-based classes, they by necessity take on a content and language integrated learning (CLIL) quality (Coyle et al., 2010), due to their being open to the full range of DWE second and third year students, with TOEIC scores ranging from 400 to 945!

What I have attempted to point out in this section is that to really develop effective ELF users among Japanese university students, they need to be mixed in with highly proficient peers from other countries, whether those be inner, outer or expanding circle users. A good example of this would be my own recent Language and Culture class, in which there were 40 Japanese DWE students mixed in with five American undergraduates, two French students and two Italian Master's students. While one of the American undergraduate students was quite dominating when the floor was opened to discussion and comments, it was the two Italians who demonstrated a more sophisticated knowledge of the field and depth of analysis. By listening to their modest, intelligent comments, and their clear but quite Italian pronunciation, the DWE students had an opportunity to see that not all international students behave like Americans. It would be wonderful if Chukyo could attract more such highly qualified expanding circle students. Several years ago we had a fair number of bright students from Finland via the International Student Exchange Program (ISEP), but in recent years, as more Japanese universities have begun to participate in ISEP, these students have opted to attend the more prestigious top-tier Japanese institutions which offer more programs in English.

One final point here is that the idea of becoming effective ELF users is not only limited to the higher level students. While it may be the higher level students who are the ones who can benefit most from entering EMI programs overseas, many of our mid- to lower level students, those who can achieve at least the modest TOEIC level of 500, go overseas on 'semester' programs. These programs are more ESL/skills oriented, but the students – even those who go to the USA or Canada – end up mainly with friends from other expanding circle contexts such as Korea, China, Turkey, Greece, Saudi Arabia, Brazil, Thailand, etc. Hence they are in fact learning to become effective ELF users with other NNSs, although at a more conversational, less academic level. Thus the following practical recommendations for a revised curriculum in Japan pertain to them as well.

Practical Suggestions for Developing Effective ELF 'Users'

This section includes practical recommendations for curricular reform in Japan – and is pertinent to other expanding circle contexts (particularly *outside* of the Northern European context, where proficiency levels are so high) as well. It is also mentioned below whether the particular recommendation applies to the higher level 'honors' type students within the DWE, or to all students.

(1) Raise students' awareness of the global use of English today, where NNSs outnumber NSs, as well as the rich variation of WE. Also,

make them aware that their L1 is an asset, rather than a source of 'interference'. (All students)

(2) Expose students to a wide range of Englishes through YouTube and other listening work, and stress the plurilingual nature of many NNS users of English and their impressive 'repertoire' of languages. (All students)

(3) Prioritize negotiation and accommodation skills, and communication strategies (what to do in case of breakdown, repair strategies, etc.), over grammatical accuracy and native-like pronunciation. This does not imply, however, that 'anything goes'. (All students)

(4) Raise awareness that rather than having knowledge of British or American culture, students should develop 'meta-cultural competence' (Sharifian, 2009) and appreciate cultural diversity. (All students)

(5) Create opportunities to have more meaningful, 'high stakes' interaction with international students from around the globe, beginning with other expanding circle contexts, via incorporating formalized Skype-based activities into the curriculum (goals can be differentiated by pre-streaming of students into regular and honors classes).

(6) Develop reading skills at a higher, more academic level, as well as increasing the amount of CLIL offerings over straight skills-based curriculum as in Bayyurt and Sifakis (2013) (more pertinent to higher level students). Consider having specific EMI majors within the curriculum, such as Global Comparative Politics and Global Management Studies.

(7) Encourage well-established international scholars among the local (Japanese in this case) faculty to teach in English – with some code-switching if needed. (For benefit of honors track and international students)

(8) In spite of their culturally derived reticence (King, 2013), create a safe environment for Japanese students to have more confidence to put themselves forward to express opinions and take part in group discussions. (For all students, but crucial for higher level students)

(9) Strengthen the writing component within EMI-based seminars and other coursework, to teach students to do the type of documented research work that would be expected at the global university. (All students, but more required for higher level students)

(10) Hire part-time staffers who are also relatively[7] active researchers themselves (and if possible, already somewhat WE aware) and who are thus more able to train students in how to do presentations and essays work which is better documented and more academically oriented. (For all students, but particularly needed for higher level students)

(11) Develop teacher training and awareness-raising programs for part-time and full-time faculty which make them aware of the advantages of a WEE-informed outlook, and which provide examples of

actual classroom practices that focus on developing English 'users' rather than 'learners'.
(12) Strengthen overseas study and exchange programs, particularly among other expanding circle partner institutions with strong EMI programs. (For higher level students)

Conclusion

It is clear from the example of Chukyo University, and several other universities attempting to internationalize and compete in the field of globalized higher education, that 'WEE' – the World Englishes Enterprise – can provide key insights into how to enhance the curriculum to better prepare our students to succeed in overseas study, going toe-to-toe with students from around the world, and from all three of Kachru's circles. By having a less native-speakerist (Houghton & Rivers, 2013), less mainstream ELT/EFL-informed focus, and setting goals for our students which will help them function as effective ELF users in their future professions, we can develop students who are much better equipped for what they will encounter in the real world. Such a critical posture which questions the usefulness of outdated yet deeply entrenched nativist approaches to English is essential. Hence a curriculum that focuses on traditional English as a 'foreign' language (EFL) approaches to English language teaching, from a four-skills based (speaking, listening, reading, writing) perspective, are clearly outdated. Curriculum and classwork must be developed which is content- based within various disciplines such as political science, international relations, management, cultural studies, gender studies, etc., and where students from a context such as Japan must compete and cooperate toe-to-toe with students from around the world. For this reason, Chukyo itself is carefully considering moving in such a direction, where in the future we may no longer have an English Department, or even a Department of World Englishes, but smaller, more focused majors (within a larger 'Department of International Studies') designed according to particular content areas, with the majority of content classes conducted in English. This reorganization may not show a lack of appreciation for the reality of WE, but may demonstrate that the global importance of English has been recognized, and all students will be required to spend the second semester of their freshman year overseas, and study within an EMI environment.

Indeed, major obstacles need to be cleared, and it will require ongoing effort by WE-aware scholars to help make this a reality. At the same time, universities in Japan that would like to truly compete globally must make a substantial effort to increase their content-based EMI coursework offerings, and to prepare their own 'honors' program students to take an active part in such classes in Japan. We are a long way from realizing this goal, but by observing the successes and failures of our own efforts, and collaborating with colleagues in Japan and other expanding circle contexts (e.g. Greece, Spain, Turkey, UAE, China, Korea) who adopt a similar critical perspective and are facing the same challenges, I am optimistic that much progress can be made in the coming years. For those of us working in Japan, we must also act quickly, since in the global race for the best students Japan is currently lagging behind many of its European and other Asian competitors, and risks losing out in the long run. I hope this chapter, and others in this volume, can help broaden the circle of scholars and teachers who better understand the reality of Global Englishes.

Notes

(1) In actuality, EIL work by Larry Smith and others preceded World Englishes, but was less discussed until a recent reinvigoration of the field by McKay, Sharifian and Matsuda.
(2) This point was originally made by S.N. Sridhar in his comments at the 16th IAWE Conference in Vancouver.
(3) There is some debate among what Mufwene (in D'Angelo, 2004) refers to as 'language militants' that English may be a killer language (Pakir, 1991), but in general he argues that English coexists in harmony with other local languages, and it is not English itself, but other economic and policy factors, which leads to the decrease in use of certain languages.
(4) Some exceptions were Malaysia and Hong Kong, which have more complicated language policy issues.
(5) The institution where he was a colleague of Kachruvian scholar and poet laureate Edwin Thumboo.
(6) In subsequent years we were able to bring in Philippine scholar Danilo Dayag from De La Salle University for the 2006 academic year, and Indian scholar Anamika Sharma for the 2009/2010 academic years, further exposing our students to educated English users from Kachru's outer circle.
(7) Since many tertiary level adjunct ELT practitioners in Japan do virtually no publishing, by 'relatively active' I mean those who show some intellectual curiosity about recent developments in applied linguistics/ELT, attend perhaps one (local) conference every several years and publish one paper every several years.

References

Bamgbose, A. (1982) Standard Nigerian English: Issues of identification. In B. Kachru (ed.) *The Other Tongue: English Across Cultures* (pp. 148–161). Champaign, IL: Illinois University Press.
Bayyurt, Y. and Sifakis, N. (2013) Transforming into an ELF-aware teacher: Insights from a self-education program. In P. Vettorel (ed.) *New Frontiers in Teaching and Learning English*. Cambridge: Cambridge Scholars.
Bjorkman, B. (2014) *English as an Academic Lingua Franca*. Berlin: De Gruyter.
Bolton, K. (2005) Where WEs stands: Approaches, issues and debate in world Englishes. *World Englishes* 24 (1), 69–84.
Bolton, K. (2012) The World Englishes enterprise. Keynote address, *18th Conference of the International Association for World Englishes*, Hong Kong.
Canagarajah, A.S. (2000) *Resisting Linguistic Imperialism in English Teaching*. Hong Kong: Oxford University Press.
Coyle, D., Hood, P. and Marsh, D. (2010) *CLIL: Content and Language Integrated Learning*. Cambridge: Cambridge University Press.

D'Angelo, J. (2002) World Englishes and critical thinking. *Journal of College of World Englishes* 1, 59–66.
D'Angelo, J. (2004) Salikoko Mufwene on global English: Myths and facts. *Journal of College of World Englishes* 6, 29–32.
D'Angelo, J. (2010) Developmental World Englishes and 'Philipson Continued': Review of 16th IAWE Conference, Vancouver. *Asian Englishes* 13 (1), 78–81.
D'Angelo, J. (2012) Curriculum and world Englishes: Additive language learning as SLA paradigm. In E. Low and A. Hashim (eds) *English in Southeast Asia* (pp. 289–306). Amsterdam: John Benjamins.
D'Angelo, J. (2015a) Nurturing EMI in broad-based Japanese higher education: The case of Chukyo University. *WASEDA Working Papers in ELF* 4, 219–228.
D'Angelo, J. (2015b) A broader concept of world Englishes for educational contexts: Applying the WE Enterprise to Japanese higher education curricula. Unpublished PhD thesis, North-West University, South Africa.
D'Angelo, J. (2017) The status of ELF in Japan. In J. Jenkins, W. Baker and M. Dewey (eds) *The Routledge Handbook of English as a Lingua Franca* (pp. 165–175). London: Routledge.
Dogancy-Aktuna, S. and Hardman, J. (2008) *Global English Teaching and Teacher Education: Praxis and Possibility*. Alexandria, VA: TESOL Publications.
Gill, S.K. (2004) Internationalise! The Story of Language Policy, Standards, and Academic Competence in Higher Education. Plenary lecture, the 43rd Japan Association of College English Teachers Conference (JACET). Chukyo University, 3 September 2004.
Honna, N. (2008) *English as a Multicultural Language in Asian Contexts: Issues and Ideas*. Tokyo: Kuroshio.
Houghton, S. and Rivers, D.J. (2013) *Native Speakerism in Japan: Intergroup Dynamics in Foreign Language Education*. Bristol: Multilingual Matters.
JAFAE (2016) *Homepage of the Japan Association for Asian Englishes*. See http://www.jafae.org/en/ (accessed 29 July 2017).
Jenkins, J. (2014) *English as a Lingua Franca in the International University*. London: Routledge.
Kachru, B. (2005) *Asian Englishes: Beyond the Canon*. Hong Kong: Hong Kong University Press.
Kachru, Y. (2003) Context, competence and curriculum in World Englishes. *First Conference on World Englishes in the Classroom*, Chukyo University, Nagoya, Japan, 7 December.
Kalocsai, K. (2014) *Communities of Practice and English as a Lingua Franca: A Study of Erasmus Students in a Central European Context*. Berlin: De Gruyter.
King, J. (2013) *Silence in the Second Language Classroom*. Basingstoke: MacMillan.
Lehtonen, T., Lönnfors, P. and Virkkunen-Fullenwider, A. (1999) *English or Not English, That Is the Question! Teaching Through English at the University of Helsinki*. Helsinki: University of Helsinki Press.
Mauranen, A. (2012) *Exploring ELF: Academic English Shaped by Non-native Speakers*. Cambridge: Cambridge University Press.
McKay, S. (2002) *Teaching English as an International Language*. Oxford: Oxford University Press.
McVeigh, B. (2002) *Japanese Higher Education as Myth*. Armonk, NY: M.E. Sharpe.
Murata, K. and Iino, M. (2014) Japanese students' changing views of communicative competence through ELF experiences. Paper delivered at the 7th conference of English as a Lingua Franca, The American College of Greece, 5 September 2014.
Nihalani, P. (2002) Personal communication. July 24, 2002.
Nishii, Y. (2015) E-mail correspondence from Chukyo student one one-year overseas study in Finland.

Pakir, A. (1991) The range and depth of English-knowing bilinguals in Singapore. *World Englishes* 10, 167–179.
Phillipson, R. (2010) *Linguistic Imperialism Continued*. London: Routledge.
Sharifian, F. (ed.) (2009) *English as an International Language: Perspectives and Pedagogical Issues*. Bristol: Multilingual Matters.
Schneider, E. (2007) *Postcolonial English*. Cambridge, CUP.
Sponseller, A. (2015) Poster session on EMI at Hiroshima University. *JALT College and University Education SIG Conference*, Sugiyama University, Nagoya, Japan, 26 September.
Sridhar, S.N. (2010) Comments made during Q&A session at *16th Conference of the International Association for World Englishes*, Simon Fraser University, 25–27 July.
Suzuki, T. (1978) *Words in Context*. Tokyo: Kodansha International.
UniRank (2017) *Top Universities in Japan*. See www.4icu.org (accessed 26 July 2017).
Vettorel, P. (2014) *English as a Lingua Franca in Wider Networking*. Berlin: DeGruyter.
Wachter, B. and Maiworm, F. (eds) (2008) *English-Taught Programmes in European Higher Education*. Bonn: Lemmens.

9 Talking the Talk but Not Walking the Walk? Preparing Teachers for Global Englishes Pedagogy

Ali Fuad Selvi

In recent years, we have been witnessing the emergence of 'critically oriented paradigms' (e.g. World Englishes, English as lingua franca and English as an international language, collectively known as 'Global Englishes') that inform language teaching (and teacher education) by merging the gap between the deeply inherent values and practices in English language teaching vis-à-vis the present-day sociolinguistic realities of today's world where English has a wide variety of uses, users, functions and contexts. At the heart of this line of inquiry are the '-informed' '-based' or '-aware' teacher education models built upon critically oriented paradigms (e.g. ELF-aware teacher education, EIL teacher education, WE-informed teacher education). Despite the great attention these paradigms have received in recent years, their prominence is often stuck into 'pedagogical implications', which teacher candidates learn 'about', rather than internalize and situate at the heart of their knowledge base informing their everyday practices as teachers. In this chapter I highlight the essential link between language pedagogy and second language teacher education in the process of equipping transnational/transcultural users of English with a repertoire of knowledge, skills, dispositions and attitudes to be able to function in today's glocalized world.

Introduction

For the past couple of decades, we have been witnessing the burgeoning of an unprecedented phenomenon situated at the crossroads of sociolinguistics, education, economy, politics and intercultural communication – the spread of English as a global/international language. Fueled with inexorable forces of (in)voluntary migration, transnational mobility, border-crossing practices, global economic growth and technological innovations, the English language has gained new 'homes' and a diverse set of roles, functions, uses and users around the world (Marlina, 2014; Selvi, 2016). Today, it goes without saying that English is (and will probably continue to remain for a foreseeable future) a pressing issue and a crucial item on educational agendas of the countries across the globe.

From the perspective of language education, the shift (from a 'foreign' language) towards an 'international' language necessitates reflecting upon, interrogating, negotiating and reconceptualizing the widely established values and practices in English language teaching (ELT) (Selvi & Rudolph, 2017, 2018). More specifically, the 'glocal' or fluidly global–local trajectory of English (i.e. being a global language with a wide variety of local impacts and a symbiotic relationship between them) complicates different aspects of ELT enterprise, and generates a list of plausible questions, such as: What is 'English'? How does it interact with other languages and linguistic repertoires available to its users? Who is a competent English 'speaker'? What does successful communication using English language entail? When teaching/learning English, 'whose language' are we talking about? If language and culture are inseparable entities, 'whose culture' are we teaching/learning? If English traveled to 'strange shores' (Marlina, 2014), found new homes and molded into new forms (i.e. language varieties), 'which language variety/ies' should be taught to learners, vis-à-vis other linguistic/cultural semiotic tools available in the local context or in the communicative interaction? 'Which approaches' are the best in addressing these issues in pedagogy? And finally, who is a 'qualified' teacher of English?

Wrestling with this set of vital questions, scholars in the fields of ELT and applied linguistics have embarked upon three interrelated ventures in a recursive fashion: (1) they called for a paradigm shift in ELT so as to meet the complex, glocal, fluid and dynamic issues surrounding using, learning and teaching English as a global language (Matsuda, 2012; McKay, 2002); (2) they worked on developing a number of different frameworks to come up with substantial and sustainable responses to (in)form ELT practices, namely e.g. English as a lingua franca (ELF)-aware pedagogy (Bayyurt & Sifakis, 2015), Global Englishes (GE) language teaching (GELT) (Galloway & Rose, 2015), English as an international language (EIL) pedagogy (Matsuda, 2012; Selvi & Yazan, 2013) or World Englishes (WE)-informed ELT (Matsuda, 2017); and (3) finally, as a natural byproduct of these endeavors, they underscored the vitality of teacher education in transforming these idea(l)s into innovations and new practices in teacher education (Doğançay-Aktuna & Hardman, 2008; Matsuda, 2017; Selvi, 2016).

These interrelated ventures have been serving as a catalyst in transforming our deeply ingrained notions and understanding of the 'native speaker' (NS) as a goal and benchmark for learning and a model of competence (Cook, 2002), instructional quality and competencies (Braine,

2010; Selvi, 2011, 2014) and cultural bases for language (Cortazzi & Jin, 1999). Furthermore, they are situated at the crux of efforts to move beyond categorical dichotomies of uniform experience to define being/becoming a language learner, user and teacher as well as marginalization and privilege manifested through their cultural, ethnic, national, professional and even gender-oriented identities (Rudolph *et al.*, 2015, 2018). Collectively, it is hoped that these endeavors will transform the gap between values and practices in ELT, and contribute to the development of a sustainable language pedagogy vis-à-vis the sociolinguistic realities of today's world where English has a wide variety of uses, users, functions and contexts. However, scholars agree that transformation and innovation in present-day classrooms depend on reconfiguration of the principles and practices of second language teacher education (Doğançay-Aktuna & Hardman, 2008; Matsuda, 2006, 2017; Selvi, 2016). In the following section, I will, therefore, highlight the importance of second language teacher education in general, and discuss how it actually informs local teacher education practices in particular.

Teacher Education in/for a New Glocal Linguistic Order

The essential link between a reconceptualized look at English and the pertinent language pedagogy is perhaps best captured in the widely quoted words of McKay (2002: 1), who asserted that 'the teaching and learning of an international language must be based on an entirely different set of assumptions than the teaching and learning of any other second or foreign language'. A corollary to this statement is the understanding that the principles and practices governing English language teacher education are to be aligned with this position. Table 9.1 presents a list of benefits attributed to second language teacher education programs in preparing teachers who can meet the diverse and changing needs of their language learners.

In order to spearhead a transformational change in language classrooms (and beyond), a change in teacher education is imperative.

Table 9.1 The importance of second language teacher education programs

• Affords a safe space for transformation
• Provides a more sustainable model (cf. conference presentations or one-time workshops)
• Engages teacher-learners over time
• Creates multiple opportunities for exposure, practice and support from multiple perspectives
• Packages professional transformation in the sustained nature of teacher preparation
• Encapsulates the potential of influencing more teachers
• Creates opportunities for teacher educators to take an active role in designing national/regional curricula and thereby to work with teachers with whom they may not have access

Source: Adapted from Matsuda (2017).

Therefore, there has been a growing interest among scholars in infusing the principles of GE into teacher education programs in various forms. Often collocated with such words as '-informed' or '-aware' (e.g. ELF-aware teacher education, EIL teacher education, WE-informed teacher education), these models are structured around the principles of GE[1] or infuse principles undergirding GE into the existing structures and practices through courses, units/modules in a course, course assignments or discussions. Responding to Matsuda's (2017: xiv) call for 'embrac[ing] an entirely new way of thinking about English language teaching and learning based on a newly acquired set of knowledge', second language teacher education programs have been putting an emphasis on such topics as historical spread and current use of (glocal) Englishes (Matsuda, 2009; McKay, 2012), cultural issues and aspects (Kubota, 2004), language proficiency (Jenkins, 2006; McKay, 2012), language user/teacher identity (Canagarajah, 2004; Kumaravadivelu, 2012a), (post-)methodology (Kumaravadivelu, 2006) and the diversity of uses and users today (Matsuda, 2006). Regardless of the form and structure, these programmatic efforts aim to contribute to the knowledge base of language teachers who can equip their transnational/transcultural users of English with a repertoire of knowledge, skills, dispositions and attitudes to be able to function in today's glocalized world.

Despite the increasing attention the critically oriented paradigms have received in recent years, the transformation of/in second language education may still be defined by such terms as slow, superficial, partial, incomplete and even short-lived, and therefore characterized by the paucity of sustainable practices for in- and pre-service teachers (Matsuda, 2009). As a result, the prominence of GE principles is often stuck into 'pedagogical implications', which teacher candidates 'learn about', rather than internalize and situate at the heart of their knowledge base informing their everyday practices. Ultimately, there exists an immediate need for systematic investigations to 'scrutinize existing teacher education practices as well as to forge new pathways in the creation of sustainable professional spaces and structures for the teachers of a global language' (Selvi, 2016: 261).

Mapping the Scene: A Close(r) Look at the Local Context

The inexorable spread of English as a global language permeates into the different spheres of life, including the educational curricula around the world. This understanding brings a diverse set of important implications for second language (teacher) education. Departing from this realization, I will now turn to the contexts of Turkey and Northern Cyprus since the English language stands out as a major area of scrutiny not just for the specialists in national education systems but also for teacher educators, policy makers and even parents. More specifically, I will present, discuss and critique a list of major 'faultlines' informing English language teacher education practices in these countries. The discussion will be specifically organized within the broader framework of GE, and the extent to which teacher education programs respond and are susceptible to the changes in our understanding of the present-day status of English as a global language.

Practices and Innovations in Teacher Education: A Top-down Approach

Regardless of the 'level' (pre-kindergarten, elementary, secondary or post-secondary), 'content area' (e.g. English, math, social sciences, special education, etc.) and 'setting' (public or private), individuals who aspire to work in educational institutions as teachers across Turkey and Northern Cyprus are required to go through a minimum of four years of undergraduate education offered by faculties of education in these countries.[2] The overarching aim of English language teacher education programs in this context is to prepare qualified teachers with excellent command of English as well as professional knowledge, skills and dispositions to serve language learners with whom they work on an everyday basis. Participants who finish these programs (predominantly from Turkish and Turkish Cypriot backgrounds) often take positions as English teachers/instructors at various levels and settings, or curriculum, materials and test developers, although some of them also assume positions in which they utilize their advanced language skills (e.g. translation/interpretation, tourism and international business) in Turkey, Northern Cyprus and even beyond.

From a curricular standpoint, the English language teacher education programs in this context consist of the following domains: (1) advanced language skills in English; (2) a compulsory second foreign language; (3) educational sciences; (4) English literature; (5) linguistics; (6) English language teaching (methodology, pedagogy and specialization); and (7) other courses (compulsory to all students irrespective of their academic departments). Table 9.2 showcases a curricular snapshot of English language teacher education programs in Turkey and Northern Cyprus. More interestingly, the curricula followed in these programs are designed by the *Yükseköğretim Kurumu*[3] (abbreviated as YÖK, Higher Education Council) in Turkey. This actually means that the envisioned knowledge base of English language teachers is predefined within the parameters determined by the Higher Education Council in a top-down and standardized manner (Selvi, 2016). This leaves no agency for individual English language teacher education programs contributing to the local teacher workforce at various levels and settings.

A closer look at these institutions and their teacher education curricula reveals a clear paucity of dedicated courses focusing on the GE pedagogy. Even a perfunctory scrutiny of curricula adopted by the English language teacher education programs in Turkey and Northern Cyprus

Table 9.2 A curricular snapshot of English language teacher education programs in Turkey and Northern Cyprus[a]

Language skills-oriented courses	Foreign languages[b]	Educational sciences	English literature	Linguistics	English language teaching	Other courses[c]
Contextual Grammar & Composition	French or German (Beginner & Intermediate)	Introduction to Education	Introduction to Literature	Linguistics	ELT Methodology	Turkish: Written Communication
Listening & Pronunciation		Educational Psychology	English Literature	Translation Studies	Teaching Language Skills – Speaking and Listening	Turkish: Oral Communication
Advanced Reading & Writing		Classroom Management	Drama Analysis	Language Acquisition	Instructional Technologies & Materials Development	Principles of Kemal Atatürk I
Oral Communication Skills		Turkish Educational System and School Management	Novel Analysis	Contrastive Turkish-English Structure	Teaching English to Young Learners	Principles of Kemal Atatürk II
Oral Expression & Public Speaking		Guidance	Schools of Modern Thought	The English Lexicon	Teaching Language Skills – Reading and Writing	First Year on Campus Seminar
Advanced Writing & Research Skills					Community Service Practice	Introduction to Information Technologies and Applications
					English Language Testing & Evaluation	
					Materials Adaptation & Development	
					School Experience	
					Practice Teaching	

Notes: [a]Based on the curriculum of the Teaching English as a Foreign Language program at Middle East Technical University, Northern Cyprus Campus. Source: https://ncc.metu.edu.tr/efl/curriculum.
[b]Students studying in English language teacher programs are required to take a minimum of three courses in a particular foreign language besides English. The readily available courses are often French and German.
[c]These courses are taken by all students (irrespective of their academic departments) in a given institution of higher education.

reveals that only three out of 61 teacher education programs have a specific course which specifically aims to support teacher-learners on GE principles. In all of these programs that have a course on GE, teacher educators utilize the 'elective course' option to circumvent the top-down approach adopted by the Higher Education Council, since the council has less control and influence in elective courses offered by respective departments. On the one hand, the existence of these courses – no matter how small they may be in terms of numbers – contributing to the professional development of teacher candidates should be viewed as a promising and important initial step towards a better future for teacher education curriculum aligned with the present-day sociolinguistic realities of our glocalized world. From a contextual standpoint, such courses bear the potential of making contributions to the individuals' ambidexterity both as a language 'user' and a language 'teacher'. As a language user, individuals gain a redefined sense of goal in language learning and success in language communication and interactions. As a language teacher, they get exposed to the historical trajectory delineating a move from 'the English language' to 'Global Englishes' and will begin to establish links and connections to language teaching practices.

On the other hand, it needs to be stated that this well-intended move brings about two major obstacles. First, the symbiotic relationship between a dedicated course on GE and the rest of the program needs to be well established so that this course will be an organic part of the broader curriculum (in)forming the professional knowledge base of teacher candidates. Secondly, although the utilization of 'elective' course status allows teacher educators to create a novel space in a narrowly predefined curriculum, it suggests that a course on GE (a) exists not as part of the 'core' curriculum, and (b) is subject to institutionalized constraints of individual programs and faculty members. Thus, in cases where programmatic dynamics concerning the program students (e.g. course sequence, graduation requirements, etc.) or teacher educators (e.g. the absence of competent teacher educators, teaching load in a given semester) create constraints, these 'elective' courses will not be offered. Collectively, these factors raise serious concerns and questions marks over sustainability in professional development from the perspective of GE.

Teacher Educators and the Issues of Reluctance, Resistance and Unawareness

English language teacher education, especially at pre-service levels, is a collaborative endeavor distributed across various stakeholders (e.g. teacher candidates, teacher educators, teacher-learners, mentor teachers, language learners) and contexts (e.g. university-based teacher education programs, school-based practicum sites). The multiplicity of individuals understandably brings about a multitude of positions, degrees of commitment, involvement and engagement with the GE paradigm (Selvi, 2016). Within the scope of second language teacher education, teacher educators have a special role and importance since they are the primary stakeholders involved in and 'charged with a series of tasks and roles including (but not limited to) organizing, implementing and (re)designing the programs that prepare teacher-learners for their future professional tasks' (Selvi, 2016: 262). Therefore, their worldviews, philosophies and agency underpinning their approaches and practices bear a critical importance. In other words, these individuals and what they choose (not) to include in their courses have a direct relevance and influence on the being and becoming of the individuals they work with. As I argued elsewhere, there may be different reasons and rationales behind the reservations held by teacher educators towards the GE pedagogy (Selvi, 2017). To be more specific, teacher educators may:

- not be informed about the GE pedagogy and its connections to second language teacher education (i.e. unawareness);
- be in epistemological and conceptual disagreement with the principles of the GE pedagogy (i.e. disagreement, rejection and resistance); and
- acknowledge the GE pedagogy and its principles but see no value in them within the scope of second language teacher education (i.e. reluctance).

My anecdotal evidence and personal interactions as a teacher educator working in this context suggest that all of these issues (i.e. reluctance, resistance and unawareness) currently exist in the local second language teacher education context. However, for those teacher educators working along the lines of GE, they offer an opportunity to reflect upon the sources of these issues at various levels and to devise innovative ways to create spaces affording negotiation of GE principles in second language teacher education programs. To be more specific, GE-oriented teacher educators may operationalize their efforts at programmatic, curricular and personal levels, as follows:

- *Programmatic level.* Carefully investigate institutional affordances and constraints embedded in teacher education programs with an intention to eliminate structural challenges and to create spaces for infusion GE-oriented courses and related experiences.
- *Curricular level.* Develop, enhance and diversify novel options and solutions in the teacher education curriculum and related experiences.
- *Personal level.* Establish constructive, bi-directional and active channels of communication to engage in intellectual and professional dialogue with major stakeholders involved in second language teacher education with an ultimate goal of reconciling their rejection, resistance, reluctance and/or ignorance.

Teacher Educators and Global Englishes: Preliminary Reflections from a National Survey

In the remainder of this section, I intend to share the preliminary results of an ongoing national survey focusing on second language teacher educators from the perspective of the GE pedagogy in the contexts of Turkey and Northern Cyprus. But why teacher educators? There are three fundamental reasons behind scrutinizing teacher educators and their views and practices. First and foremost, they are the primary agents in organizing, implementing and (re-)designing teacher education programs in general. Thus, they are equipped with institutional power to devise new tools and processes and modify existing ones. Secondly, they often play influential roles in national and/or regional curriculum design, review and revision projects, and they get involved in in administration, which collectively suggests that their sphere of influence also transcends (both pre- and in-service) teachers beyond their immediate contexts (Matsuda, 2017). Finally, as Matsuda (2009: 171–172) insightfully reminds us, 'in spite of the increasing attention given to the teaching of EIL ..., we know much less when it comes to the question of how such ideas as World Englishes and EIL are dealt with in teacher preparation programs'. Departing from these realizations, I embarked upon a national survey investigating the views, practices and levels of engagement of teacher educators about the GE pedagogy. To be more specific, I aimed to develop a more systematic investigation of teacher educators' commitment (or lack thereof) in aligning their practices conducive to the contextualized lived experiences of individuals negotiating identity within and across borders (Motha *et al.*, 2012) and providing teacher candidates with the contextually sensitive knowledge, skills and dispositions within societies and ELT located therein (Selvi & Rudolph, 2018). The major points of inquiry in this national survey included the following questions:

(1) What is teacher educators' stance on the current status of English as a global language?
(2) How familiar are teacher educator with Global Englishes as a paradigm?
(3) What is teacher educators' current level of engagement with the principles of Global Englishes?

The national survey of teacher educators involved nearly 400 teacher educators in 61 institutions of higher education located in the contexts of Turkey and Northern Cyprus. As described earlier, these educators come from various disciplinary backgrounds (e.g. English language teaching, linguistics, literature and educational sciences) to work with teacher candidates in these programs. The survey instrument included a total of 39 items, organized in four sections, namely: (1) teacher educators' views on the current status of English (16 items); (2) teacher educators' familiarity with GE (four items); (3) teacher educators' engagement with GE (10 items); and (4) demographic information (nine items). The data for the current project were collected electronically through Google Forms and the current response rate at the time of writing this manuscript is around 25%.

A great majority of teacher educators who participated in this national survey recognized the current status of English as a global language (97%) and pointed to 'sociopolitical reasons' as the main force behind the status it holds today (89.6%). Although they predominantly acknowledged the 'global' status of the language, two out of every three respondents associated the language with inner circle countries (57.2%) and the cultures of inner circle countries (50.3%). Nevertheless, they believed that it is used to communicate beyond inner circle English speakers (76.7%); therefore, the ultimate goal of learning is to become a proficient speaker in it, rather than to speak like a native speaker (76.6%). In general, teacher educators reported a moderate familiarity with GE principles and pedagogy. For those who viewed themselves as familiar with the GE pedagogy, when asked about the sources of their familiarity they reported: (a) reading relevant research in the field; (b) interactions with colleagues and/or collaborators in other institutions; and (c) interactions with colleagues and/or collaborators in their programs. Along the same lines, those who viewed themselves as unfamiliar with the GE pedagogy reported: (a) lack of opportunity (e.g. time, resources, etc.); (b) relevance; and (c) its absence from their previous academic background, as the primary reasons behind their unfamiliarity.

From the perspective of language teaching practices, only one in five teacher educators believed in the aforementioned words of McKay (2002: 1), who argued that 'the teaching and learning of an international language must be based on an entirely different set of assumptions than the teaching and learning of any other second and foreign language'. Although teacher educators have reservations about the reconceptualization of the established set of assumptions informing second/foreign language teaching, they nevertheless considered integrating GE principles into teacher education as a 'high priority', which was also manifested in the fact that three out of five teacher educators reported engagement with GE principles and pedagogy at some level. Courses on ELT methodology, teaching language skills, linguistics and other 'big picture' courses (e.g. applied linguistics, sociolinguistics, language policy, etc.) were often cited as spaces where GE principles found a presence in teacher education programs. As summarized in Figure 9.1, teacher educators' engagement with the GE pedagogy and the interplay between GE and language teaching practices can be best captured using a continuum. On the one end of the spectrum, teacher educators acknowledged that they were not engaged with GE in any way. However, the teacher educators who reported some kind of engagement with the GE pedagogy (nearly 60% of the

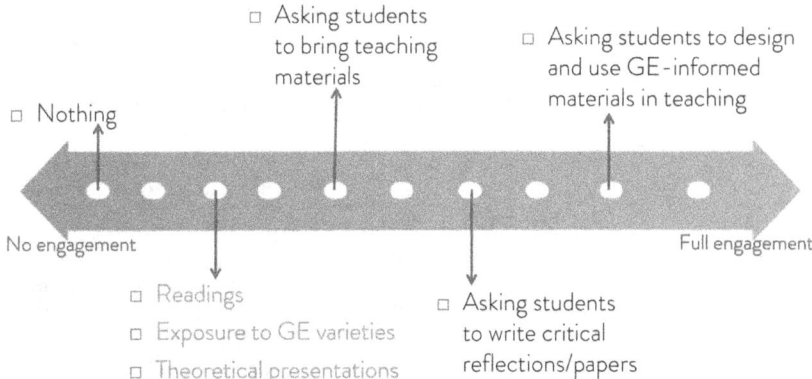

Figure 9.1 The engagement continuum: Teacher educators and their engagement in GE

participants) varied in terms of degrees and forms. While some viewed GE as a set of principles to design and utilize GE-informed materials in language teaching, others required their students to write critical reflections or simply bring teaching materials related to it. It should be noted that a great majority of teacher educators utilize readings, exposure to GE varieties, and theoretical presentations to engage their teacher candidates with the GE pedagogy. Furthermore, teacher educators find different ways to integrate GE into the broader experience of their teacher education programs such as integrating GE-related topics into reading circles, workshops and talks given by invited speakers, and sharing web links for articles and videos related to GE.

Viewed through the tripartite conceptualization of Bayyurt and Sifakis (2015),[4] teacher educators' engagement may be viewed within the category of 'theory', with relatively little or no emphasis on 'application' and 'evaluation', since the 'theory' level encompasses being 'informed' about and/or 'aware' of the information related to GE principles and pedagogy in diverse contexts.

Implications and Conclusions

Diverse uses, users, functions and contexts of English as an international lingua franca serve as a powerful catalyst promoting an 'epistemic break'[5] (Kumaravadivelu, 2012b) in ELT. To be more specific, it calls for reconceptualization of the existing assumptions undergirding major pillars of ELT enterprise, namely material design, ownership, cultures and cultural ideology, norms, role models, instructors, language assessment, curriculum, language ideology, recruitment and workplace practices. As summarized in Table 9.3, GE language teaching stands out as a plausible and sustainable alternative to traditional ELT.

Table 9.3 The shift from ELT to GE language teaching (GELT)

	ELT	GELT
Target interlocutor	Native English speakers	Native English speakers and non-native English speakers
Owners	Native English speakers	Native English speakers and non-native English speakers
Target culture	Fixed native English culture	Fluid cultures
Teachers	Non-native English speaking teachers (same first language) and native English speaking teachers	Non-native English speaking teachers (same and different first language), native English speaking teachers
Norms	Native English and concept of standard English	Diversity, flexibility and multiple forms of competence
Role model	Native English speakers	Successful ELF users
Materials	Native English and native English speakers	Native English, non-native English, ELF, and ELF communities and contexts
First language and own culture	Seen as a hindrance and source of interference	Seen as a resource
Ideology	Underpinned by an exclusive and ethnocentric view of English	Underpinned by an inclusive Global Englishes perspective

Source: Galloway and Rose (2015: 208).

The major principles and practices surrounding the GE pedagogy inform 'how the teaching and learning of English can be undertaken in such a way as to maintain linguistic diversity while providing equal access to the acquisition of English' (McKay & Bokhorst-Heng, 2008: 21). As I argued elsewhere (Selvi & Yazan, 2013: 39), EIL (and at the same time, GE) pedagogy:

- is a radical shift from the traditional conceptualization of ELT;
- is sensitive to the local teaching context and culture of learning;
- is sensitive to achieving balance between local and global concerns;
- offers a viable alternative to the NS framework in terms of norms and cultural tendencies in the curriculum, methods, material design, assessment, teacher qualities and identity;
- recognizes and promotes the plurality of present-day local and global English uses, users and contexts;
- equips learners with a repertoire of sociolinguistic and cultural strategies to better function as competent users in cross-cultural encounters;
- encourages English speaking ownership and participation in (mostly digital) global discourse communities;
- recognizes the importance of local teachers in designing and providing socially sensitive, diverse and rich opportunities for ELT;

- creates a global pedagogical space where multiple identities, realities, varieties, voices and cultures co-exist;
- examines sociocultural identity in respect of diverse teaching contexts of use and profiles of users; and
- redefines the notion of proficiency, authenticity, acceptability and appropriateness in the learning, teaching and assessment of the language.

In reconceptualizing language learning, use, instruction and identity beyond the NS episteme, teacher educators and teacher education programs have an indispensable role and importance. More specifically, second language teacher education necessitates: (1) competent teacher educators who have teaching experience in and expertise about GE practices; (2) teacher education practices that consolidate the interrelation among teacher-learners' past histories, present realities and future trajectories within the parameters of the GE framework; and (3) teacher-learners whose agency is acknowledged, practiced and developed in respect of their imagined instructional settings (Selvi, 2013).

A closer look at the second language teacher education landscape in the contexts of Turkey and Northern Cyprus revealed macro-level systemic challenges (e.g. top-down imposition of teacher education curricula) and micro-level programmatic constraints (e.g. a paucity of dedicated courses focusing on the GE pedagogy; the issues of reluctance, resistance and unawareness towards the GE pedagogy). Furthermore, based on the preliminary findings gleaned from the national survey focusing on the Turkish and Northern Cypriot contexts, it could be summarized that the teacher educators recognize the current global status of English as a global language as well as the importance of the GE paradigm as part of English language teacher education. However, their level of engagement varies extensively, and it is often limited within non-institutionalized forms and structures (e.g. the dearth of a dedicated course on GE, programmatic decisions promoting GE, etc.). Collectively, the research results clearly indicate the need for extra training on GE as well as GE-informed second language teacher education since it has been reported that they are moderately familiar and engaged with the GE principles within existing curricular impositions and constraints. Otherwise, in the current state of affairs, integrating GE principles into second language teacher education programs or organizing second language teacher education programs around the principles of GE is left at the discretion and conscience of individual teacher educators.

It needs to be reiterated that there is a great opportunity and an immediate need to align second language teacher education practices with the present-day sociolinguistic realities of the glocalized world in which the English language has a multitude of uses, users, forms, varieties and functions, operating in a dynamic fashion with other languages and linguistic repertoires available to its users (cf. translanguaging, García & Wei, 2014; Selvi, forthcoming). Although the major points of discussion in this discussion (i.e. top-down impositions on teacher education; programmatic affordances and constraints; the issues of reluctance, resistance and unawareness; and varying levels of commitment, involvement and engagement with the GE pedagogy) are contextualized and rooted in the specific educational contexts of Turkey and Northern Cyprus, their significance may extend to other contexts where similar discussions, tensions and opportunities exist.

In closing, the progressive trajectory towards a pluricentric orientation to the ideas, theories, values and practices (in)forming the 'English language', 'English language teaching' and 'English language teacher education' demands the involvement of various stakeholders comprising the ELT enterprise, and teacher educators have a paramount role and importance in this picture. Therefore, it is expected for teacher educators, irrespective of their contexts, to reflect upon their knowledge, beliefs, experiences and practices with regards to GE principles. This will be a concrete first step in developing (in)formal, innovative, sustainable and collaborative practices contributing to the knowledge base of English language teachers going through teacher education programs in these contexts.

Notes

(1) The term Global Englishes refers to an umbrella term that unites both localized and globalized versions of English as an international language (EIL), World Englishes (WE) and English as a lingua franca (ELF) paradigms (Galloway & Rose, 2015). Due to its inclusionary scope, the term has been adopted throughout the manuscript.
(2) In order to address the growing teacher shortage and meet the increasing demand in certain content areas (e.g. English), alternative routes to teacher certification have been developed and implemented in Turkey and Northern Cyprus. These programs have been eliminated from the discussion in this manuscript. Interested readers may refer to Seferoğlu (2004) for a more comprehensive discussion about these programs.
(3) Established in 1982, YÖK is a governmental body charged primarily with the task of planning, regulating, directing and supervising education provided by the institutions of higher education in Turkey.
(4) Built upon the principles of transformative learning theory (Mezirow, 1991; Sifakis, 2007), the model proposed by Bayyurt and Sifakis (2015) identifies three major phases in critically oriented (GE-informed/aware) teacher education programs and courses. These phases include: (1) *theory* – which refers to being 'informed' about and 'aware' of the principles underpinning GE principles and pedagogy; (2) *application* – which entails the ability to develop instructional plans and practices within the parameters of GE, conducive to the dynamics of the local context; and (3) *evaluation* – which encompasses 'self' and 'peer' evaluation with an ultimate aim of reflecting upon and critiquing instructional plans and practices by relying on GE principles.
(5) Defined as 'thorough re-conceptualization and a thorough re-organization of knowledge systems' (Kumaravadivelu, 2012a: 14), the term 'epistemic break' refers to a meaningful break from the NS episteme which defines theoretical principles, classroom practices, the publication industry or the job market. He argues that 'in order

for our profession to meet the challenges of globalism in a deeply meaningful way, what is required is no less than an epistemic break from its dependency on the current West-oriented, Center-based knowledge systems that carry an indelible colonial coloration' (Kumaravadivelu, 2012a: 14).

References

Bayyurt, Y. and Sifakis, N.C. (2015) Developing an ELF-aware pedagogy: Insights from a self-education program. In P. Vettorel (ed.) *New Frontiers in Teaching and Learning English* (pp. 55–76). Newcastle: Cambridge Scholars.

Braine, G. (2010) *Nonnative Speaker English Teachers: Research, Pedagogy and Professional Growth*. New York: Routledge.

Canagarajah, S. (2004) Subversive identities, pedagogical safe houses, and critical learning. In B. Norton and K. Toohey (eds) *Critical Pedagogies and Language Learning* (pp. 116–137). Cambridge: Cambridge University Press.

Cook, V. (2002) *Portraits of the L2 User*. Clevedon: Multilingual Matters.

Cortazzi, M. and Jin, L. (1999) Cultural mirrors: Materials and methods in the EFL classroom. In E. Hinkel (ed.) *Culture in Second Language Teaching and Learning* (pp. 196–219). Cambridge: Cambridge University Press.

Doğançay-Aktuna, S. and Hardman, J. (2008) *Global English Teaching and Teacher Education: Praxis and Possibility*. Alexandria, VA: TESOL Publications.

Galloway, N. and Rose, H. (2015) *Introducing Global Englishes*. Abingdon: Routledge.

García, O. and Wei, L. (2014) *Translanguaging: Language, Bilingualism and Education*. London: Palgrave Macmillan.

Jenkins, J. (2006) Points of view and blind spots: ELF and SLA. *International Journal of Applied Linguistics* 16, 137–162.

Kubota, R. (2004) Critical multiculturalism and second language education. In B. Norton and K. Toohey (eds) *Critical Pedagogies and Language Learning* (pp. 30–52). Cambridge: Cambridge University Press.

Kumaravadivelu, B. (2006) *Understanding Language Teaching: From Method to Postmethod*. Mahwah, NJ: Lawrence Erlbaum.

Kumaravadivelu, B. (2012a) Individual identity, cultural globalization, and teaching English as an international language. In L. Alsagoff, S.L. McKay, G. Hu and W. Renandya (eds) *Principles and Practices for Teaching English as an International Language* (pp. 9–27). London: Routledge.

Kumaravadivelu, B. (2012b) *Language Teacher Education for a Global Society: A Modular Model for knowing, Analyzing, Recognizing, Doing, and Seeing*. New York: Taylor & Francis.

Marlina, R. (2014) The pedagogy of English as an international language (EIL): More reflections and dialogues. In R. Marlina and R.A. Giri (eds) *Pedagogy of English as an International Language: Perspectives from Scholars, Teachers and Students* (pp. 1–19). New York: Springer.

Matsuda, A. (2006) Negotiating ELT assumptions in EIL classrooms. In J. Edge (ed.) *(Re-)locating TESOL in an Age of Empire* (pp. 158–170). Basingstoke: Palgrave Macmillan.

Matsuda, A. (2009) Desirable but not necessary? The place of World Englishes and English as an international language in English teacher preparation programs in Japan. In F. Sharifian (ed.) *English as an International Language: Perspectives and Pedagogical Issues* (pp. 169–189). Bristol: Multilingual Matters.

Matsuda, A. (2012) *Principles and Practices of Teaching English as an International Language*. Bristol: Multilingual Matters.

Matsuda, A. (2017) *Preparing Teachers to Teach English as an International Language*. Bristol: Multilingual Matters.

McKay, S.L. (2002) *Teaching English as an International Language*. Oxford: Oxford University Press.
McKay, S.L. (2012) Principles of teaching English as an international language. In L. Alsagoff, S.L. McKay, G. Hu and W. Renandya (eds) *Principles and Practices for Teaching English as an International Language* (pp. 28–46). London: Routledge.
McKay, S.L. and Bokhorst-Heng, W. (2008) *International English in its Sociolinguistic Context: Towards a Socially Sensitive EIL Pedagogy*. London: Routledge.
Mezirow, J. (1991) *Transformative Dimensions of Adult Learning*. San Francisco, CA: Jossey-Bass.
Motha, S., Jain, R. and Tecle, T. (2012) Translinguistic identity-as-pedagogy: Implications for teacher education. *International Journal of Innovation in English Language Teaching and Research* 1 (1), 13–27.
Rudolph, N., Selvi, A.F. and Yazan, B. (2015) Conceptualizing and confronting inequity: Approaches within and new directions for the 'NNEST' movement'. *Critical Inquiry in Language Studies* 12 (1), 27–50.
Rudolph, N., Yazan, B. and Rudolph, J. (2018) Negotiating 'ares,' 'cans,' and 'shoulds' of being and becoming in English language teaching: Two teacher accounts from one Japanese university. *Asian Englishes*, 1–16. Advance online publication. doi:10.1080/13488678.2018.1471639
Seferoğlu, G. (2004) A study of alternative English teacher certification practices in Turkey. *Journal of Education for Teaching* 30, 151–159.
Selvi, A.F. (2011) The non-native speaker teacher. *ELT Journal* 65, 187–189.
Selvi, A.F. (2013) Towards EIL teacher education: Exploring challenges and potentials of MATESOL programs in the United States. In N.T. Zacharias and C. Manara (eds) *Contextualizing the Pedagogy of English as an International Language: Issues and Tensions* (pp. 42–58). Newcastle: Cambridge Scholars.
Selvi, A.F. (2014) Myths and misconceptions about the non-native English speakers in the TESOL (NNEST) movement. *TESOL Journal* 5, 573–611.
Selvi, A.F. (2016) The role of teacher education at a crossroads of tensions and opportunities. *Asian Englishes* 18, 258–264.
Selvi, A.F. (2017) Preparing teachers to teach English as an international language (EIL): Reflections from Northern Cyprus. In A. Matsuda (ed.) *Preparing Teachers to Teach English as an International Language* (pp. 115–129). Bristol: Multilingual Matters.
Selvi, A.F. (forthcoming) Incorporating global Englishes in K-12 classrooms. In. L. de Oliveira (ed.) *The Handbook of TESOL in K-12*. Chichester: Wiley.
Selvi, A.F. and Rudolph, N. (2017) Non-native English teachers' professional identities: Implications and challenges for teacher education. In J.D. Martinez Agudo (ed.) *Native and Non-native Teachers in English Language Teaching: Professional Challenges and Teacher Education* (pp. 257–272). Boston, MA and Berlin: De Gruyter.
Selvi, A.F. and Rudolph, N. (2018) *Conceptual Shifts and Contextualized Practices in Education for Glocal Interaction: Issues and Implications*. Singapore: Springer Nature.
Selvi, A.F. and Yazan, B. (2013) *Teaching English as an International Language*. Alexandria, VA: TESOL Press.
Sifakis, N.C. (2007) The education of the teachers of English as a lingua franca: A transformative perspective. *International Journal of Applied Linguistics* 17, 355–375.

10 Practices of Teaching Englishes: Pedagogical Reflections and Implications

Zhichang Xu

The paradigm shift from monolithic English to global Englishes has had an impact on English language teaching. New curricula and theories surrounding World Englishes have been introduced into English studies programmes worldwide. This chapter explores issues related to the curriculum, pedagogy and assessment of a postgraduate unit, namely 'Practices of Teaching Englishes for Intercultural Communication'. This unit is offered in an Australian university to Master's students majoring in applied linguistics with a general linguistics stream and an English as an international language stream. The curriculum involves relevant World Englishes frameworks, lesson observations and teaching practices. The pedagogy incorporates World Englishes theories into practices of English language teaching for intercultural communication. The assessment consists of lesson plan development, teaching practices and reflective portfolios. The chapter begins with an introduction to the paradigm shift from English to Englishes. It then reviews relevant notions and theories based on which the curriculum, pedagogy and assessment of the postgraduate unit are designed and implemented. The data for this chapter consist of discussion forums regarding teaching World Englishes in multilingual contexts, and portfolios of lesson observations and teaching practices by the students. It also explores the implications for incorporating World Englishes into English language teaching practices.

Introduction

The spread of English over the past few centuries has been a result of early waves of migration during the 16th and 18th centuries, different forms of colonization during the 18th and the 19th centuries, and new waves of globalization over the last two centuries largely due to the unprecedented advancement in transport and technology. Globalization necessitates accessible means of translingual and intercultural communication. Current conceptualizations of globalization are characterized by 'global mobility', 'cultural blending', 'local functionality', 'super-diversity' and 'heterogeneity' (Xu, 2013: 3–8).

The English language has undergone two major processes of change and variation, namely the localization or nativization of English and the globalization of English. The former process has resulted in different forms and functions of English, particularly different varieties of English, or World Englishes (WE). The latter process has given rise to emerging paradigms of English as an international language (EIL) and English as a lingua franca (ELF). The global spread of English has also brought about new realities in relation to the 'glocalization' of English. One aspect of these new realities is that English is increasingly learned and used in multicultural contexts by multilingual speakers rather than in homogeneous contexts by monolingual speakers. The current default context for intercultural communication is likely to involve the use of different varieties of English, commonly used as a lingua franca, and it is often characterized as being mobile and dynamic, blended with multiple languages and cultures, location based, super-diverse and heterogeneous by nature. In addition, various new types of competence, apart from linguistic competence (cf. Noam Chomsky, 1965) and communicative competence (cf. Dell Hymes, 1972), have been developed to align with the new realities, e.g. intercultural communicative competence (Byram, 1989, 1997), multidialectal competence (Canagarajah, 2006) and metacultural competence (Sharifian & Jamarani, 2013).

As far as the English language is concerned, there has been a noticeable paradigm shift from a monolithic English to global Englishes. English has become and increasingly been recognized as a pluricentric language, with legitimate variations in lexis, syntax, discourse, pragmatics and cultural conceptualizations among different varieties of English. In the context of English language teaching (ELT), the paradigm shift reflects how people perceive decontextualized 'correctness' versus contextualized 'appropriateness', particularly in multilingual contexts. In addition, one of the fundamental aspects of the paradigm shift in relation to ELT is the shifting goals for teaching and learning the language, from 'manufacturing native or near-native speakers of English to developing and mentoring effective and strategic translanguaging users of English in multilingual communication contexts' (Xu, 2017: 704).

In response to the paradigm shift and the diversifying needs of English learners, teachers and users in the era of globalization, there is a need to revisit and re-examine the curriculum, pedagogy and assessment of ELT practices. This chapter introduces a unit titled 'Practices of Teaching Englishes for Intercultural Communication', which is offered in an Australian university to Master's students majoring in applied linguistics, and which explores issues related to the curriculum, pedagogy and assessment of the unit.

Literature Review

The unit of 'Practices of Teaching Englishes for Intercultural Communication' involves awareness and relevant perspectives of WE, and their implications for developing various types of competence in relation to the curriculum, pedagogy and assessment for ELT. Therefore, this section reviews relevant perspectives of teaching WE, and developing new competences for intercultural communication.

'We are currently witnessing the enormously dynamic, ongoing expansion of English, which started out in the colonial period since the seventeenth century, gained in strength after decolonization in the second half of the twentieth century, and, interestingly enough, gained even more momentum in the early twenty-first century' (Schneider, 2014: 9). The term 'Word Englishes', as it currently stands, refers to the varying varieties of the English language that have been developed and used throughout the world. Proshina (2014: 2) refers to it as a 'dynamic cline, an element of the world Englishes family', not as an 'interlanguage'. According to Seargeant (2010: 97), the term is used 'for the diversity of varieties around the world today', and it indicates 'the multiplex nature of English by adopting a plural noun'.

Over the last decades, research and relevant practices in WE have given rise to an emerging academic discipline and paradigm. As a discipline, WE demonstrates the following characteristics: (1) it has been increasingly acknowledged and required in the education system worldwide, with 'the appearance of the named subject (e.g. "World Englishes") with a relatively standardized content across different universities' in relation to the 'creation of teaching materials' (textbooks, assessment procedures, etc.); (2) it has been influenced by a series of historically specific events (such as WE conference series and the journals of *World Englishes*, *English World-Wide* and *Asian Englishes*) related to the research and teaching of a particular body of knowledge; (3) the knowledge of WE has been organized and articulated discursively and systematically to reflect the 'nature of the phenomenon (or phenomena) under investigation', and the 'discourse and practice conventions of the community which construct a research agenda around it'; (4) it has been researched, validated and practised following certain models and a 'methodological and theoretical framework' in the 'shaping of specific fields of knowledge'; and (5) it has been employing differing 'conventions related to *language* and *discourse*' in the way that 'linguistic (and other semiotic) resources' are used to frame knowledge, e.g. the descriptive approach (as opposed to the prescriptive approach) focusing on empirical and corpus-based studies (Seargeant, 2012: 131–132).

As a paradigm, WE 'shook the 20th century' for at least two decades, and it 'revolutionized the linguistic, sociocultural, and educational world, and has had a great impact on theory and practice of the new millennium' (Proshina, 2014: 1). The acronym WE serves as a symbol of the principle of inclusivity that is the cornerstone of the World Englishes paradigm. It is 'inclusive of all varieties and variants of English, of many cultures and ethnicities, of many topics and subjects, of various approaches and perspectives' (Proshina, 2014: 2). Proshina (2014: 1) has summarized the salient features of the WE paradigm, including: (1) diversity of Englishes; (2) pluricentricity of the language; (3) domineering of a dynamic functionality over a static prescriptive approach; (4) change of the goal of ELT and learning; (5) change of the native-speaker concept; and (6) integration of ELT with intercultural communication studies.

Regarding teaching WE, Kachru (1992: 359–361) points out that 'the changing sociolinguistic profile of English' and 'the global uses of English in linguistically, culturally, and economically diverse contexts' are the major reasons, as they provide 'refreshing new data and new insights'. Kachru also points out that teaching WE depends on 'the level of the class and the specific goals of teaching ... particularly for training professionals and for teaching advanced students'. According to Kachru, the following points deserve attention: (1) the *sociolinguistic profile* of English in 'its world context with discussion of selected major varieties, their users and uses'; (2) *variety exposure*; (3) *attitudinal neutrality* in terms of focusing on one specific variety and at the same time emphasizing the *awareness* and *functional validity* of other varieties; (4) the *range of uses* from educated varieties to the pidgins and basilects; (5) *contrastive pragmatics* in relation to the local conventions of culture, e.g. strategies used for persuasion, phatic communion and apologies; and (6) the *multidimensionality of functions*, e.g. in the media, in literary creativity, in administration and in the legal system (Kachru, 1992: 360–361).

Regarding WE-informed requirements for ELT teachers, Kirkpatrick (2007: 195–196) has summarized a list, including: (1) being multilingual and multicultural; (2) providing an appropriate and attainable model for their students; (3) understanding how different varieties of English operate; (4) understanding how English has developed and spread across the world in specific contexts; (5) understanding how the roles of English interrelate with other local languages; (6) evaluating ELT materials critically; (7) catering for the specific needs of their students; and (8) contributing to the extracurricular life of their students. Kirkpatrick (2007: 196–197) argues that 'well-trained, multilingual and culturally sensitive and sophisticated teachers can best teach today's learners of English, the overwhelming majority of whom are bilingual and who are learning in culturally diverse contexts for an extraordinarily complex range of needs, stretching from local to international'. In addition, informed by WE, Xu (2010: 178–188) has explored the implications for ELT in a local context, proposing that ELT in the classroom should: (1) address the needs of both students and teachers; (2) contextualize the learning and teaching experiences; (3) maximize the L1, or language-other-than-English experiences in learning and teaching English; and (4) raise the awareness of identity (re-)construction of students and teachers while developing their bilingual/multilingual competence.

The review of WE as a discipline and a paradigm, and the teaching of WE in current practices, show that the paradigm shift does not only exist at the conceptual or theoretical level, but it also has pedagogical implications for the curriculum, pedagogy and assessment of ELT practices. One of the implications is to develop different types of competence for English learners and users to manage their intercultural communication in multicultural contexts.

As far as the 'competence' of English learners and users is concerned, Byram (1997) theorizes intercultural communicative competence as comprising attitudes, knowledge and skills. Such 'attitudes' include curiosity and openness, readiness to suspend disbelief about other cultures and belief about one's own without being judgmental. The required 'knowledge' is 'of social groups and their products and practices in one's own and in one's interlocutor's country, and of the general processes of societal and individual interaction' (Byram, 1997: 51). In addition, Byram (1997) suggests that essential skills for intercultural communication include those of interpreting and relating, discovery and interaction, and critical cultural awareness and political education.

In the current superdiverse, multicultural context, Canagarajah (2006) points out that people also need to be aware of new varieties of English, and this awareness has become part of what Canagarajah terms the 'multidialectal competence'. In addition, Sharifian (2013: 8) proposes the notion of 'metacultural competence', defining it as a 'competence that enables interlocutors to communicate and negotiate their cultural conceptualisations during the process of intercultural communication'. The metacultural competence comprises three essential components, including: (1) conceptual variation awareness; (2) conceptual explication strategy; and (3) conceptual negotiation strategy. Given that new types of competence are identified and developed, there is a need to revisit the curriculum, pedagogy and assessment to make necessary alignments for good ELT practices.

The following section introduces the unit of 'Practices of Teaching Englishes for Intercultural Communication', in particular the curriculum, pedagogy and assessment of the unit, followed by pedagogical reflections based on the analysis of the unit-related data, and implications for ELT.

Practices of Teaching Englishes for Intercultural Communication: The Unit

'Practices of Teaching Englishes for Intercultural Communication' is a postgraduate unit which introduces students to the practical aspects of teaching WE in multicultural contexts. This unit covers diverse topics that equip students with knowledge and skills to teach WE, including instructional language in a WE lesson, curriculum development for WE courses, intercultural pedagogy and assessing multidialectal and intercultural competencies.

The students for this unit are mostly international and Australian domestic postgraduate students majoring in applied linguistics, and also students majoring in education, and interpreting and translation studies. Towards the second half of the unit, students are provided with opportunities to observe lessons within the program of EIL, to develop their own WE-oriented lesson plans, to practise teaching WE and to engage in critical reflections and evaluations of their observations and their own teaching practices.

The curriculum

The curriculum of the unit 'Practices of Teaching Englishes of Intercultural Communication' comprises three sections over a 12-week semester, including: (1) an introduction and theoretical input regarding WE-informed materials development, pedagogy and assessment; (2) lesson observation practicum and mini-lesson teaching practicum; and (3) discussion forums and portfolio-based reflections as part of the unit assessment.

The introduction and theoretical input part of the curriculum covers the first four weeks, involving weekly readings, lectures and tutorial discussions, primarily based on publications regarding teaching WE and curriculum development (e.g. Alsagoff et al., 2012; Baumgardner, 2006; Kachru, 1992; Kirkpatrick, 2007; Marlina & Giri, 2014). This part of the curriculum involves discussions surrounding the paradigm shift from English to Englishes, and issues of teaching WE in relation to materials development, pedagogy and assessment.

The second part of the curriculum, namely lesson observation practicum and mini-lesson teaching practicum, consists of two weeks of lesson observations and four weeks of mini-lesson teaching practices. For the lesson observations, students are provided with a list of classes within the EIL programme, so that they choose any two classes, each for one hour, to observe. These classes are undergraduate units, including 'Englishes for global communication', 'Language and globalization' and 'Writing across cultures'. A list of guiding observation questions is provided to the students, including: (1) What have you learned from the lessons? (2) To what extent do the lessons reflect the principles of teaching WE? and (3) Is there anything you would have done differently? How and why?

For the mini-lesson teaching practices, students are required to practise teaching a 20-minute mini-lesson in pairs (i.e. co-teaching by two students) in class to fellow course participants. Guiding questions for the mini-lesson teaching practices include: (1) How is your lesson (including 'learning activities') aligned with the WE perspectives? (2) What are the challenges you have experienced in conducting a WE-oriented lesson? and (3) What are your strategies in coping with the challenges?

The third part of the curriculum consists of discussion forums and portfolio-based reflections as part of the unit assessment. There are two major online discussion forums, including an ongoing asynchronous forum running throughout the 12-week course, and a specific synchronous forum scheduled for Week 5 during the two hours of the weekly lecture and seminar time. The ongoing forum covers topics that are explored on a weekly basis, and it serves a complementary role in relation to the weekly lectures and seminars. Examples of the forum discussion topics include: sharing your experiences of learning and teaching English; commenting on Kachru's 'six fallacies' regarding the uses and users of English; discussing whether English represents a repertoire of cultures; providing possible sources for English teaching materials; unpacking challenging issues in ELT; tips for teaching English in multilingual and multi-varietal societies; exploring pedagogical implications of WE; and aligning WE with location-based testing. The Week 5 discussion forum forms part of the theoretical input, where students and the lecturer relate to their own understandings of the relevant notions and theories regarding their respective English learning and teaching experiences, so that they can unpack the principles and theories of teaching WE in multicultural contexts. Examples of discussion forum topics include: models of ELT, namely the 'native-speaker' model, 'nativized English' model and EIL model; and criteria for recruiting English language teachers worldwide.

The pedagogy

The teaching and learning approach for this unit involves active experiential learning, lectures, seminars and tutorials, online discussion forums, class observations and mini-lesson teaching practices. Such a wide-ranging teaching approach facilitates learning, practical exploration and collaborative peer learning; provides experiential learning with active learner involvement in a practical environment; and encourages students to take responsibility for organizing and directing their learning with support from their unit lecturer. The medium of instruction is primarily English; however, multilingualism and code-switching practices are also encouraged during pair work or small group discussions if students share similar linguistic and cultural backgrounds. Students' first language and cultural experiences are appreciated and valued throughout the teaching and learning activities of the unit.

The assessment

The unit assessment consists of three major tasks, including: (1) developing a lesson plan; (2) co-teaching (in pairs) a mini-lesson of approximately 20 minutes in class; and (3) constructing a practicum portfolio based on the lesson observations and mini-lesson teaching practices.

Informed of the paradigm shift from English to Englishes, and relevant WE theories and perspectives during the first four weeks, students are assessed in the form of a 'lesson plan' development. They are provided with a template for lesson planning, where they are expected to specify lesson topics or themes, lesson aims and objectives, and materials and resources. They are also expected to design relevant WE teaching and learning activities and sequence the activities within a 20-minute lesson timeframe.

The mini-lesson teaching practice task focuses on three stages, namely: mini-lesson planning; mini-lesson teaching; and reflections on the mini-lesson, primarily in terms of aligning practices of teaching with WE theories and perspectives. The assessment criteria include: (1) clarity of lesson aims and objectives; (2) quality of teaching and learning materials; (3) effectiveness of class instructions; (4) engagement with students; (5) alignment with World Englishes; and (6) self-reflections.

The end-of-semester practicum portfolio assessment task is one of the major tasks of the unit, and it consists of two sections. The lesson observation portfolio section is for the students to present what they have learned from the lessons, and their reflections and suggestions for WE alignments of the observed lessons. The mini-lesson teaching practices section is for the students to reflect critically on their own teaching materials development and pedagogical considerations, including challenges they anticipate and experience, and strategies they develop accordingly throughout the mini-lesson teaching practices.

Pedagogical Reflections and Implications

This section comprises unit-related data analysis, and the data are derived from selected discussion forums and students' reflections in their portfolios. As stated in the subsection on 'The curriculum', the data for this chapter are derived from the two discussion forums and student portfolio-based reflections. The ongoing asynchronous forum (hereafter coded as Forum 1) contains a total of 130 posts from both the lecturer and students and it contains a total of 21,582 words. The Week 5 synchronous forum (hereafter coded as Forum 2) contains a total of 90 posts from the lecturer and students and it contains a total of 17,958 words. The majority of the Forum 1 and Forum 2 discussion topics are related to teaching WE for intercultural communication in terms of the curriculum, pedagogy and assessment. The portfolio-based reflections data (hereafter coded as Portfolio data) are derived from 35 international and Australian domestic postgraduate students. The reflections are primarily based on their lesson observations and mini-lesson teaching practices in terms of the alignment of the lessons and practices with WE theories and perspectives. Each student is expected to provide reflections of approximately 3500 words, including 1500 words on the observed lessons and 2000 words on their own mini-lesson practices.

A close examination of the Forum 1 and Forum 2 discussions and the students' portfolio reflections has led to the following pedagogical reflections and implications for ELT in the era of global Englishes.

Incorporating up-to-date theories and perspectives into English language teaching practices

For many of the students, the notion of WE is a revelation. They are aware of British English and American English, and they are also aware of the many different varieties of English; however, they are not yet fully aware that WE as a discipline has developed vigorously over the past few decades, and relevant theories and practices have turned the discipline into a paradigm of thinking, doing and being, and they have pedagogical implications for ELT, learning and use, particularly in multicultural contexts. Therefore, it is important to introduce and incorporate up-to-date theories and perspectives of WE, alongside other relevant areas of research, e.g. EIL and ELF, into ELT practices, so that students and teachers are up to speed on the latest developments of the ELT-related fields of research and practices.

The following data analysis shows how WE-informed students discuss models for English teaching, which is one of the topics for the Forum 2 discussions of the unit. It is apparent that after introducing WE and the paradigm shift from English to Englishes, students have become knowledgeable and passionate about new models of teaching English, such as the EIL model and the ELF model, as shown in the selected data excerpts below:

> Ideally, the EIL model of teaching English would be the most suitable to adopt in a multicultural context due to it encompassing every variety of English. Hence, the students would not be subjected to the unrealistic goal of having to achieve native-like competence. ... In my opinion, I feel that the EIL model could be adopted to raise awareness among students of the differences between varieties [of English] but at the same time it needs to be modified to focus more on the concept of communicative competence whereas the goal here is to boost communication skills instead of achieving the target varieties. (Forum 2 data, by an international student from Singapore)

The following data excerpt, also from Forum 2, shows how an international student from Indonesia reflected on the 'benefits' and 'downsides' of the ELF model for teaching English:

> Benefits: English as a lingua franca model facilitates the students not only to learn the linguistic aspects but also a wide range of varieties of English and communication strategies. This will certainly help the students/learners to communicate effectively with people from the countries of the same Kachruvian circle or other circles. In addition, for those who are aiming to participate or work in a global community, this teaching model will be a strong bridge for them to achieve their target.
>
> Downsides: This model seems 'too ideal'. To apply this model in regions that are equipped with technology and excellent facilities such as books or other teaching materials will be very easy and beneficial for both the students and the teachers. However, when it comes to applying this in under-privileged regions, applying such a model will be a real challenge. Students who are not aware of technology will be limited in terms of their understanding of other cultures and other varieties of English. Teachers, when having difficulty in finding teaching materials, will also face obstacles in achieving the target of this model of teaching. (Forum 2 data, by an international student from Indonesia)

The data analysis above shows that introducing and incorporating up-to-date theories and perspectives, such as WE, EIL and ELF, into the classroom may serve as a catalyst that engenders a chain of reactions from the students in relation to their local and global experiences of ELT, learning and use. They may also come up with novel ideas and suggestions for new curriculum development, pedagogy and assessment, e.g. new models for ELT.

Adopting a holistic approach for real-world challenges in relation to ELT practices

A holistic approach to ELT practices is proposed because ELT is commonly contextualized globally and implemented locally. Each ELT class may have its own local make-up of teachers and students. The needs and experiences of the teachers and students in terms of their teaching, learning and use of English should be taken into holistic consideration when ELT curriculum and pedagogy are designed and implemented in a wide range of contexts.

As far as the unit-related data analysis is concerned, one of the topics for Forum 2 is to identify the issues and real-world challenges of ELT in varying contexts. The following data excerpts show various issues and challenges; for example, the local cultures of the students and teachers in certain contexts can be loosely connected with, or rather detached from the English teaching and learning materials.

> In the Saudi context, desires, wants and needs are the main reasons to learn and acquire English. The main challenging issue, in my opinion, is that we don't use our culture to express our ideas and thoughts as the syllabus itself is adapted from different countries such as the UK. For example, when teaching children 'How are you?', the answer must be 'Fine, thank you'. In fact we ask the same question but the answer would be 'Fine, may God bless you' in order to match our local culture. This is how I learnt English. So, I believe that taking the local culture into consideration in teaching English is very important and then exposing the students to different Englishes. (Forum 2 data, by an international student from Saudi Arabia)

The suggestion made by the student in the above excerpt, which is 'taking the local culture into consideration in teaching English is very important and then exposing the students to different Englishes', shows how a holistic approach works in such a context, in that local cultures should be incorporated into the curriculum to reflect the local experiences of the students and the teachers.

Another real-world challenge is to view the 'strong influence' of a 'native-speaker model' on people's mindsets critically; for example, a domestic student from Australia has articulated such a challenge in the Australian context in one of the Forum 1 discussions:

> I think that one of the challenging issues of EIL in many ELT contexts is convincing people that teaching EIL is a worthwhile endeavour. Despite the ever increasing internationalisation of English, the native speaker model is still very prominent in many contexts and has a strong influence on people's mindsets. If educational boards, teachers, parents and students themselves wish to have students learn to speak like a 'native speaker', then schools may struggle to get the political, financial, educational and social support to implement EIL pedagogy into ELT classrooms. (Forum 1 data, by a domestic student from Australia)

It is commonly understood that 'native-speakerism' has been prevalent and resilient due to historical, economic and political reasons, as well as the globalization of popular culture and ubiquitous social media communication. British English and American English still dominate ELT industries across the world, particularly in East Asia and the Asia-Pacific region. The suggestion here is to make people aware of the side-effects of native-speakerism, and manage to change people's mindsets from native-speakerism to the WE paradigm or an EIL pedagogy. This can be a joint effort made holistically among researchers, teachers and learners, as well as language-in-education policymakers and other stakeholders of ELT.

Revisiting and reconceptualizing ELT curriculum, pedagogy and assessment to align with the paradigm shift from English to Englishes

It is apparent that the demographics of English language learners, teachers and users are changing, alongside the shifting and super-diverse multicultural contexts. Traditionally, British English and American English have been adopted unconditionally as the exclusive standard 'native-speaker' English, based on which ELT curriculum, pedagogy and assessment are constructed and implemented. Over the past few decades, new varieties of English have been recognized and codified due to the advanced research in the discipline of WE. Local cultures and norms of English language use have increasingly become relevant to the learners and teachers of English. Therefore, ELT curriculum, pedagogy and assessment need to be revisited and reconceptualized to align with the paradigm shift from English to Englishes.

The students in the postgraduate unit are also aware of the paradigm shift, and its implications for English language teaching and learning. For example:

> To shift from a traditional paradigm to the new paradigm of world Englishes, it is important to provide information for students in any age about expectations of English learners. For example, producing understandable and appropriate sentences is more demanding than producing absolute correct ones. This means a teacher should mention that English has varieties which imply that there is no absolute 'correct' English but appropriate English. In addition, we should also avoid achieving an impractical goal in learning English such as speaking like native speakers. As a result, students can be more confident to speak English without worrying excessively about making mistakes. (Forum 2 data, by an international student from Indonesia)

Another international student has also articulated a major implication of the paradigm shift explicitly.

> In my opinion, one of the major implications of this new paradigm shifting from the traditional pedagogy is that the aim now focuses more on communication and exposure to various cultures, instead of simply learning one of two designated 'standard' dialects (i.e. either General American or RP English). In the World Englishes paradigm, the bastardised variants of English, as well as English spoken by non-native speakers, are all regarded as having equal importance in terms of intercultural interaction and communication. (Forum 2 data, by an international student from Saudi Arabia)

With regard to curriculum, pedagogy and assessment for WE-informed practices, the students have also shared their opinions and experiences. The following data excerpts show how they can be reconceptualized from the students' perspectives, when they reflect on their observed lessons and mini-lesson teaching practices. For example:

> One aspect that we wanted to bring into the lesson was the sharing of culture, as EIL curricula should promote cross cultural awareness, through things such as cross cultural comparison. English is not bound to Anglo-culture, and can be used as a communication tool by any user of English to communicate their own cultures and values. The students' own knowledge, experience and culture are excellent sources of English varieties, cultural conceptualisations and for cultural content in EIL materials, and comparative culture is an effective way of learning to talk about themselves and their own culture. ... It is one of the main goals for EIL to create awareness, sensitivity and respect towards such differences, and materials must be developed to support this. (Portfolio data, by a domestic student from Australia)

The above excerpt shows that the curriculum should be developed with the aim of raising students' 'awareness, sensitivity and respect' towards English varieties and different cultural conceptualizations.

In terms of pedagogy, one of the domestic students, who is an in-service teacher, reflected on his new understanding of 'learner-centredness' in the English language classroom, in terms of the medium of instruction, and his 'personal challenge' of the 'handover' of control to the learners in teaching multicultural learners of English.

> Although my teaching approach is a learner-centred one, the fact that I have up to now insisted on the use of English only in the class ensure that I remain in control at all times. While I have been interested in my learners and have encouraged them to talk about their experiences and cultures, I have always encouraged this in English only. I see now that this approach has been broadly undemocratic, and places me always as the authoritative expert. I suspect my friends would not be surprised to learn that I have been a control freak in the classroom! This lesson then would also be a personal challenge because it required me to handover control to the learners. (Portfolio data, by a domestic student from Australia)

In terms of assessment, students have commented on the relevance of assessment tasks to the students' learning experiences. One of the students suggests, as shown in the excerpt below, that different forms, such as portfolios and projects, as alternative means of assessment, may help allow the learner to 'bring more of their learning to the assessment task':

> I like the idea of portfolios and projects as alternative (or additional?) means of assessment. They avoid the stress and pressure of having to perform on a one-off test, because they take place over a longer period of time, and they are perhaps more likely to show the true capabilities of the learner than the 'snap shot' of a test. Portfolios and projects are also more likely to demonstrate what a learner is capable of in a way that tests may not. ... Portfolios and projects are also more democratic in the sense that

they allow the learner to bring more of their learning to the assessment task. It is also possible that a learner may bring something unexpected (to the Assessor's eye) that is perhaps less likely with one-off, discrete-item tests. (Forum 1 data, by a domestic student from Australia)

The revisit or reconceptualization of ELT practices implies a WE alignment and location-based teaching and learning. Xu (2014: 145–154) suggests that WE curriculum, pedagogy and assessment tasks should be aligned with one another, and that they should be informed by updated theories surrounding the developments of the English language and ELT practices. Tomlinson (2010: 614) proposes a number of criteria for a good test or examination of English, and some of them are also applicable to WE-aligned curriculum and pedagogy, e.g. providing a valuable learning experience for the learners, using the varieties of English and the topic content suitable for the learners, improving and assessing the learners' performance of contextualized communication tasks, and having a positive washback effect on the teaching and learning process.

Raising awareness of the global perspectives and acting locally in teaching English as a glocal (global and local) language

English has become an international language, commonly used as a lingua franca. Such realities should be reflected in ELT practices. Raising awareness of teaching and learning English as a glocal language among the students becomes important, because English is no longer a monolithic language, but has embedded global cultures, norms and perspectives. Both teachers and students in the ELT classroom and beyond should adopt pedagogy and principles that enable them to develop global and local perspectives in association with the teaching, learning and use of English. The following excerpts show students' awareness and how they perceive English in its global and local sense.

> I am glad to have had the opportunity to deliver this lesson within this unit. It feels like I have crossed a threshold. This is my personal experience of the 'paradigm shift'. This is no longer an abstract, academic construct. It is deeply personal and required – forces – me to question ideas and beliefs I had assumed were given, that is, that English should be the only language used in the classroom, that learners should be discouraged from translating as it leads to interference, and that my role as gatekeeper of the language is a noble and worthy one. However, this is a good thing. It is humbling but at the same time invigorating. (Portfolio data, by a domestic in-service teacher student)

With an enhanced awareness of the WE paradigm, students tend to challenge their beliefs and assumptions, such as that English should exclusively be used in the ELT classroom and that students' mother tongues or their mental translation processes during English learning lead to interference. Teaching English as a 'glocal' language helps teachers and students to become more open-minded and knowledgeable about their changing roles as learners, teachers and users of English in multilingual contexts. For example:

> I have felt threatened by EIL. However, the principles of EIL are both local and global. The teacher who knows their learners' L1 has an undoubted advantage in many ways. However, not every teacher will speak the language on every learner. An English classroom in China or Korea, for example, may have a European or African ex-patriot. EIL is about acknowledging, embracing and inviting other languages and cultures into our classrooms. As teachers, we do not have to be masters of all these languages, but we need to be open about our changing roles and to be comfortable that we may not always have the answer. (Portfolio data, by a domestic in-service teacher student)

The following is a compilation of students' views from Forum 1 data and the portfolio reflections data that show their awareness that English is a pluricentric language and that it should be learned and taught as one.

> English represents cultures as long as people speak their own Englishes. (Forum 1 data, by an international student from Japan)

> Sometimes I desire standardisation or the so-called Standard English, but I know for sure there is no consensus on this. (Forum 1 data, by an international student from Indonesia)

> The development of an awareness of language variation is one of the most important principles that need to be considered and developed by teachers and then pass to students as many people travel to different places that present different Englishes. (Portfolio data, by an international student from Saudi Arabia)

> I think it is important for students of English to be aware and familiar with different varieties, but I also think it would be beneficial if all English users have the awareness and respect of the use of different varieties of English. (Forum 1 data, by an international student from China)

> Given the international aspect of English, it is important to educate all users of English about the rich variety of Englishes around the world, not just the traditional 'native speaker' varieties, in order to facilitate good communication between all the English speakers of the world. (Portfolio data, by a domestic student from Australia)

> Having delivered the mini-lesson I believe there may be a place for me at the WE table after all. ... I now feel obliged to respond to the changing sociolinguistic profile of English and to push my professional boundaries. ... The paradigm of WE emphasises the 'inclusivity and pluricentricity in approaches to the linguistics of English worldwide'. Having previously contributed to the othering of English, I now want to be part of the

'one-ness' and 'worldliness' of English that a WE framework can provide. This is my own humble attempt to start thinking globally but acting locally; one class at a time. (Portfolio data, by a domestic in-service teacher student)

Developing new competence for intercultural communication in multicultural contexts

English is no longer solely viewed as a skill, but as a range of varying competences developed and adopted for intercultural communication. ELT has been focusing on the linguistic competence and communicative competence of learners of English. However, with the paradigm shift, new types of competence have been identified in relation to adopting English for intercultural communication. Back in the 1990s, Kachru (1992: 360–361) proposed that teaching WE should reflect the 'changing sociolinguistic profile of English', focusing on 'variety exposure', 'awareness and functional validity', 'contrastive pragmatics' and 'multidimensionality of functions'. In terms of the new requirements for ELT teachers, Kirkpatrick (2007: 195–196) proposes that teachers should have multilingual and multicultural backgrounds or experiences, and that they can serve as an 'appropriate and attainable model' with an understanding of how different varieties of English operate in multilingual and multicultural contexts. In addition, House (2012) has suggested principles of developing intercultural competence to heighten English users' 'pragmatic fluency' and their 'interactional awareness' (House, 2012: 186); in particular, she suggests that ELT should 'provide learners with the linguistic means for realizing their full interpersonal competence, i.e. achieve their own goals and remain polite ... increase speakers' meta-pragmatic knowledge and awareness' (House, 2012: 200). In more recent years, metacultural competence has been proposed for teaching EIL (Sharifian, 2014; Xu, 2017). 'The traditional approaches in ELT that focused on developing fluency in one or two varieties of English no longer prepare learners for facing the sociolinguistic reality of the use of the language in the twenty first century' (Sharifian, 2014: 45). Xu (2017: 711) puts forward three principles, including: (1) acknowledge the paradigm shift in relation to the current use and users of English; (2) anticipate different cultural conceptualizations that are embedded in English when using EIL for intercultural communication; and (3) acquire and accomplish new literacy, proficiency and competence to engage in intercultural communication in EIL.

The following data excerpts from Forum 1 show that students are also aware of the importance of developing new competence for ELT practices.

> I really like the idea of creating space in the classroom to raise awareness to intercultural variation and I especially like the idea of helping students to acquire and practice strategies to help with metacultural competence.

These are skills that should really start in primary and secondary schools. The explication and negotiation strategies are not only important for speakers of different cultures and varieties of English, they are essential life-skills – in the playground, at work, at the bus stop and between governments ... they are essential skills for harmonious day-to-day living! (Forum 1 data, by a domestic student)

In my opinion, by adopting EIL, we can guide and teach the students simultaneously in terms of their cultural awareness and metacultural competence, and therefore the students are not only equipped with communicative competence but also the broad understanding of a wider cultural conceptualization among different English speakers. (Forum 1 data, by an international student from Indonesia)

When being engaged in intercultural communication contexts, competencies such as intercultural communicative competence, multidialectal competence, and meta-cultural competence are all needed in such contexts where different varieties of English are being used and heard. However, the meta-cultural competence is the most important one as it helps interlocutors to negotiate and co-construct meanings in such contexts. (Forum 1 data, by an international student from Oman)

The above data analysis and reflections show that incorporating WE research into ELT has significant implications. The English language has been changing, giving rise to a paradigm shift. New research and theories enable ELT practitioners to engage in new practices in relation to curriculum, pedagogy and assessment. They also enable English language learners and users to engage in ELF communication in local and global contexts more successfully. Two major implications include raising people's awareness of the shifting sociolinguistic profiles of the English language and developing relevant competence for successful intercultural communication in multicultural contexts.

Conclusion

This chapter takes into consideration the paradigm shift from English to Englishes, and it has explored the curriculum, pedagogy and assessment of 'Practices of Teaching Englishes for Intercultural Communication', a unit which is offered in an Australian university to Master's students majoring in applied linguistics. Through a review of the relevant literature and the unit-related data analysis, this chapter offers a number of pedagogical reflections and implications for WE-informed ELT practices. These include: (1) incorporating up-to-date theories and perspectives into ELT practices; (2) adopting a holistic approach for real-world challenges in relation to ELT practices; (3) revisiting and reconceptualizing ELT curriculum, pedagogy and assessment to align with the paradigm shift from English to Englishes; (4) raising awareness of the global perspectives and acting locally in teaching English as a glocal (global and local) language;

and (5) developing new competence for intercultural communication in multicultural contexts.

References

Alsagoff, L., McKay, S.L., Hu, G. and Renandya, W.A. (eds) (2012) *Principles and Practices for Teaching English as an International Language*. New York: Routledge.

Baumgardner, R.J. (2006) Teaching World Englishes. In B.B. Kachru, Y. Kachru and C.L. Nelson (eds) *The Handbook of World Englishes* (pp. 661–679). Malden: Blackwell.

Byram, M. (1989) *Cultural Studies in Foreign Language Education*. Clevedon: Multilingual Matters.

Byram, M. (1997) *Teaching and Assessing Intercultural Communicative Competence*. Clevedon: Multilingual Matters.

Canagarajah, S. (2006) Changing communicative needs, revised assessment objectives: Testing English as an international language. *Language Assessment Quarterly* 3, 229–242.

Chomsky, N. (1965) *Aspects of the Theory of Syntax*. Cambridge, MA: MIT Press.

House, J. (2012) Teaching oral skills in English as a lingua franca. In G. Alsagoff, S. McKay, G. Hu and W.A. Renandya (eds) *Principles and Practices for Teaching English as an International Language* (pp. 186–205). New York: Routledge.

Hymes, De. (1972) On communicative competence. In J.B. Pride and J. Holmes (eds) *Sociolinguistics: Selected Readings* (pp. 269–293). Harmondsworth: Penguin.

Kachru, B.B. (1992) Teaching World Englishes. In B.B. Kachru (ed.) *The Other Tongue: English across Cultures* (2nd edn) (pp. 355–365). Champaign, IL: University of Illinois Press.

Kirkpatrick, A. (2007) *World Englishes: Implications for Intercultural Communication and English Language Teaching*. Cambridge: Cambridge University Press.

Marlina, R. and Giri, R.A. (eds) (2014) *The Pedagogy of English as an International Language: Perspectives from Scholars, Teachers, and Students*. Cham: Springer.

Proshina, Z.G. (2014) Language revolution behind the cultural curtain. *World Englishes* 33 (1), 1–8.

Schneider, E.W. (2014) New reflections on the evolutionary dynamics of world Englishes. *World Englishes* 33 (1), 9–32.

Seargeant, P. (2010) Naming and defining in world Englishes. *World Englishes* 29 (1), 97–113.

Seargeant, P. (2012) *Exploring World Englishes: Language in a Global Context*. New York: Routledge.

Sharifian, F. (2013) Globalisation and developing metacultural competence in learning English as an international language. *Multilingual Education* 3 (7), 1–11.

Sharifian, F. (2014) Teaching English as an international language in multicultural contexts: Focus on Australia. In R. Marlina and R.A. Giri (eds) *The Pedagogy of English as an International Language: Perspectives from Scholars, Teachers, and Students* (pp. 35–46). Cham: Springer.

Sharifian, F. and Jamarani, M. (2013) Language and intercultural communication: From the old era to the new one. In F. Sharifian and M. Jamarani (eds) *Language and Intercultural Communication in the New Era* (pp. 1–19). New York: Routledge.

Tomlinson, B. (2010) Which test of which English and why? In A. Kirkpatrick (ed.) *The Routledge Handbook of World Englishes* (pp. 599–616). New York: Routledge.

Xu, Z. (2010) *Chinese English: Features and Implications*. Hong Kong: Open University of Hong Kong Press.

Xu, Z. (2013) Globalization, culture and ELT materials: A focus on China. *Multilingual Education* 3 (6), 1–19.

Xu, Z. (2014) Teaching and assessing EIL vocabulary in Hong Kong. In R. Marlina and R.A. Giri (eds) *The Pedagogy of English as an International Language: Perspectives from Scholars, Teachers, and Students* (pp. 143–156). Cham: Springer.

Xu, Z. (2017) Developing meta-cultural competence in teaching English as an international language. In F. Sharifian (ed.) *Advances in Cultural Linguistics* (pp. 703–720). Cham: Springer.

11 Reform and Opportunities: China English in Chinese Higher Education

Yue Chen and Cong Zhang

The English language has been involved in Chinese society since the 17th century, and it has been taught in government institutes in China since 1862. From then on, the status of English, along with its educational practices, has been one of the most discussed topics in Chinese society. Especially in the past 50 years, with the Reform and Opening-up Movement in the late 1970s and increasing global exchanges, the English language has developed fast in China, from a banned language in the 1960s to a required foreign language in Chinese higher education in the 21st century. The English language in China is now frequently investigated as China English under the framework of World Englishes. However, questions such as who first proposed the concept of China English, how the concept has been developed in the past decades and how China English affects Chinese higher education still await a clear answer. Therefore, this chapter adopts a historical approach to investigating the development of English education in China by tracing the status of English in different time periods throughout history and reviewing scholars' discussions of China English. It also attempts to help English teachers and scholars visualize how China English has been integrated into China's higher education system from three perspectives: English curriculum, pedagogy and assessment. Pedagogical practices and suggestions for future research are provided at the end.

Introduction

English, widely used in international communication and business exchange, has been involved in Chinese society since the 17th century (Bolton, 2002), and it was first taught in Chinese schools in the 19th century (You, 2010). The status of China English has gained increasing attention in recent World Englishes scholarship (e.g. Fang, 2017a). The idea of World Englishes holds that there is no 'one standard English'; English spoken by native speakers is no longer the norm. Rather, English used in other countries should also be regarded as a legitimized variety of English, such as Indian English, Jamaican English and Singaporean English. Under this framework, English in China has been considered an emerging variety of English (He & Li, 2009; Wang, 1991). With the development of World Englishes over the past decades, scholars in China began to investigate the involvement of China English in Chinese higher education (Wu, 2016), and China English should not be overlooked in China's higher education system given the large number[1] of English language learners in China (Yang, 2006).

Traditional native-norm oriented teaching and assessment in college education does not fulfill the need to cultivate global citizens who use English for cross-cultural communications (Fang, 2017b). Inspired by the development of World Englishes theories, instructors are now beginning to ask questions such as what lesson(s) English instructors in China could learn from World Englishes theories and whether China English is teachable. Researchers are exploring the unique features of China English, and instructors are trying to develop pedagogical tools to integrate China English into their classrooms with both English majors and non-English majors (He & Li, 2009; Lv, 2009). This chapter presents a historical review of the development of English education in China, along with interactions between China English and English education in Chinese colleges and universities.

A Historical Review of English in China's Education System

English has had a long history in China's society and education system. During the past 380 years, the status of English in China has fluctuated with various political and social events as influential factors. Table 11.1 highlights some of the key events and periods in order to portray the development of English in China's education system. These periods will be illustrated in the following paragraphs. For a detailed account of the history of English in China, see Adamson (2004) and Bolton (2003).

China's first contact with the English language occurred in 1637 when four ships under the command of Captain John Weddell arrived in Macao and Guangzhou (Bolton, 2002) and, 200 years later, the Opium War and the treaties signed afterwards became milestones in the spread of English in Mainland China. By that time, Pidgin English was being used not only between the British and local Chinese residents but also among Chinese residents whose dialects were not mutually comprehensible (Cole, 2007). However, the spread of English in China was accompanied by a large amount of resistance on different levels, from peasants to government officials. One of the most significant social/peasant movements was the Taiping Rebellion in the mid-19th century (Adamson, 2004), which discouraged intercultural communication and prevented any further spread

Table 11.1 Major historical events in English entering China's education system

Period	Starting time	Events	Status of English	References
First contact	1637	Four British ships' arrival in China to see the Emperor	No real influence on the use of the English language in China	Bolton, 2002
A more profound early contact	1664	The establishment of a British trading port in Guangzhou	Pidgin English promoted by business contacts	Pride & Liu, 1988
Spread of English	The Opium War	Treaties with the British on their privilege to do business in five trading ports in China	English entering China's society	Gil & Adamson, 2011
Resistance	Mid-19th century	Taiping Rebellion	Spread of English in China prevented	Adamson, 2004; Pepper, 2000
Boosted development	Late 1800s	Self-strengthening Movement	English taught at school; international students sent to foreign countries	Adamson, 2004; Orton, 2009; Teng & Fairbank, 1954
Down times	1949	Establishment of the People's Republic of the China and Cultural Revolution	Russian, rather than English, being emphasized in foreign language teaching	Adamson, 2007; Yao, 1993
Fast development	1978	Reform and Opening-up Movement; Olympic Games in Beijing; Globalization	English learning promoted and respected	Gao, 2012; Gil & Adamson, 2011; Hu, 2005; Wolff, 2010; Xiong, 1982

of the English language in China. After the decade-long resistance to the spread to English in China, scholars and government officials in the Qing Dynasty started to realize the importance of studying foreign languages in order to strengthen their own rule; they provided suggestions for setting up colleges to teach foreign languages. In 1862, *Tongwen Guan* (同文馆) was founded to provide training for foreign languages, and English was the first foreign language taught. As the first foreign language institute established in China, the establishment of *Tongwen Guan* marks the start of formal English education in China. It was also during this period, in 1872, that the Chinese government sent its first group of international students to the United States for a planned 15 years of study (Palm, 2014). Although the plan died mid-way and the students were recalled to China in 1881, these students not only brought home advanced technology but also the communicative tools of the English language. Since then, the English language experienced a boosted development until the establishment of the People's Republic of China (PRC).

On 1 October 1949, the PRC was established; since that time, after which English education in China has gone through various fluctuating stages with ups and downs along the road. Between 1949 and 1955 the PRC Government launched its first Five-Year Plan a national social and economic development plan during which English classes were banned in secondary schools and reduced in universities and colleges. Russian, rather than instead of English, became the main foreign language taught at all levels. In the early 1950s, English was rarely found in the school curriculum in China (Adamson, 2004, 2007). Especially after the Korean War broke out in mid-1950, English was recognized as an enemy language, since America became China's direct opponent on the Korean battlefields. During the Korean War, a nationwide anti-America movement was launched in China, and the English language was almost completely excluded from Chinese people's lives and the Chinese educational system.

The already weakened status of English education became even worse during the Cultural Revolution between 1966 and 1976. During the Cultural Revolution, English education was on the verge of extinction. College entrance exams ceased, and only a few universities still maintained English courses. The content of these courses was about cultivating communist servants. For example, one of the lessons in the university English textbook was about worshipping Chairman Mao Zedong, the first Chairman of the PRC. During the Cultural Revolution, students had to spend more time in factories and thus spent less time studying English. English by that time was taught in order to serve the communist government, and all of the textbooks and teaching materials were developed locally by native Chinese speakers. Foreign films, books and broadcasts were all banned during the Cultural Revolution (Yao, 1993). English was associated with Western bourgeoisie, and people who spoke foreign languages were investigated as potential foreign spies.

After the Cultural Revolution came the historically significant Reform and Opening-up Movement in China. The new paramount leader in China, Deng Xiaoping, called for economic modernization and emphasized the learning of English as 'the touchstone for getting ahead' (Xiong, 1982: 275). Due to the open economic policy, an increasing number of foreign companies and investors came to China to look for opportunities. English was no longer seen as an enemy language or the representation of Western bourgeoisie; instead, English became a label of internationalization and modernization. It is also during this post-Cultural Revolution era that college education was resumed with English as an independent major in Chinese higher education. By the early 1980s, English courses were taught in different types of schools and in different ways (Hu, 2005). For example, English major students usually spent four years at universities with 16–18 class sessions per week devoted to different English courses, such as reading, speaking, writing, literature and linguistics, and for non-English majors in arts and sciences, English was a required subject for two years with four class sessions every week (Xiong, 1982). By the end of the 20th century, English education in Chinese universities and colleges had recovered from the Cultural Revolution and became systematic. English was brought back to the higher education system, in planned curricula, national exams and classroom teaching in China (see Adamson & Morris, 1997, for more details).

The development of English education in China in the 21st century demonstrates the changes in the status of English in China from an educational tool to a representation of China's international stature, especially because of China's hosting of various international events. On 13 July 2011, Beijing, the capital of China, was announced as the host of the 2008 Olympic Games. In the preparation for the Olympics, China experienced an 'English fever' (Wolff, 2010: 53), when the government unprecedentedly supported both formal and informal education in English (Gao, 2012). Roughly 90,000 taxi drivers in Beijing learned English in preparation for the Summer Olympic Games (Beijing 2008), and approximately 600,000 residents of the city in total have taken English courses or learned some everyday English since then.

During the first 10 years of the 21st century, English began to hold an instrumental function in both formal and informal education systems in China (Gil & Adamson, 2011). English was taught at different academic levels from kindergarten to graduate programs, with an increasing popularity in both public education systems and private language schools. At that time, to encourage the study of English at post-secondary levels, the Ministry of Education required that all non-English major students pass the College English Test Band Four (CET-4) in order to get their degrees. University students were encouraged to pass CET-6 for better job opportunities, such as, employment in international companies (Lam, 2002). For English majors, there is another equivalent national standardized test – the Test for English Majors (TEM). English majors were required to pass TEM Band Four (TEM-4) to graduate, and they were also encouraged to take TEM Band Eight (TEM-8) for better job opportunities. Although CET-4 or TEM-4 is no longer a graduation requirement for college students in some universities, passing these standardized tests is still considered an indication of English mastery by many Chinese students and teachers. In addition to the national standardized tests on English proficiency, the English language was also suggested as the medium of instruction in some subjects in China's higher education. In September 2001, the Ministry of Education issued curricula suggesting that all universities and colleges use English as the medium of instruction for information technology, biotechnology, finance, foreign trade, economics and law (Gil & Adamson, 2011; Gill, 2003). These top-down policies from the government made English education one of the most important subjects in higher education in China for both English majors and non-English majors. English has become the most popularly taught and researched foreign language in China, and Chinese scholars started to investigate the English used by Chinese speakers in order to develop the concept of China English.

Contextualizing China English

Along with the wide spread of English in China, the features of the Chinese variety of English started to draw scholars' attention for analysis. Research on English in China started in the mid-1960s (Han, 2007), and it is from the late 1970s onwards that scholars began to distinguish between China English and Chinglish (Xu, 2017). Chuangui Ge was the first to use 'China English' in publications. Ge (1980) argued that when translating expressions that are unique in China into English, the words used in the translation should not be called Chinese English or Chinglish, but China English. Examples of such expressions include '四书' (Four Books), '五经' (Five Classics), '八股文' (eight-legged essay), '人民公社' (people's commune) and '四个现代化' (four modernizations). Although Ge did not provide a specific definition for China English, it can be inferred that Ge used China English to refer to the lexis expressing concepts that are unique in China. Almost one decade later, Huang (1988) first suggested the concept of '汉化英语' ('*Han Hua Ying Yu*', which literally means 'Chinesized English'); later, in 1991, he confirmed that '汉化英语' could be the Chinese translation of 'China English'. Huang defined *Han Hua Ying Yu* as 'Chinese-colored English which is correct, has Chinese characteristics, fits Chinese way of thinking and civilization, and enriches English through Chinese way of thinking and civilization' (Huang, 1991: 88). The 1980s mark the beginning of Chinese scholars' explicit investigation into China English.

China English was been defined and discussed by multiple scholars during the 1990s. In 1991, Rongpei Wang defined China English as

'English used in China by Chinese people, taking standard English as its core, and having Chinese characteristics' (Wang, 1991: 3). He was acknowledged as the first to define 'China English' (Du & Jiang, 2001; Jia, 2013; Jia & Xiang, 1997; Li, 1993). Wang's definition is one of the most frequently cited early definitions of China English. Addressing the user population and the interaction between Standard English and the Chinese varieties, this definition functions as a starting point where other definitions began to develop. Wang (1991) was also the first to describe explicitly why English in China should be called 'China English' instead of 'Chinese English' and 'Chinglish': 'Since "Chinese English" has already been considered to have derogatory connotation, while "Chinglish" is obviously regarded as bad English … we might as well name it "China English" that may not denote negative meaning' (Wang, 1991: 4). Since then, scholars (e.g. Eaves, 2011; He & Li, 2009; Henry, 2010) have suggested that Chinglish should be perceived as a term loaded with social stigma that it is not welcomed in China, while Chinese English is identified as an interlanguage that needs to be improved.

A couple of years later, Wang's definition was refined by Li (1993). Li (1993) argued against Wang's (1991) definition on two points: first, China English is 'used in China by Chinese people' (Li, 1993: 3); secondly, China English takes 'standard English' as its core. According to Li, China English was not only English used in China by Chinese people; rather, it could also be used outside China. Li also stated that the term 'standard English' was tricky in itself because there was no such thing as 'standard English'. Therefore, Li proposed a new definition for China English:

> China English takes normative English[2] as its core, expresses the unique things in Chinese society and culture through transliteration, borrowing, and semantic regeneration, yet is neither interfered nor influenced by the Chinese language. China English is mainly constituted by transliterated words, borrowing words, and its unique syntactic and discourse patterns. (Li, 1993: 19)

Li's definition of 'China English' can be considered a milestone in the definition and research of China English because, for the first time, into the definition of China English was added the existence of its unique syntactic and discoursal features. This is recognized as an important aspect of the definition by many scholars later on.

Despite the aforementioned popularity and wide citation of Li's definition of 'China English' (Du & Jiang, 2001; Gao, 2006; Han, 2007; He & Li, 2009; Jia, 2013; Jia & Xiang, 1997), the definition was not accepted without criticism. For example, Xie (1995) criticized Li's (1993: 19) definition on the grounds that '"China English" is neither interfered nor influenced by the Chinese language'. Xie (1995) argued that English in China would unavoidably be interfered with and influenced by Chinese language and culture, which provide English with Chinese characteristics. Based on that, he described 'China English' as:

> a variety of English used by Chinese people in inter-cultural communication that is interfered and influenced by the Chinese language, way of thinking, and culture. It is based on Standard English and can be used in English communication, but how frequently this variety of English is used in communication and how effective it can be is related to the English proficiency of speakers of this variety of English. (Xie, 1995: 10)

Two key points can be taken from Xie's definition, which are: (1) China English is the result of the Chinese language interfering with English; and (2) only Chinese people can say 'China English' – in other words, if native speakers of English use English to express China-specific things, such expressions should not be considered as 'China English', which echoes Rongpei Wang's (1991) definition.

Several years later, their opinion (Wang, 1991; Xie, 1995) that 'China English' can only be spoken by Chinese people triggered a rebuttal from Jia and Xiang (1997), who argued that it is the first language that influences people's use of English. In other words, whether they are Chinese people or not, as long as they acquired Chinese first, their way of using English will be different from native speakers of English. Therefore, Jia and Xiang came up with a definition for China English as 'English that is used by people who speak Chinese, takes standard English as its core, and has Chinese characteristics that are unavoidable yet beneficial to the spread of Chinese culture' (Jia & Xiang, 1997: 11).

The period from the late 1980s to the late 1990s witnessed a heated discussion about the definition of 'China English'. Besides polishing the definition of China English, scholars (e.g. Li, 1993) also discussed the choice of terminology between China English and Chinese English. Li (1993) offered one of the most popular definitions of China English, but he was hesitant to use the term 'China English' and felt that 'using "China English" seems not safe enough' (Li, 1993: 19), because 'in English, "noun + English" is usually used to refer to the varieties that are inferior to legitimized ones, e.g. Hong Kong English. Standard varieties of English are usually named as "adjective + English" such as British English, American English, and Australian English' (Li, 1993: 19). Xu (2017) also suggests the use of 'Chinese English' to describe the variety of English used in China. However, Li (1993) decided to use 'China English' in the end, probably because he recognized that 'people have thought of "Chinese English" to denote negative meaning' (Li, 1993: 19). At present, the majority of scholars investigating this Chinese variety of English use the term China English for similar reasons. The various debates on the terminology and definition of China English have prompted more scholars to join in with this research in the 21st century.

Scholars have found more common ground with one another and most definitions contain two common elements – 'based on standard English' and 'have Chinese characteristics'.

In 2003, Jin defined China English as:

> English that takes international normative English as its core, expresses the culture, ideology, and tradition that are unique in China through transliteration, borrowing, and semantic regeneration as well as China-specific expressions such as Chinese-flavored lexis, sentences, and way of writing. (Jin, 2003: 66–67)

In 2004, Zhang described China English by pinpointing its main features:

> (1) China English expresses China-specific things that do not have counterparts in native English; (2) mainly serves the purpose of exporting Chinese culture in international communication and the communicators are mainly people who use English as their tool of communication and are from different cultural backgrounds; and (3) follows the rules and conventions of standard English and takes into consideration the way of thinking and cultural backgrounds of speakers of standard English. (Zhang, 2004: 74)

This is the first time that the features of China English were clarified, followed by Gao (2006).

Gao (2006) described the features of China English in a more detailed way:

> (1) China English is the product of English globalization and nativization; (2) has the ownership of English, and is one important part of World Englishes; (3) is a standard and reasonable performance variety; (4) can reflect the characteristics of Chinese society and culture; (5) has two main functions – is used both in international communication and in intranational areas such as economy, international business, diplomacy, politics, science and technology, tourism and media; and (6) can be seen mainly from the lexical, sentential and discoursal level, among which lexical characteristics are the most prevalent and obvious; lies in the combination of phonology, lexis, and semantics. (Gao, 2006: 59)

Gao's description of the characteristics of China English, for the first time, makes it explicit that China English is a performance variety of English. Comparing the two descriptions of Zhang (2004) and Gao (2006), it can be seen that while Zhang (2004) described China English as being mainly used internationally, Gao (2006) added that it could also be used intranationally. This is a step forward in the research into China English.

A more recent and more comprehensive definition of China English came from He and Li (2009). After investigating the linguistic features of China English, they defined China English as:

> a performance variety of English which has the standard Englishes as its core but is colored with characteristic features of Chinese phonology, lexis, syntax, and discourse pragmatics, and which is particularly suited for expressing content ideas specific to Chinese culture through such means as transliteration and loan translation. (He & Li, 2009: 83)

In their widely cited article, four sets of linguistic features were identified and analyzed, as shown in Table 11.2. Their analysis of the linguistic features in China English triggered heated discussions as to how China English differs from other Englishes linguistically: some scholars mention phonology, lexis, spelling and grammar (Wang, 1991); some present characteristics in lexis, syntax and discourse (Kirkpatrick & Xu, 2002; Li, 1993; Xie, 1995; Xu, 2010); and others describe the phonological, lexical and discourse patterns (Du & Jiang, 2001; He & Li, 2009; Jiang et al., 2003).

Despite its distinct linguistic features, it is still questionable whether China English is a full member of the World Englishes family or still in its infancy (see Yang & Zhang, 2015). Since China English has not received full recognition by Chinese speakers of English (Fang, 2016), it is being studied as a performance variety with a noticeable number of studies on college students' attitudes towards China English. For example, Edwards' (2017) survey results show that Chinese students in Hong Kong are showing a more positive attitude towards China English, but they are still more willing to accept it than to speak it themselves. Similar conflicted and

Table 11.2 Linguistic features in China English

Phonological features	Lexical features	Syntactic features	Discourse pragmatic features
• Replacement of /θ/ with [s] and /ð/ with [d]; • Insertion of final [ə]; • General lack of voiced fricatives; • Certain types of diphthong simplification; • Avoidance of weak forms for function words; and • A tendency to pronounce multisyllabic words or word groups with syllable-timing.	• Transliteration; • Loan translation or calque.	• Idioms made up of four morphosyllables; • Parallel structure; • Topicalization of adjuncts; • The null subject parameter.	• Inductive writing; • Use of patterns of discourse.

Source: Developed by He and Li (2009).

complicated attitudes are also seen in He and Li (2009: 85), where the majority of both students and teachers of college English in China prefer an 'exonormative' model of English as the teaching model. Such contradictory attitudes indicate that China English is still in its development stage as a member of World Englishes, and should not be treated as a fully localized variety of English in education settings.

Even though different scholars disagree about the specific linguistic features of China English and hold different attitudes towards it, such a historical review and analysis of the current scholarship show that the development of the English language in China can be traced in three stages, which are Chinese Pidgin English (CPE), Chinese English as an interlanguage, and China English (CE) as a developing variety of English (Ge, 1983; Li, 1993; Wei & Fei, 2003). Although China English is still a developing variety of English, its existence should not be overlooked and should be revealed in the educational system in China. After identifying the developing stages of China English, scholars began to explore the practical sphere of this concept in order to apply this concept to the Chinese education system.

China English in English Education

A careful look at the linguistic features of China English and the history of English education in China helps instructors and scholars to visualize how China English can be included in China's higher education system. Despite the common agreement among Chinese scholars that China English is an inevitable and unarguable fact (Li, 2008), integrating China English into Chinese higher education is still a challenge. Most English teachers in Chinese universities are unfamiliar with the concept of China English. Li (2008) argues that even for scholars and professors in China who have heard of the term China English, the differences between Pidgin English, Chinglish, Chinese English and China English are not explicitly clear, which may cause the conscious or unconscious avoidance of including China English in their teaching. Another problem identified in the literature is the lack of representation of Chinese culture in current college English curricula, where the emphasis is still on the culture of inner circle countries (e.g. He & Li, 2009). Therefore, the integration of China English could come from three aspects: English curriculum, pedagogy and assessment.

Curriculum

To involve China English in the English curriculum in China's English education is not easy. From the very beginning of English's involvement in Chinese education, the concept of native norms has been rooted in the system. Most teaching materials widely adopted in China only discuss American and British cultures with a few addressing cultures in other inner circle countries, such as Australia, New Zealand and Canada. Few textbooks or materials cover the discussion of Chinese culture in English. Cong (2000) points out that there is an unbalanced coverage of cultural aspects in English teaching across different levels in China: much attention is given to English-speaking world, with little attention given to Chinese culture. This underrepresentation may come from teachers' misunderstanding of intercultural communication, where teachers focus too much on the import of Western cultures while ignoring the export of Chinese culture in the interaction with people from all over the world.

The initial attempt to invite China English into English classrooms in China is to acknowledge the legitimacy of China English in the educational curriculum. Jia and Xiang (1997) suggest that the existence of China English should be fully acknowledged before decisions are made on what features are inevitable or helpful for students' progress and what should be overcome or avoided in the students' learning. The goal of English language teaching in terms of cultural aspects in the era of World Englishes should include an understanding of other cultures, an expression of learners' own culture, and the teaching of English as an international language (Li, 2008). The emphasis in curriculum is no longer merely on the linguistic features of standard English, but rather to cultivate international communicators. This shift of emphasis will help release the tension between a high standard of native-like proficiency and the students' struggle to achieve it, and will also bring instructors to realize the legitimacy of China English.

After acknowledging the necessity of including China English in the Chinese higher education curriculum, scholars, especially scholars in Mainland China, started to develop various methods in order to improve the situation and to increase the involvement of China English in Chinese universities. One suggestion that is widely discussed in the existing literature is with regard to textbooks. Feng (2009) suggested that college English textbooks should include texts from a large variety of genres produced by writers from different language/culture backgrounds, especially texts produced by Chinese writers or writing about Chinese culture. Du (1998) also suggests the inclusion of diverse materials, such as English works produced by Chinese scholars, translated works from Chinese to English, and English-speaking scholars' works on China and/or Chinese culture. Wen (2016) provided two textbook examples: *New Standard College English* and *iEnglish*. Both textbooks, published by Foreign Language Teaching and Research Press, introduce diverse culture topics, cultivating students' multicultural competence. Including texts on Chinese culture, both traditional and current, can help increase students' sense of ownership over the English language, raise their awareness of the existence of China English, and facilitate their learning of English because of their increase in confidence and culture identity.

Another suggestion to enhance the curriculum for teaching China English is teacher training. Equipping teachers with a knowledge of China English is of vital importance. The focus should be on drawing the boundaries of World Englishes, which means informing in-service teachers about what World Englishes can bring and what it cannot. The conflict between the descriptive nature of World Englishes and the prescriptive nature of teaching is actually more about opportunities than about tension. As is suggested in the existing literature, Chinese scholars are aware of the existence of China English and the necessity of its inclusion in the college English curriculum, so the question becomes figuring out practical tools teachers can use in their own classrooms (Lv, 2009; Shen, 2012; Yan & He, 2010). These practical tools, along with World Englishes theories, should be introduced to teachers at the same time.

Pedagogy

As regards classroom pedagogies, much of the literature on China English includes a detailed discussion on pedagogical approaches and classroom activities. Such discussions prepare both pre- and in-service teachers for a classroom with the presence of China English not only as the production of students but also as part of the teaching materials. Wen (2012) provides a pedagogical model for the teaching of English as an international language, which encourages teachers to balance linguistic, cultural and pragmatic components in their teaching. This model details what to teach and what to expect from students, and can serve as an example for practitioners who want to include China English in their classrooms. Cultural sensitivity, tolerance and flexibility are to be achieved under this model. Similarly, Nuske (2017) advocates the multilingual-normative approach to helping English language learners increase their tolerance towards variation across performed varieties of English. Such an approach centers instruction on the specific performative purpose that English serves in learners' linguistic resources. In teaching Chinese college students, a largely linguistic-homogeneous student population, teachers could have students participate in internet-mediated collaborative projects with peers who speak other English varieties. Instructors, in this case, would help students realize how mutual understanding can be achieved through various communicative strategies such as negotiation and accommodation.

Specific suggestions include the use and teaching of China English vocabulary in college English classrooms (Feng, 2009; Shen, 2012). As was described in the previous section on curriculum, such vocabulary can serve as a starting point to introduce the concept of China English to students and encourage them to view China English through a positive lens. The teaching of China English expressions can go beyond traditional cultural practices in China, such as '风水' (fengshui) and '四书五经' (Four Books and Five Classics). Including expressions about modern cultural practices in China like '改革开放' (reform and opening up), '一国两制' (one country, two systems) and '一带一路' (One Belt, One Road) in the teaching will also help students and teachers better prepare themselves for the use of China English in an equal communication with English users from other countries. It provides students with language they can use to talk about their own cultures and their own Englishes.

Another suggestion for classroom activities is from Lv (2009), who suggests that teachers should have the courage to teach China English. Instead of always teaching students how the British talk in Great Britain or how Americans talk in the United States, teachers could also show students how communication emerges in English with both Chinese and non-Chinese in China to show them how the language is used in real communication in international business or sports interviews. With careful guidance in these activities, students will be able to produce their language and to express their own ideas and thoughts in English, rather than to merely memorize the paragraphs in textbooks. Including China English in the classroom will provide students with the opportunities and courage to practice what they have learned and make progress in mastering the language.

Assessment

Another area that can be tackled in order to involve China English in the Chinese education system is assessment. Under the World Englishes framework, teachers are expected to be tolerant of students' language mistakes since some of the mistakes may be a variation of the students' own English (Lv, 2009). From a World Englishes perspective, all language learners have the right to use their own languages, and the varieties they use should be respected. For example, when responding to students' use of non-standard English, teachers could ask them to explain what they mean and help them find the expressions that are the most proper in a given context, instead of correcting all the 'mistakes' students make without showing them other options they could take in different linguistic contexts. While teaching students the expected or academically acceptable English needed to pass standardized tests, it is suggested that instructors should be aware of the students' use of their own varieties of English. In other words, we could equip the learners with the idea that they are successful multicompetent speakers rather than failed native speakers by acknowledging their own power and the rights of their own languages (Cook, 1999). Through communication and negotiation, instructors will be able to keep a balance between teaching the standard English that is more commonly used in a given discourse community and helping the students maintain their own identity through the language they use.

Therefore, the goal of assessment in English classrooms should be to help students decide which English(es) to use in specific situation(s), rather than to test whether the learners represent native norms in their use of English. For example, Fang (2015, 2017b) suggests some assessment tasks based on an approach called ToPIC (Teaching of Pronunciation for Intercultural Communication). These tasks are designed to focus on various linguistic skills beyond grammatical correctness, and these performative activities target accommodation strategies and communication skills. Such tasks will not only enable language learners to realize the importance of their own cultural and linguistic background, but will also help direct language educators' attention away from what the students are lacking and towards what they are capable of. This form of assessment opens up opportunities for China English to be included in the education system and to be valued as an element to be taught and researched by scholars in China.

Conclusion: Recommendations for Future Research

The large number of English language learners and the long history of English-Chinese interactions make the implementation of China English in Chinese higher education interesting and challenging at the same time. However, this tension, when viewed from the World Englishes perspective, is more an opportunity for Chinese scholars and students to establish themselves in international communication than an obstacle to learning the English language. Scholars have investigated the linguistic features of China English, examined students and instructor's attitudes towards China English in higher education, and suggested feasible pedagogical tools to include China English in college classrooms.

Future research is needed on the theoretical foundation of China English since there is still some debate as to whether or not China English falls under the paradigm of World Englishes, given that it has not yet been fully localized. Such theoretical development could also contribute to the development of English as a foreign language (EFL) theories and World Englishes theories because China has the largest EFL learner population in the world and China is increasing its involvement in global exchanges. In addition, the investigation of pedagogical tools to teach China English to Chinese students can help promote the learning and teaching of English in the Chinese context in a more effective and culturally meaningful way. Instruction focusing on performance will facilitate fluent communication between Chinese speakers of English and speakers of English from other countries, and pedagogical inspirations from the Chinese context can help with the development of pedagogical tools in other EFL contexts. The rich context of Chinese higher education, the ongoing reform and debate, as well as the continuous exploration of China English all contribute to the scholarship and pedagogy of English in Chinese universities and colleges.

Notes

(1) According to a recent estimate (Wei & Su, 2012), a total of 390 million people in China had learned English as a foreign language.
(2) According to Li (1993: 19), normative English referred to 'English that follows the common rules of English, and is intelligible to and accepted by native speakers of English'.

References

Adamson, B. (2004) *China's English: A History of English in Chinese Education*. Hong Kong: Hong Kong University Press.
Adamson, B. (2007) Depoliticisation in the English curriculum. In A. Feng (ed.) *Bilingual Education in China: Practices, Policies, and Concepts* (pp. 34–48). Clevedon: Multilingual Matters.
Adamson, B. and Morris, P. (1997) The English curriculum in the People's Republic of China. *Comparative Education Review* 41 (1), 3–26.
Bolton, K. (2002) Chinese Englishes: From Canton jargon to global English. *World Englishes* 21, 181–199.
Bolton, K. (2003) *Chinese English: A Sociolinguistic History*. Cambridge: Cambridge University Press.
Cole, S. (2007) *The Functionalist Account of English in China: A Sociolinguistic History*. See http://homes.chass.utoronto.ca/~cpercy/courses/eng6365-cole.htm.
Cong, C. (2000) '中国文化失语':我国英语教学的缺陷 [Chinese culture deficiency: Weaknesses in English teaching in China]. *Guangming Daily*, 19 October.
Cook, V. (1999) Going beyond the native speaker in language teaching. *TESOL Quarterly* 33, 185–209.
Du, Z. (1998) 中国英语问题及其他 [Issues of China English and others]. *Foreign Language Education* 19 (3), 6–14.
Du, R. and Jiang, Y. (2001) 近二十年'中国英语'研究述评 ['China English' in the past 20 years]. *Foreign Language Teaching and Research* 33 (1), 37–41.
Eaves, M. (2011) English, Chinglish or China English? *English Today* 27 (4), 64–70.
Edwards, J.G.H. (2017) China English: Attitudes, legitimacy, and the native speaker construct: Is China English becoming accepted as a legitimate variety of English? *English Today* 33 (2), 38–45.
Fang, F. (2015) An investigation of attitudes towards English accents at a Chinese university. Unpublished doctoral thesis, University of Southampton.
Fang, F. (2016) 'Mind your local accent': Does accent training resonate to college students' English use? *Englishes in Practice* 3 (1), 1–28.
Fang, F. (2017a) World Englishes or English as a lingua franca: Where does English in China stand? An ideological negotiation and attitudinal debate of the use and function of English in the Chinese context. *English Today* 33 (1), 19–24.
Fang, F. (2017b) English as a lingua franca: Implications for pedagogy and assessment. *TEFLIN Journal* 28 (1), 57–70.
Feng, W. (2009) 大学英语教材中'中国英语'特色的建设 [Building China English in college English textbooks]. *Theory and Practice of Education* 29 (8), 43–45.
Gao, C. (2006) 世界英语理论与中国英语研究综述 [World Englishes theory and the study of China English]. *Foreign Language Teaching Abroad* 4, 55–60.
Gao, S. (2012) The biggest English corner in China. *English Today* 28 (3), 34–39.
Ge, C. (1980) 漫谈由汉译英问题 [On problems in Han-English translation]. *Chinese Translators Journal* 2, 1–8.
Ge, C. (1983) *Translation Theory and Translation Skills*. Beijing: China Translation Publishing.
Gil, J. and Adamson, B. (2011) The English language in Mainland China: A sociolinguistic profile. In A. Feng (ed.) *English Language Education Across Greater China* (pp. 23–45). Bristol: Multilingual Matters.
Gill, S.K. (2003) Medium-of-instruction policy in higher education in Malaysia: Nationalism versus internationalization. In J.W. Tollefson and A.B.M. Tsui (eds) *Medium of Instruction Policies: Which Agenda? Whose Agenda?* (pp. 135–152). Mahwah, NJ: Lawrence Erlbaum.
Han, L. (2007) '中国英语'研究现状分析 [An analysis of current research on China English]. *Foreign Languages and Their Teaching* 223 (10), 28–32.

He, D. and Li, D. (2009) Language attitudes and linguistic features in the 'China English' debate. *World Englishes* 28 (1), 70–89.

Henry, E.S. (2010) Interpretations of 'Chinglish': Native speakers, language learners and the enregisterment of a stigmatized code. *Language in Society* 39, 669–688.

Hu, G. (2005) English language education in China: Policies, progress, and problems. *Language Policy* 4 (1), 5–24.

Huang, J. (1988) 应当肯定'西译汉化'现象的积极面 – 兼论'汉化英语'的出现和发展 [The goodness of Chinesenization in Chinese-English translation – The emergence and development of Chinesenized English]. *Chinese Translators Journal* 1, 39–47.

Huang, J. (1991) 再论《应当肯定'西译汉化'现象的积极面》– 兼答周式中同志 [A further discussion on 'The goodness of Chinesenization in Chinese-English translation']. *Foreign Language Teaching* 12 (3), 87–90.

Jia, G. (2013) 中国英语再研究 [A restudy of China English]. *Contemporary Foreign Language Studies* 3, 8–13.

Jia, G. and Xiang, Y. (1997) 为中国英语一辩 [Defending China English]. *Foreign Languages and Their Teaching* 101 (5), 11–12.

Jiang, Y., Du, R. and Wang, H. (2003) 有关"中国英语"的问题 – 对"中国英语'质疑"一文的回应 [On 'China English' – A response to 'Addressing queries on China English']. *Foreign Language Education* 24 (1), 27–35.

Jin, H. (2003) 中国英语与中式英语讨论 [A discussion on China English and Chinglish]. *Journal of Guangdong Polytechnic Normal University* 5, 66–70.

Kirkpatrick, A. and Xu, Z. (2002) Chinese pragmatic norms and 'China English'. *World Englishes* 21, 269–279.

Lam, A. (2002) English in education in China: Policy changes and learners' experiences. *World Englishes* 21, 245–256.

Li, H. (2008) China English and college English teaching and learning. *Journal of Jiangxi Institute of Education (Social Sciences)* 29 (1), 47–48.

Li, W. (1993) China English and Chinglish. *Foreign Language Teaching and Research* 4, 18–24.

Lv, L. (2009) '中国英语'对高校英语跨文化教学的启示 [China English's implication on cross-cultural instruction in Chinese higher education]. *China Adult Education* 10, 155–156.

Nuske, K. (2017) 'I mean I'm kind of discriminating my own people': A Chinese TESOL graduate student's shifting perceptions of China English. *TESOL Quarterly* 52, 360–390.

Orton, J. (2009) English and the Chinese quest. In J. Lo Bianco, J. Orton and G. Yihong (eds) *China and English: Globalization and the Dilemmas of Identity* (pp. 79–97). Bristol: Multilingual Matters.

Palm, D. (2014) Learning the 'superior techniques of the barbarians': China's self-strengthening movement. In D.C. Chau and T.M. Kane (eds) *China and International Security: History, Strategy, and 21st-century Policy* (pp. 39–58). Santa Barbara, CA: ABC-CLIO.

Pepper, S. (2000) *Radicalism and Education Reform in 20th-century China: The Search for an Ideal Development Model*. Cambridge: Cambridge University Press.

Pride, J.B. and Liu, R. (1988) Some aspects of the spread of English in China since 1949. *International Journal of the Sociology of Language* 1988 (74), 41–70.

Shen, Y. (2012) 世界英语语境中中国英语的客观存在及其对高校英语教学的启示 [The existence of China English in the World Englishes framework and its implications for English education in universities]. *Education Exploration* 257 (11), 63–64.

Teng, S. and Fairbank, J. (1954) *Research Guide for China's Response to the West: A Documentary Survey, 1839–1923*. Cambridge, MA: Harvard University Press.

Wang, R. (1991) 中国英语是个客观存在 [China English is an objective reality]. *Journal of PLA Foreign Languages Institute* 1, 1–8.

Wei, R. and Su, J. (2012) The statistics of English in China: An analysis of the best available data from government sources. *English Today* 28 (3), 10–14.
Wei, Y. and Fei, J. (2003) Using English in China. *English Today* 19 (4), 42–47.
Wen, Q. (2012) 英语国际语的教学框架 [A pedagogical model for the teaching of English as an international language]. *Curriculum, Teaching Material and Method* 32 (1), 77–81.
Wen, Q. (2016) Teaching culture(s) in English as a lingua franca in Asia: Dilemma and solution. *Journal of English as a Lingua Franca* 5 (1), 155–177.
Wolff, M. (2010) China's English mystery – the views of a China 'foreign expert'. *English Today* 26 (4), 53–56.
Wu, J. (2016) Retrospection and expectation: A review on studies of China English. *US-China Education Review* 6, 268–272.
Xie, Z. (1995) 中国英语：跨文化语言交际中的干扰性变体 [China English: Interference variety in cross-culture communication]. *Modern Foreign Languages* 70 (4), 7–11.
Xiong, Z.B. (1982) The forum: Further comments on English education in China. *TESOL Quarterly* 16, 273–277.
Xu, Z. (2010) Chinese English: A future power? In A. Kirkpatrick (ed.) *The Routledge Handbook of World Englishes* (pp. 282–298). New York: Routledge.
Xu, Z. (2017) Researching Chinese English: A meta-analysis of Chinese scholarship on Chinese English research. In Z. Xu, D. He and D. Deterding (eds) *Researching Chinese English: The State of the Art* (pp. 235–266). Cham: Springer.
Yan, Y. and He, S. (2010) '中国英语'视角下的大学英语 [College English under the China English perspective]. *Theory and Practice* 12, 106–108.
Yang, C. and Zhang, L.J. (2015) China English in trouble: Evidence from dyadic teacher talk. *System* 51, 39–50.
Yang, J. (2006) Learners and users of English in China. *English Today* 22 (2), 3–10. doi:10.1017/S0266078406002021
Yao, X. (1993) Foreign languages in Chinese higher education. *Language Learning Journal* 7 (1), 74–77.
You, X. (2010) *Writing in the Devil's Tongue: A History of English Composition in China*. Chicago, IL: Southern Illinois University Press.
Zhang, Y. (2004) 谈标准英语, 中国英语和中式英语 [A study of Standard English, China English and Chinese English]. *Journal of Jimei University* 5 (1), 72–77.

12 Global Englishes-oriented English Language Education

Handoyo Puji Widodo and Fan (Gabriel) Fang

The development of English as a global language (EGL) has provoked lively and ongoing debates as to how we shall view English from a critical ecological perspective. What we mean by a critical ecological perspective is that we have to observe and recognize the use of English sociopolitically situated in different geographical locations in which English users come from different linguistic and cultural backgrounds. Global Englishes (GE) is an ecological approach that recognizes the use of language in different social and cultural domains in which different languages and cultures coexist. Recent years have witnessed a large number of non-native English speaking users and learners around the globe. This showcases the changing sociolinguistic landscape of English as a global lingua franca (Galloway & Rose, 2018). This also suggests that the ownership of English belongs to anyone who uses this language regardless of their nativeness or *otherness*. With this changing sociolinguistic landscape in mind, the role of English as a second or foreign language becomes outdated and even problematic because speakers of English use this language for different social purposes (e.g. transnational friendship and diplomatic relations) and are educated in different socio-institutional contexts. In addition, non-native speakers of English put much effort into re-appropriating the use of English in different ways that involve their first language/mother tongue as a linguistic resource. The reappropriation of English challenges non-native speakers/users of English to contextualize their English use at sociopragmatic and discoursal levels.

The use of English as a global language, a lingua franca (ELF) and an international language (EIL) and its implications for English language education has been the locus of scholarly discussion and debates in recent years (e.g. Renandya & Widodo, 2016; Widodo *et al.*, 2017). In reality, the number of English learners and teachers in countries where English is seen as an additional language exceeds that of those in countries where English is regarded as a native language or second language. Against this backdrop, issues of language ideology and attitudes towards different linguistic and discoursal aspects of the English language, linked to English language policy, curriculum, pedagogy and assessment, have emerged. This suggests that critical GE perspectives should be taken into account when language teachers and teacher educators design and enact English language policy, curriculum, pedagogy and assessment in contemporary language education, which should move beyond the native speakerism zone (Holliday, 2006). To keep this in mind, the goal of reframing or recontextualizing English language policy, curriculum, pedagogy and assessment is to help English language learners build and enhance their critical awareness of how the use of English is sociopolitically situated in different sociolinguistic landscapes. Grounded in the critical GE paradigm, we help English learners make a negotiable transition from language learners to language users as well as to recognize their first language or native language not as a hindrance but rather as a resource for building and developing their English language repertoire.

Although the issue of GE has been much discussed and researched in the extant literature, few books and edited volumes are concerned with how English language policy, curriculum, language pedagogy and language assessment are designed and implemented through the lens of GE. One main reason for the lack of research in this area may lie in difficulties in terms of how to design language curricula, teach English and assess learners' English ability from the perspective of GE. Additionally, enmeshed in institutional cultures, many language curriculum designers, language practitioners and assessment designers still have strong beliefs in the ideology of native speakerism. Another reason is that the notion of GE remains underpracticed because of a lack of GE resources for teachers. In order to promote the inclusion of critical GE perspectives in English language education, there is an urgent need for a volume that includes contributions from scholars and language practitioners who are working in different countries with students of different levels of English ability. Therefore, in this edited volume, we emphasize that through a critical GE lens, the use of English in different sociolinguistic situations challenges us as language teachers and teacher educators to rethink what using and learning EGL means to learners who are trying to reach a certain level of English repertoire or to be recognized as competent users of English in today's globalized communities.

This volume focuses on a wider range of contexts and covers language policy, curriculum, pedagogy and the less-researched area of assessment from the GE perspective. Incorporating GE into language policy, curriculum, pedagogy and assessment practices calls for a reframing of our pedagogical practices that takes into account the use of Englishes in intercultural and multicultural encounters where people have different first languages and cultural backgrounds (Fang & Baker, 2018). This edited book provides fresh and critical insight into how GE perspectives are translated into pedagogical practices. It interweaves both theoretical developments and practical guides for language researchers and practitioners in the areas of TESOL and applied linguistics.

Global Englishes-oriented Language Policy, Curriculum, Pedagogy and Assessment: The Road Ahead

Asia is a context where English plays different but key roles in socio-economic mobility and cultural assimilations and has a sociopolitical status in which the use and learning of English have different social motivation orientations (Murata & Jenkins, 2009; Widodo et al., 2017). Although many language ideologies and empirical studies have shown that it is far more complicated to view English simply as a language per se, many people still perceive the importance of English as being attached to their own personal development. For example, people would like to pass international Standard English examinations (e.g. IELTS and TOEFL), pursue an English-medium career and further education, and travel abroad. The critical perspective of GE in the Asian context urges readers to go beyond this volume to think of all the relevant issues addressed therein. However, we also admit that this volume only represents certain contexts in Asia, and we hope that these discussions and debates can be extended to a wider context.

We emphasize that the inclusion of GE in language policy, curriculum, pedagogy and assessment can be a point of departure for re-appropriating our English language education. This is because such elements are the core of language education against the backdrop of globalization today. As regards language policy and curriculum, it is not an easy task to change the current language policy in general, which will in turn lead to reluctance to apply the notion of GE in many language curricula. At present, the idea of incorporating GE into language classrooms has been promoted by some practitioners who have a background knowledge of GE (see D'Angelo, this volume; Xu, this volume). At this stage, we hope that more bottom-up policies will support GE-oriented English language education in multilingual contexts with policies that recognize the importance of GE. With some policies and curricula that promote GE, we believe that GE-oriented education will be implemented in a wider context. Thus, from an educational perspective, the chapters of this edited volume problematize the essentialist view of language use and the dichotomy between the language use by non-native speakers of English and that by native speakers. We recognize an urgent need for enhancing teacher and learner awareness of the sociolinguistically fluid use of English by non-native speakers who are socially nurtured and by native speakers who are biologically endowed with English as their mother tongue or native language. GE-oriented English language education promotes the inclusion of GE as a manifest of linguistic and ecological diversity in language policy, curriculum, pedagogy and assessment. Linguistic and ecological diversity is here defined as a representation of language use by different speakers of English regardless of their nativeness inheritance.

Pedagogically speaking, GE-oriented pedagogy is enacted in Asian settings, as reported in many chapters of this volume. The theory of GE can hardly stand alone without the application of GE-oriented pedagogy, and the issue of how to incorporate GE into language classrooms has been discussed by many scholars, with proposals including Global English Language Teaching (Galloway & Rose, 2018) and Teaching of Pronunciation for Intercultural Communication (Fang, 2016). However, the adoption of GE-oriented pedagogy really depends on whether teachers have pedagogical content knowledge (PCK) of GE, whether they can design a syllabus on their own (this is challenging but critical as it also relates to assessment) and, if so, whether they are willing to translate GE into their own classroom (in many cases, they are aware of GE, but they do not know how to implement a GE-oriented pedagogy). Because language materials shape how language teachers and students engage in in-class and out-of-class activities or tasks, it is of paramount importance for us to design or develop GE-oriented language materials. In this respect, language teachers as materials designers should take into account: (1) GE as guiding theory; (2) authenticity of English use in inner, outer and expanding circle contexts; (3) GE-related topics; (4) GE knowledge and language awareness; (5) GE-oriented assessment in various contexts; and (6) GE awareness-raising tasks or activities. Language teachers as materials designers or developers can also take into account student and teacher prior knowledge and experience. Therefore, introducing the notion of GE to language teachers and learners can be a starting point for implementing GE-oriented language curriculum and materials.

The biggest gap in GE in terms of English language education probably lies in language assessment, with few proposals for GE-informed assessment methods. To our knowledge and observation, English language assessment in many settings still tests English as a *language* per se based merely on fixed standard native-speakerism norms. This neglects the nature of the English language used as a global language for international and intercultural communication in many emergent contexts, as discussed here in this volume. Language assessment will be hopefully made more GE-oriented when language policies and curricula recognize GE. We therefore see some examples in this volume of some GE-oriented approaches to language assessment. However, international standardized tests are still acting rather slowly to keep pace with language development and the current linguistic landscape. For example, international tests such as TOEFL, IELTS and TOEIC are claimed to be gatekeepers for the majority of English language learners if they want to study abroad (Jenkins, 2014). Although recognized, research on assessment in relation to GE is still scarce, and native speakerism is still quite dominant in a wide range of English language teaching (ELT) practices. We can see this from the fact that many TOEFL and IELTS providers (especially for the speaking section) employ native speakers of English although they are not specialized in language assessment. In addition, we problematize IELTS and TOEFL because they represent tests of English as an international language while the English that is being normed remains native speakerism-oriented. Although various proposals have been made to change the monolithic framing of native speakerism-oriented language assessment, it has a long way to go, particularly for international standardized tests to be made more GE friendly (see Jenkins & Leung, 2019; McNamara, 2012). In other words, we acknowledge that GE has been growing in theory, but its penetration is slow in the field of English language pedagogy and assessment.

Future Directions for Research on Global Englishes

Now it is high time for us to think about researching the notion of GE in English language education. This research agenda aims to socialize GE as a critical ecological approach to reframing and enacting language policy, curriculum, pedagogy and assessment that recognize more variation in English use in different geographical locations. Here are some research agendas in which language researchers and practitioners may be interested:

(1) critical discourse studies that examine language policy and curriculum documents, such as curriculum guidelines, syllabi and textbooks, through a critical GE lens;
(2) critical content analysis studies that look into ideological values of Anglophone varieties of English in commercial ELT textbooks;
(3) classroom-based research that examines how GE can be introduced and incorporated into the ELT classroom, especially in the Asian context (e.g. Sung, 2015);
(4) ethnographic classroom studies that explore the implementation of various GE-oriented activities which enhance learner awareness of GE and variation in English use;
(5) case studies that explore policymakers' perceptions of GE-driven policy on English language education;
(6) action research and design-based studies that investigate the design, use and evaluation of GE-oriented curriculum materials, such as textbooks and assessment papers;
(7) experimental studies that examine language teachers' and students' beliefs about GE in language teaching and learning.

Of course, there are more research agendas examining GE and ELT for which we can aim so as to promote the incorporation of GE into English language education. We are situated in a fluid context of English use, so we have to take larger social and political matters into account within dynamic language change, use and development. It is important to keep in mind that there is a need for more research on GE in language education to invigorate GE-oriented language education.

Closing

We feel that some previous publications will need to be updated as the field of GE is moving and changing fast (and, of course, publications related to GE have also mushroomed in recent decades). The trend of developments in GE has gained a breakthrough in the last decade, but there seems to be a lack of monographs or edited volumes to embrace the different aspects related to GE together, particularly in relation to the issues of curriculum, pedagogy and assessment. It is hoped that this book contributes and 'fills the gap' by interweaving the issues of language curriculum design, language pedagogy and language assessment together.

By problematizing what the use and learning of English as a global language means, we raise the ideas of innovation and change to reformulate our English policy and curriculum, re-appropriate our pedagogy, and administer language tests as well as language assessments that reflect on the use of English in different settings. Thus, this edited volume provides fresh impetus for exploration of GE in English language education at both micro (classroom and school) and macro (nationwide) levels. With this in mind, policymakers, curriculum developers, researchers, teacher trainers/educators and practicing teachers involved in this pedagogical arena will reap benefits by reading this volume. We see that WE and ELF will invigorate the design and enactment of English language policy, curriculum, pedagogy and assessment, as well as having a significant impact on how English language education is innovated and informed by the GE paradigm in different socio-educational contexts. Let us reiterate that our volume aims to achieve the following goals:

- to explore and unpack what English language education means in changing GE in which other languages affect the use of English in multilingual and multicultural contexts;
- to develop awareness of how curricular, pedagogical and assessment practices are informed by different dimensions of GE and how these practices are shaped by sociopolitical and institutional forces;
- to develop awareness of how critical GE perspectives inform the design and enactment of English language curriculum, pedagogy and assessment;
- to translate the notion of GE into practices of English language curriculum, pedagogy and assessment.

The current volume exemplifies different scholarly work which necessitates the idea of moving English language education beyond the (so-called but rather unrealistic) comfort zone of native speakerism. With all the contributions, this volume will be one of the key teacher and researcher references discussing and problematizing English language policy, curriculum, pedagogy and assessment together encapsulated in the GE paradigm. We believe that this edited volume is a timely contribution to GE and English language pedagogy for people working in multi-contexts in Asia and beyond. This book can be of great interest to university librarians and to people who are in the field of research on GE in practice.

References

Fang, F. (2016) 'Mind your local accent': Does accent training resonate to college students' English use? *Englishes in Practice* 3 (1), 1–28.
Fang, F. and Baker, W. (2018) 'A more inclusive mind towards the world': English language teaching and study abroad in China from Intercultural citizenship and English as a lingua franca perspectives. *Language Teaching Research* 22 (5), 608–624.
Galloway, N. and Rose, H. (2018) Incorporating Global Englishes into the ELT classroom. *ELT Journal* 72 (1), 3–14.
Holliday, A. (2006) Native speakerism. *ELT Journal* 60 (4), 385–387.
Jenkins, J. (2014) *English as a Lingua Franca in the International University: The Politics of Academic English Language Policy*. Abingdon and New York: Routledge.
Jenkins, J. and Leung, C. (2019) From mythical 'standard' to standard reality: The need for alternatives to standardized English language tests. *Language Teaching* 52 (1), 86–110.
McNamara, T. (2012) English as a lingua franca: The challenge for language testing. *Journal of English as a Lingua Franca* 1 (1), 199–202.
Murata, K. and Jenkins, J. (2009) *Global Englishes in Asian Contexts: Current and Future Debates*. London: Palgrave Macmillan.
Renandya, W.A. and Widodo, H.P. (eds) (2016) *English Language Teaching Today: Building a Closer Link Between Theory and Practice*. Cham: Springer.
Sung, C.C.M. (2015) Implementing a Global Englishes component in a university English course in Hong Kong. *English Today* 124, 42–49.
Widodo, H.P., Wood, A. and Gupta, D. (eds) (2017) *Asian English Language Classrooms: Where Theory and Practice Meet*. New York: Routledge.

Index

Note: References in *italics* are to figures, those in **bold** to tables; 'n' refers to chapter notes.

academic English 13, 38–39, 40
accommodation xii
Adamson, B. 177
Airey, J. 39
Anderson, B. 16
Asian use of English 2
assessment 47, 164, 169–170, 189–190, 197–198
Association of Southeast Asian Nations (ASEAN) 91

Bachman, L.F. 67–68
Bayliss, A. 46
Bayyurt, Y. 136, 151, 154n4
beliefs about language teaching 3, 10, 11–12
　changes in TEFL 11
　cultural essentialism 16–17
　early learning of English 19–20
　English as an international language 17–18
　English competence for economic success 18–19
　Euro- and US-centrism 15–16
　ideal learner and learning 21–22
　legitimate varieties of English 12–13
　monolingual approach to pedagogy 20–21
　native speakerness 13–14
　whiteness 14–15
　conclusion 22
bilingual education 20, 46, 48, 86, 87
Bokhorst-Heng, W. 152
Bolton, K. 126, 177
British National Corpus (BNC) 55

Brown, J.D. 12–13, 64, 66, 69, 71, 73, 74
Brunei *see* language selection and assessment in Brunei Darussalam; misunderstandings in international communication in Brunei
Byram, M. 158, 161

Canagarajah, A.S. 125
Canagarajah, S. 90, 100, 158, 161
Canale, M. 67
Canilao, M.L.E. 101n4
CDC (Curriculum Development Council, Hong Kong) 113
Chalhoub-Deville, M. 65
Childs, M. 77, 78
China English (CE)
　definitions 181–186
　linguistic features 182, 184–186, **185**
　terminology 181, 182, 183
China English in Chinese higher education 6–7, 176–177, 186
　assessment 189–190
　curriculum 186–188
　English in Chinese society 176–177, 186, 190n1
　foreign language teaching 179
　pedagogy 188–189
　teacher training 187–188
　textbooks 187
　recommendations for future research 190
　see also China: historical review of English education; language needs in Chinese higher education

China: historical review of English
    education 177, **178**
  Taiping Rebellion 177, 179
  Qing Dynasty 179
  People's Republic of China (PRC) 179
  Cultural Revolution 179
  Reform and Opening-up
    Movement 180
  standardized tests 180–181
  English as medium of instruction 181
  see also China English in Chinese
    higher education; language needs
    in Chinese higher education
Chinese English 181, 182, 183, 186
Chinese Pidgin English (CPE) 186
Chinglish 181, 182, 186
code-meshing 90
code-switching 20, 28, 87, 89, 91, 95,
  96–97, 100
communicative ability 18
communicative language teaching 11, 18
Cong, C. 187
contrastive rhetoric (CR) research 17
Corpus of Contemporary American
  English (COCA) 55
critical ecological perspective 194
critical pedagogy (CP) 88
critical period hypothesis 19
cultural diversity 136
cultural essentialism 16–17
Cummins, J. 20
Curriculum Development Council, Hong
  Kong (CDC) 113

D'Angelo, J. 126, 127, 138n3
Davidson, F. 65–66, 77, 79
Davies, A. 59–60, 67, 70
Dayag, Danilo 138n6
Deng Xiaoping 180
Dogancy-Aktuna, S. 128
Du, Z. 187

EAP *see* English for academic purposes
early learning of English 19–20
economic benefit myth 18–19
Edwards, J.G.H. 185, 186
EFL *see* English as a foreign language
EGL *see* English as a global language
EIL *see* English as an international
  language
Elder, C. 59–60, 77

ELF *see* English as a lingua franca
ELT *see* English language teaching
EMI *see* English as medium of
  instruction
English as a foreign language (EFL) 1,
  65, 66, 89, 190, 194
English as a global language (EGL) 11,
  35–38, 194
English as a glocal language 142, 144,
  153, 158, 170–172
English as a lingua franca (ELF) xi,
  158, 194
  complexity xii
  definitions xii, 2, 45
  research xiii, 12
  teaching 47, 48
  users not *learners* 124
  see also English as an international
    language
English as a native language (ENL) 88,
  91, 100
English as a second language (ESL)
  65, 194
English as an additional language 194
English as an international language
  (EIL) 17–18, 88, 124, 158, 194
  defined 64
  pedagogy 188
  see also English as a lingua franca
English as medium of instruction
  (EMI) 28
  in China 181
  code-switching 28
  defined 41n1
  and EAP 40
  research 28
  study destinations 29
  see also World Englishes enterprise in
    Japan
English for academic purposes (EAP)
  38–39, 40, 47
English language competence 67–68
English language proficiency 66, 67–69, 70
English language teaching (ELT) xii,
  1–3, 165–166
ENL *see* English as a native language
epistemological racism 15
ESL *see* English as a second language
Euro-centrism 15–16
expanding circle countries 12, 17–18
expanding circle Englishes 65, 66

Fang, F. 2, 189–190
Feng, W. 187
Ferguson, C. xi
foreign language learning 19–20, 179

Gall, M.D. *et al.* 31
Galloway, N. **152**
Gao, C. 184
Ge, C. 181
Gill, S.K. 134
Global English Language Teaching 7, 197
Global English Standard (GES) 74
Global Englishes (GE) xi, xiii, 64, 89–90
  defined xii, 2–3, 64, 154n1, 194
  expanding circle Englishes (EC) 65, 66
  and language testing 65–66
  and teacher educators 149–151, *151*
Global Englishes-oriented education 194–196
  future directions for research 198–199
  language assessment 197–198
  language policy and curriculum 196–197
  materials 88, 91, 94, 95, 98, 99, 197
  outer circle Englishes (OC) 65, 66
  pedagogy 197
  conclusion 199–200
globalization 11, 27–28, 104–105, 124, 157–158
Graddol, D. 17
Grin, F. *et al.* 18, 19

Harding, L. 60, 77
Hardman, J. 128
He, D. 185, **185**, 186
higher education *see* language needs in Chinese higher education
Hino, N. 127
Holliday, A. 13
Hong Kong *see* teaching English as a local/global language in Hong Kong
Hong Kong English (HKE) 110, 111, 112, 114, **115**, 116, 117
Hong Kong Examinations and Assessment Authority (HKEAA) 113
Honna, N. 127, 128
House, J. 172

Hu, G.W. *et al.* 30
Huang, J. 181
human capital 17

ideal learner and learning 21–22
IELTS (International English Language Testing System) 46, 66, 197, 198
Iino, M. 131
ILTA *see* International Language Testing Association
imagined communities 16
immersion education 20
individual racism 14–15
inner circle countries xi, 12, 15, 17
inner circle Englishes 65, 66
institutional racism 14
intercultural awareness and competence 88–89, 172–173
intercultural communication xii, 33–35
  see also Practices of Teaching Englishes for Intercultural Communication
intercultural communicative competence 158, 161
international English tests 66
International Language Testing Association (ILTA)
  Code of Ethics (2000) 79–80
  Guidelines for Practice (2007) 80
International Student Exchange Program (ISEP) 135
ISELPTs (international standardized English language proficiency tests) 4, 64–65, 66–67, 69
  alternative models 74–76
  change strategies 77–80
  difficulty/slowness of change? 76–77
  English language competence 67–68
  English language proficiency 67–69, 70, 71
  Global English standard 74
  Global Englishes and language testing 65–66
  'Native-speaker standard' 70–73
  purpose of the chapter 66–67
  scores 77
  why learn English? 73
  conclusion 80–81

JACET Conference 2004, Nagoya 134
Jamarani, M. 158

Japan *see* World Englishes enterprise in Japan
Japan-U.S. Training and Exchange Program for English Language Teachers (JUSTE) 15
Japanese Association for World Englishes (JAFAE) 128
Jenkins, J. xii, 54, 60, 89, 91
Jia, G. 183, 187
Jin, H. 184

Kachru, B.B. xi, 90, 125, 127, 128, 160, 172
Kachru, Y. 128
Kirkpatrick, A. 47, 90–91, 116, 160, 172
Kobayashi, Y. 15
Kubota, R. 17–18
Kumaravadivelu, B. 14, 151, 154–5n5

language ideology *see* beliefs about language teaching
language materials 70–71, 197
   for GE-oriented education 88, 91, 94, 95, 98, 99, 197
   in Philippine multicultural classrooms 88, 91, 94, 95, 98, 99
language needs in Chinese higher education 4, 27–28
   Chinese as added skill 36–38
   code-switching for intercultural communication 33–35
   core prompt interview questions 32, 40–41
   English as a global language 35–38
   international students and language choice 29–30
   need for academic English training 38–39, 40
   research questions 30, 32
   study 30–33, **32**
   findings and discussion 33–35
   conclusion 39–40
language selection and assessment in Brunei Darussalam 4, 45–46
   current issues in pedagogy and assessment 46–47
   pedagogy and assesment in Brunei 48–50, **49**
   see also misunderstandings in international communication
learner-centredness 169
learning for consumption of pleasure 21

Lee, E. 20–21
Lee, J.H. 15
Leech, G. 48
legitimate language myth 12–13
Leung, C. *et al.* 47, 68
Li, D. 185, **185**
Li, H. 186
Li, W. 182, 183, 190n2
linguistic imperialism 88
linguistic interdependence principle 20
linguistic norms 13, 65
Lowenberg, P. 65
Lv, L. 189

Macaro, E. 20–21
McKay, S. 74, 88, 90
McKay, S.L. 143, 150, 152
McNamara, T. 60
maintenance bilingual instruction 20
Mao Zedong 179
Matsuda, A. 144, 149
Mauranen, A. xii
metacultural competence 136, 158, 161, 172
misunderstandings in international communication in Brunei 50
   research methodology 50–52, **51**
   data analysis 52
   pronunciation **53**, 53–55
   lexis 55, 55–59, **56**, **57**, **58**
   discussion 59–60
   conclusion 60–61
monolingual approach to pedagogy 20–21
monolingual fallacy 20
Mortensen, J. 35, 37
mother tongue based multilingual education (MTBMLE) 88
Mufwene, S. 126, 127, 138n3
multicompetence 20
multicultural classrooms in the Philippines 4–5, 84–85
   code-switching 87, 89, 91, 95, 96–97, 100
   English Only Policy (EOP) 86, 87, 94, 95, 97, 98
   gap between the Englishes 91–97
   Global Englishes 87–91, 98
   linguistic, cultural, socio-economic divisions 92–93
   link between Englishes 97–100
   local English versions 96–97

materials 88, 91, 94, 95, 98, 99
MTBMLE Policy 88
primacy of Standard English (SE) 85–87, 92
teacher education 91, 99
teachers' constraints 93–96
multidialectal competence 158, 161
multilingualism xii, 1–2, 18, 90
Muñoz, C. 19
Murata, K. xiii, 131

nationalism 16
native-speaker (NS) models 47, 167
'Native-speaker standard' 70–73
native speakerism 2, 13, 128, 167, 195, 197, 198
native-speakerness 13–14
native-speakers (NSs)
  defined 67
  ideology 2, 13–14, 66
  language material issues 70–71
  person issues 71–72
neoliberalism 13, 19, 22
Nevile, M. 28
Nihalani, P. 126, 128, 138n5
non-native English speaking teachers (NNESTs) 13–14
non-native speakers (NNSs) 89
Northern Cyprus 144–145, 153–154
  national survey 149–151
  practices and innovations in teacher education 145–147, **146**
Nuske, K. 188

O'Sullivan, B. 47
outer circle countries 12, 15, 16, 47
outer circle Englishes (OC) 65, 66

Palmer, A.S. 67–68
Philippines
  Bilingual Education Policy (BEP) 86
  English Only Policy (EOP) 86, 87, 94, 95, 97, 98
  Enhanced Basic Education Act (2013) 88
  Executive Order (EO) No.210 88
  Kapampangan 86, 101n2
  Tagalog 86, 87, 101n1
  see also multicultural classrooms in the Philippines
Phillipson, R. 13, 19, 20, 126

plurilingual competence 18
Practices of Teaching Englishes for Intercultural Communication 6, 157–159, 161–162
  assessment 164, 169–170
  curriculum 162–163, 170
  data analysis 164–165
  ELT theories and perspectives 165–166
  English as a glocal language 158, 170–172
  globalization 157–158
  holistic approach for real-world challenges 166–167
  intercultural communication in multicultural contexts 158, 172–173
  literature review 159–161
  paradigm shift from English to Englishes 168–170
  pedagogical reflections and implications 164–173
  pedagogy 163, 170
  conclusion 173–174
proficiency tests *see* ISELPTs (international standardized English language proficiency tests)
Proshina, Z.G. 159–160

racial micro-aggressions 14–15
racism 14–15
rate of acquisition 19
Richards, J.C. 64
Rivers, D.J. 14
Rose, H. **152**
Ross, A.S. 14
Rubdy, R. 91

Sakai, S. 127, 128
Schmidt, R. 64
Seargeant, P. 159
second language acquisition (SLA) research 19
second order contact xii
Seferoglu, G. 154n2
Seidlhofer, B. 89
Selvi, A.F. 144, 148
Sewell, A. 116
Sharifian, F. 136, 158, 161, 172
Sharma, A. 138n6

Sifakis, N. 136
Sifakis, N.C. 151, 154n4
similects xii
Simon-Maeda, A. 15
Smith, L.E. xi, 127, 138n1
social and affective needs of learners 20
socio-economics 16
Sridhar, S.N. 125–126, 138n2
Standard English 1
  in the Philippines 85–87, 92
standardized English language tests 46–47
Study in China Program 29
Sue, D.W. *et al.* 15
Suzuki, T. 127, 128
Svartvik, J. 48
Swain, M. 67

Taylor, L. 77
teacher education 6, 141–143
  China English 187–188
  in/for a new global linguistic order **143**, 143–144
  local context 144–145
  in the Philippines 91, 99
  practices and innovations in Turkey and Northern Cyprus 145–147, **146**
  reluctance, resistance and unawareness 147–148
  teacher educators and Global Englishes 149–151, *151*
  implications and conclusions 151–154, **152**
teaching English as a local/global language in Hong Kong 5, 104–106
  attitudes towards English varieties and learning 110–112
  benchmarking localized pronunciation target 116
  bottom-up investigation and pedagogical implications 114–116
  contextualizing English learning activities 117
  currect practices in English language education 112–114
  Hong Kong English (HKE) 110, 111, 112, 114, **115**, 116, 117
  research project overview **106**, 106–107, 119n2
  shifting pedagoical foci 118
  spoken English use in Hong Kong 107–110
  teachers' speech 114, **115**
  textbooks 113
  verbal guise technique (VGT) 106, 107, 111–112, 117, 119n1, 119n3
  conclusion 118–119
Terasawa, T. 18
TESOL 14
test validity and fairness 12–13, 65–66
testing cultures 65
Three Circles model xii, 12, 15, 16, 17–18, 46, 47, 88
  see also Global Englishes (GE)
Thumboo, E. 138n5
TOEFL (Test of English as a Foreign Language) 130–131, 134, 197, 198
TOEFL 2000 project 76
TOEFL iBT (Test of English as a Foreign Language Internet Based Test) 66
TOEIC (Test of English for International Communication) 66, 130, 134, 135, 197
Tollefson, J.W. 40
Tomlinson, B. 47, 170
ToPIC (Teaching of Pronunciation for Intercultural Communication) 188–189, 197
transient multilingual communities 35
translanguaging 20, 89, 158
translingual approaches 13, 20, 89–90
Tsui, A.B.M. 40
Tupas, R. 91
Tupas, T. 91
Turkey 144–145, 153–154
  national survey 149–151
  practices and innovations in teacher education 145–147, **146**
  YÖK 145, 154n4

ultimate attainment 19
UNESCO 98
University of Maastricht 134
US-centrism 15–16

verbal guise technique (VGT) 106, 107, 111–112, 117, 119n1, 119n3
Vettorel, P. 99

Wachter, B. *et al.* 134
Wagner, J. 28

Wang, R. 181–182, 183
Waseda University 131
Watts, R.J. 18
Weddell, J. 177
Wen, Q. 187, 188
whiteness 14–15
Wigglesworth, G. 65
Wilkinson, R. 34
Wolff, M. 180
World Englishes (WE) xi, xiii, 66, 88
  accomplishments 125–126
  defined xii, 159
  as discipline and paradigm 158, 159–161, 190
  research 12
  speaker/writer and listener/reader matrix 72, **72**
  teaching 160–161, 187, 188, 189
World Englishes enterprise (WEE) in Japan 5–6, 123–124
  attracting high-level international students 132–135, **133**
  background 124–127
  College of World Englishes, Chukyo 128, 129
  Department of World Englishes 127–135
  English medium instruction 129–131
  preparing 'globalized' Japanese students 127–135
  recommendations for curricular reform 135–137
  six myths 125
  conclusion 137–138
writing practices 13, 16

Xiang, Y. 183, 187
Xie, Z. 182–183
Xiong, Z.B. 180
Xu, Z. 158, 160–161, 170, 172

Zhang, Y. 184
Zhao, T. 21

For Product Safety Concerns and Information please contact our EU Authorised Representative:

Easy Access System Europe

Mustamäe tee 50

10621 Tallinn

Estonia

gpsr.requests@easproject.com